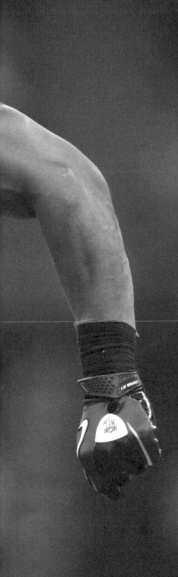

OUT OF THE BLUE

VICTOR CRUZ

WITH **PETER SCHRAGER**

OUT OF THE BLUE

A CELEBRA BOOK

CELEBRA
Published by New American Library, a division of
Penguin Group (USA) Inc., 375 Hudson Street,
New York, New York 10014, USA
Penguin Group (Canada), 90 Eglinton Avenue East, Suite 700, Toronto,
Ontario M4P 2Y3, Canada (a division of Pearson Penguin Canada Inc.)
Penguin Books Ltd., 80 Strand, London WC2R 0RL, England
Penguin Ireland, 25 St. Stephen's Green, Dublin 2,
Ireland (a division of Penguin Books Ltd.)
Penguin Group (Australia), 250 Camberwell Road, Camberwell, Victoria 3124,
Australia (a division of Pearson Australia Group Pty. Ltd.)
Penguin Books India Pvt. Ltd., 11 Community Centre, Panchsheel Park,
New Delhi - 110 017, India
Penguin Group (NZ), 67 Apollo Drive, Rosedale, Auckland 0632,
New Zealand (a division of Pearson New Zealand Ltd.)
Penguin Books (South Africa) (Pty.) Ltd., 24 Sturdee Avenue,
Rosebank, Johannesburg 2196, South Africa

Penguin Books Ltd., Registered Offices:
80 Strand, London WC2R 0RL, England

First published by Celebra,
a division of Penguin Group (USA) Inc.

First Printing, July 2012
10 9 8 7 6 5 4 3 2 1

LIBRARY OF CONGRESS CATALOGING-IN-PUBLICATION DATA:

Cruz, Victor, 1986–
Out of the blue/Victor Cruz with Peter Schrager.
p. cm.
ISBN 978-0-451-41615-5
1. Cruz, Victor, 1986– 2. Football players—United States—Biography. 3. Wide receivers
(Football)—United States—Biography. I. Schrager, Peter. II. Title.
GV939.C783A3 2012
796.332092—dc23
[B]

Set in ITC New Baskerville Std
Designed by Pauline Neuwirth

Printed in the United States of America

This book is dedicated to my dad, Michael Walker, and my grandfather, Fernando DeJesus. May you rest in peace and watch over my family and me.

CONTENTS

OUT OF THE BLUE

PROLOGUE

THIRD AND TEN.

Two minutes, twenty-seven seconds left in the first half.

The ball was on our own one yard line. We were down 7-3 to the Jets.

Antonio Cromartie, the Jets cornerback, may have been lined up across from my teammate Ramses Barden, but he was staring me right in the eye, running his mouth. It's what Cromartie does. He's a talker. He told me I was a "no name." He said that I didn't belong on the field.

Cromartie had every right to be jawing.

Up until that point, I'd done nothing the whole game. Earlier in the week, my teammate Mario Manningham and I had said a few things about Cro's Jets teammate Darrelle Revis that we probably shouldn't have. The kind of chatter that gets copied and pasted on to a bulletin board and gets guys riled up.

The New York media ran with our quotes and they ended up on the back pages of all the major newspapers in the city. I showed up to practice one morning that week and saw in big, bold letters a headline that read CRUZ SAYS TEAMS AREN'T SCARED OF REVIS ANYMORE.

I shook my head in amazement. That wasn't *quite* what I had said, but that's what ended up being printed. Welcome to New York.

But it was Cromartie who answered back, not Revis. When a reporter asked him about Mario's comments, he said, "We'll have to see on Saturday. That's even if he touches the field. He let a guy named Victor Cruz come in and take his job."

A guy named Victor Cruz.

Like it was some shameful thing.

A guy named Victor Cruz.

I was looking at Cro and he was telling me that he'd never heard of me, telling me that I wasn't worthy of lining up across from him. He was talking before, during, and after every play from scrimmage, and I was just silent. What could I say? We were getting beaten up and down the field all afternoon.

It was Christmas Eve and I was all out of sorts. We were playing the Jets at MetLife Stadium, our home building, but it was technically a Jets home game on the schedule. Things were twisted. At every other game we'd played at MetLife, we lined up on sideline to the east of the field. For this one, because we were the "visiting" team, we were on the west sideline. You wouldn't think that'd matter, but it was throwing us off. We all had to get used to the change.

There was more. The night before every home game, we sleep in the same rooms at the same hotel in Teaneck, New Jersey. For this one, though, because the Jets were staying there and had priority as the "home" team, we were forced to crash at another hotel in nearby East Rutherford. Our routines were all off.

Before kickoff, I scanned the stands—our stands—and it was just a sea of green. I looked for my mother and my girlfriend, Elaina, who always sat together in the same seats in Section 111, but they were nowhere to be found. It took me a second or two before I remembered that they were sitting behind one of the end zones, with tickets my buddy Josh got them, instead. I'd played in this stadium all season—my entire career, really—but never as a visitor. I was out of my comfort zone.

There were guys in green Santa Claus suits in the crowd, that Fireman Ed dude was on his buddy's shoulders leading the *"J-e-t-s, Jets, Jets, Jets!"* chant, and there was a bloodlust in the air unlike one I'd ever experienced in the building before.

On our first five offensive drives of the game, we punted four times and kicked a field goal. Eli threw to me just twice and I only had one catch for twenty-nine yards.

Our defense had bailed us out all afternoon. The Jets kicker missed a makeable field goal attempt that would have put them up 10-3. We were lucky to be down just four points. It had been an ugly, sloppy game. Usually, we're cool with that. That's Giants football. We win games in the trenches and we capitalize on our opponents' mistakes.

But it was late in the second quarter, heading into halftime, and we were still struggling.

THIRTEEN YEARS EARLIER, about fifteen miles north of MetLife Stadium, I was wearing double pads and a red, white, and blue mesh jersey for my Little League football team, the PAL North Firefighters. I loved that jersey and wore it with a tremendous amount of pride.

My father was a firefighter in Paterson, New Jersey, and all the other kids on the team were either sons or nephews of Paterson firefighters, too. I played center on that squad. I hiked the ball to the quarterback. I blocked opposing blitzers. I was one of the biggest cats on the team, so the head coach put me on the offensive line during the first day of practice and that was that.

I really liked playing center. I got to handle the rock every down and I was a part of the action. Running play, passing play—I was always involved. I got to hit the other kids; I got to run.

It was cool.

But, behind the scenes, my father was always telling the other coaches that I should be playing running back. He liked seeing me on the field and excelling at center, but he wanted me to get a chance at one of the skill positions. The offensive line made sense—I was one of the tallest twelve-year-olds in the league— but he never viewed me as a lineman. He saw me as a playmaker, changing the game with my speed and scoring touchdowns. I was enjoying my life as the starting center on the PAL North Firefighters, but without me ever knowing, Dad was pushing hard for his son to get a shot at any other position.

I was twelve years old and I had this weird, little kid body. I was awkward looking, with really long arms and crazy long legs. I had a big neck, too, like a giraffe. I wore thickly framed glasses and there was no meat on my bones. I was so tall that our tailback, a boy we called Little JaJa, was half my size.

He was good, though. *Really good.* Little JaJa was probably four-foot-one, but he had the biggest heart on the team. He would get the ball on a handoff and I'd pave the way for him, blocking defenders and ensuring that he'd have a clear path down the field. We had a good thing going and I loved celebrating his touchdown runs, knowing I played a role in getting our team those six points.

I was happy playing center. I remember just savoring the opportunity to wear that red, white, and blue jersey and running up and down the field with all those fans on the sidelines cheering us on. The best part of those games was always the postgame pizza parties we'd have afterward at Frank and Joe's. Win or lose, both teams would pile into the pizzeria and dive into giant pies of pizza. We'd reenact all the big plays and stuff our faces with pepperoni slices.

I blocked for Little JaJa most of the season, but my dad was always grinding his teeth about me being used out of position. He was an assistant coach on the squad and would constantly be in the ear of our head coach, Mr. Tolbert. We called Mr. Tolbert "Coach Bulldog," and if you saw Mr. Tolbert, you'd immediately know why that was his nickname. The guy was as tough as nails and he never took any crap from anyone.

"Give Victor a shot at tailback," my father would tell him. "Let Victor run the ball."

One game pretty late in the season, we were up by a few touch-downs, and after my father spent much of the second half pestering Mr. Tolbert, I got called off the field and was told to stand on the sideline.

I was upset. I never wanted to come out of a game, no matter what the score was. Coach Tolbert waved me over.

"Victor, we're putting you in at fullback," he told me. "We're up by a lot of points, so just don't fumble the ball. If you lose a few yards, that's okay. Just don't fumble the ball."

I was going to carry the rock. Finally. But I wasn't being asked to do much. The play that Coach Tolbert called was "21 Dive." I was supposed to take the ball from our quarterback, then run up the middle for a few yards and go down.

I lined up in the backfield for the first time of my life, and looked over to our sideline. Coach Tolbert was screaming, but I couldn't hear a word he was saying. I also spotted my father. His eyes were lit up. He was beaming.

It was as if he knew something I didn't.

"Hut one, hut two, hike . . ."

Nigel, our quarterback, handed me the ball and I remember just thinking, Don't fumble the ball. But after I shook one defender behind the line of scrimmage, I saw an opening over the right guard. Daylight. I shimmied left and shifted right, just like I'd seen one of my childhood idols, Emmitt Smith, do so many times before. I shed another tackle. I was past the line and in open space, now, with just one man to beat—a cornerback that I was a foot taller than.

Suddenly I was Eddie George of the Tennessee Titans, another one of my football heroes growing up. I'd seen Eddie George run over defenders on Sundays my entire life. I remember practicing his moves, always in slow motion, in my bedroom the nights before our games. In a flash, I had to decide—do I barrel over this kid or do I just burn him on the outside? I went with option one and ran over the dude.

I was gone. Sixty-four yards. Touchdown.

I'd never play center another down in my life.

I didn't realize it at the time, but my father had sprinted down the sideline, running stride for stride with me, for the entire sixty-four-yard run. When I scored, I immediately looked to the sideline for his reaction, but couldn't find him.

> MY FATHER ALWAYS BELIEVED IN ME AND ONCE I WAS GIVEN AN OPPORTUNITY, I MADE THE VERY MOST OF IT.

That was because he was in the end zone, right there next to me, jumping up and down.

I ran over and gave him a big hug. He was having even more fun than me! Little JaJa, all four feet of him, was going wild, too. For the first time, he was celebrating *my* touchdown score and not the other way around. On my way back to the sideline, I watched as my father skipped over to Coach Tolbert, a good buddy of his, shouting, "I told you so! I told you so!"

Even Coach Bulldog was smiling. And trust me, Coach Bulldog wasn't much of a smiler.

My father always believed in me and once I was given an opportunity, I made the very most of it. My dad was with me—side by side—for every single step of that run.

He's with me—side by side—on all of my big plays.

ANTONIO CROMARTIE DIDN'T know about that touchdown. He didn't know that all I was asked to do was not fumble the ball on a "21 Dive" and I ran it sixty-four yards for a score, instead. Cro didn't know that tae kwon do—not football—was my first true passion. He didn't know what I saw on the corner of East Eighteenth and Eleventh Avenue every day when I walked home from school. He didn't know how hard I'd worked just to become a guy named Victor Cruz.

He didn't know how *proud* I was to be a guy named Victor Cruz.

We were 7-7 going into the Jets game. Though we started the year out strong, our team suffered through some bad injuries and we lost a few really close games in the middle part of our season. Two weeks before the Jets game, we beat the Cowboys down in Dallas in a huge NFC East battle on a Sunday night. We were in good position to win the division, and though Michael Vick and the "Dream Team" Eagles were starting to get hot, we knew that wins over the Redskins and Jets in back-to-back weeks would all but seal up our first playoff berth in three years.

That didn't happen. We lost the previous week to the Skins. In this building. In front of our home fans. They booed us and we deserved it. We laid an egg when it mattered most. Eli didn't have his best game, I certainly didn't play very well, and the defense couldn't stop Rex Grossman and Jabar Gaffney.

In the locker room after the Washington game, we all just stared at each other with dazed looks. We'd beaten the Cowboys, one of the toughest teams in the league, but lost to the 4-9 Redskins? I remember getting dressed and muttering, "What just happened?"

Despite the loss, our Super Bowl dreams were still very much intact. We just had to win out the rest of the way. We had no other option than to win every single game on our schedule from that point on. There were two regular season games left and we'd have to win four more in the playoffs. If we could go 6-0 in the next six games, we'd be Super Bowl champions in February.

We'd be up against some stiff competition in the weeks ahead, but our goals were clear. We just had to win the next six games. Every single play from that game on, I tried to give it my all, both mentally and physically. I tried to gain as many yards as humanly possible, not get caught by anybody on any one play, and take every single pass reception to the house for a touchdown.

The Redskins loss was awful, but the Jets were just as bad in week fifteen. They went into Philadelphia and got clobbered 45-19 by the Eagles on national television. They were 8-6 heading into our game, but if they lost, they would instantly become a long shot to make the playoffs. This was a must-win game for both teams.

All week in New York and New Jersey, it was all Giants-Jets, all the time. I couldn't turn on the TV or the radio and not hear about it. Peter Rosenberg on Hot 97 started his show every day with something on the game. Greg and Rosanna on *Good Day New York* were picking sides on Thursday, and it was all the talking heads on ESPN could talk about. I was getting ready for practice that Friday morning and had ESPN 2's *First Take* show on in the background as I ate my cereal. I was just minding my business when I heard Stephen A. Smith, a guy whose voice I'd grown up listening to on TV and the radio, say my name. In that unmistakable Stephen A. Smith voice of his, he was shouting, "Victor Cruz, I'm talking to you! How *dare* you talk about Darrelle Revis like that? In your *first* year on the field? You have the *audacity* to even say Revis's name?"

It was surreal. Stephen A. Smith was doing his whole Stephen A. thing—and he was doing it about *me!*

Giants-Jets was the biggest topic in sports that week, and with all the back-and-forth in the media, the hype leading up to the game was out of control.

That whole week of practice was incredibly intense. You could even feel it from the coaching staff. We always pay attention to detail, but that week, every in-cut, every out-cut, the coaches were calling them out and making sure we were absolutely nailing our routes. It was the biggest game of the season and it was certainly the biggest game I'd ever been a part of. All the talk between our two teams only added fuel to the fire.

A few days before the game, Rex Ryan, the head coach of the Jets, said they were the better team in town. I liked how my teammate Justin Tuck responded to that. When asked about it by a reporter, Justin just smiled and said, "The fact of the matter is, I have a Super Bowl ring."

He handled it perfectly.

I've learned a lot from Justin.

But I've learned a lot from several people along the way.

AS CROMARTIE AND I stared at each other and my quarterback, Eli Manning, barked out commands over a rowdy crowd of Jets fans, I remembered the down and distance.

Third and ten.

The play that our offensive coordinator, Kevin Gilbride, called in from the sideline was a double hook route for Hakeem Nicks and me. In this instance, though, there would also be a third receiver in the set, lined up outside me, running something called a "deep in-route." Both Hakeem and I were supposed to fight off press coverage at the line of scrimmage, run about ten yards, and pivot to the outside—Hakeem going left, me going right. He was covered by Revis, an NFL All-Pro. I lined up across from Kyle Wilson, a first-round pick from 2010. Ramses, the third wideout, had Cromartie on him.

The play was designed for both Hakeem and me to pivot hard into our hook routes, coming back toward Eli around the first down marker. As we both turned and pivoted, Ramses was supposed to fly past me on the outside and down the sidelines, crossing toward the middle of the field as the third option. Getting a first down was the obvious goal of the play, but pinned against our goal line, if one of the three of us could catch the ball, gain a few yards, and give our punter, Steve Weatherford, some room for his fourth down boot—that would have been good, too.

We needed ten yards for a first down, ninety-nine yards for a touchdown, and I couldn't hear a damn thing.

As Eli settled into the shotgun, it was hard not to be impressed with his overall demeanor, his moxie. Eli was the first overall pick in the 2004 NFL Draft and he plays like it. I'm told he wasn't always as cool and confident as he is now, but I can't imagine him any other way. Every day I come to work, I'm amazed by the way Eli carries himself. As the first overall pick in the Draft, Eli Manning knew there were expectations for him. He's exceeded all of them.

I looked around the field.

Cromartie was the nineteenth pick in the 2006 NFL Draft. Revis went fourteenth overall to the Jets a year later. Hakeem was a Giants first-round pick in 2009 and the Jets took Wilson with the twenty-ninth overall selection in 2010. Even Ramses was a third-rounder.

I wasn't drafted.

Twenty-seven different wide receivers were taken in the 2010 NFL Draft, and I wasn't one of them.

My NFL Draft experience was different from that of most the guys on the field that day, and different from that of most the guys playing in the NFL, period. Though I had a really productive final two seasons at UMass, I wasn't considered a blue-chip NFL prospect. Mel Kiper and Todd McShay never argued over where I'd be drafted on *SportsCenter*.

I wasn't one of the 320 college players invited to the NFL Draft Scouting Combine that year. I had a strong Pro Day workout, though, and there were several scouts in attendance. I ran the forty-yard dash in 4.42 seconds. I jumped 41.5 inches. My agent said a few teams were interested in me and that there was a chance I could get selected on the Draft's third day.

In the days leading up to the Draft, I went on NFL.com, the league's official Web site, and studied all thirty-two teams' rosters. I clicked on "Depth Chart" for each squad and learned the names of every wide receiver on all the teams in the league. I printed out all thirty-two rosters and memorized the names of those wide receivers. On the night before the draft, I took out a yellow highlighter and marked off all the different fran- **I WASN'T** chises I could see drafting me that weekend.

But Draft weekend came and went and I never heard **DRAFTED.** my name called. I watched every second of the Draft that year—all ten hours—and remember those three days pretty well. Tim Tebow had Jeremy Schaap and the ESPN cameras in his living room, Colt McCoy had the NFL Network following his every step, and I was on my couch in Paterson, New Jersey.

In my gym shorts and a T-shirt.

Alone.

Though I was disappointed that I didn't get drafted, I wasn't really all that shocked. I understood the process and understood that I wasn't a guy who had monster statistics, or was six-foot-six, 250 pounds. I understood that there was a chance I wouldn't be drafted and that I would just have to make the most of coming in as a practice squad guy and as an undrafted rookie free agent.

Across that line of scrimmage, Cromartie, Wilson, and Revis— the three first-rounders—didn't know me. They didn't know that I stared at a phone for three days that didn't ring. They didn't know what I was about to do them and their team's playoff hopes.

THIRD AND TEN.

Our center, David Baas, snapped the ball. Eli stepped back and looked left to Hakeem, but Revis was draped all over him. Eli shifted right and looked toward his second and third options. Ramses and me.

Four yards, five yards, six—I started my hook pattern.

Just as I shifted right and began to pivot, Eli and I linked eyes.

The two of us had spent hours practicing this very route over the previous summer. Running a hook route is very difficult on the body and has to be timed perfectly. You've got to make a hard plant with one leg and your entire body has to shift, turn, and dart the other direction in one smooth motion. If you don't time the pivot perfectly, it's an interception and six points the other way. Wes Welker, the wide receiver for the New England Patriots, is probably the best at running hook routes in all of football. He and his quarterback, Tom Brady, practice the route every time they step on the field before a game or practice. Eli and I haven't been together quite as long as Welker and Brady, but we had a connection, and in the summer of 2011, we really started to gel.

During the NFL lockout, Eli called the athletic director at Hoboken High School and asked if we could use their facilities to practice. Imagine that phone call? "Hi, this is Eli Manning of the New York Giants, and I'd like to use your high school's football field." That's pretty much what happened. After the AD gave Eli the okay, he sent our entire team a mass e-mail, encouraging us all to show up.

Not everyone came. Some guys were out of town and others just weren't into it. But that e-mail was exactly what I'd been waiting for. Having missed the majority of the 2010 season with a hamstring injury, I'd been itching to get back on the field and run some routes. I sent Eli a text message right away that said, "I'm in." He responded, "Good. I can't wait to get started. Be ready to work hard."

It must have been 100 degrees out on that first day at Hoboken High. Because of the lockout, there were no coaches, no trainers, and no front-office personnel allowed on the premises. There wasn't much media on hand, either. Eli brought out his strength guy, we warmed up, and we just went at it in the heat. We ran routes on air, and then we went through everything—the terminology, the timing, the entire route tree.

There was no guarantee that I'd make the squad coming into training camp, so I listened to Eli's every word and did whatever he said. Every morning, I'd get up at seven a.m., throw on some shorts and my spikes, and drive my car to Hoboken High School. When the crowds of fans and media got out of control, we moved the practices to Bergen Catholic High School. We worked even harder there.

I never missed a session. I was usually the first one on the field, stretching. If I wasn't the first guy there, Eli was.

Hakeem, Ramses, Michael Clayton, Duke Calhoun, Sam Giguere—we ran routes from early in the morning to late in the afternoon. It was competitive, too. Eli and Sage Rosenfels, one of our backup quarterbacks at the time, stressed the importance of timing, diligence, and discipline.

I was able to step up when my number was called during the season because of how hard I worked during those days in the summer. Opportunities had never been just handed to me, and in that 100 degree heat, I knew I had to make the very most of my time with my quarterback and teammates.

AS I BROKE right, Eli wound up and unleashed a perfectly thrown ten-yard pass to my outside. I felt Wilson's right hand on the back of my jersey, but I knew I could shed him.

Cromartie was next. He had already peeled off from Ramses and came at me head-on from the left.

Wilson lunged to swipe at the ball and knock it down. I felt him overpursuing, pushed him off me, and caught the ball cleanly.

I had the first down. But I wasn't done.

Cro had an angle on me, but if I made a strong move to the inside, I was pretty sure I could take this one for a big gain.

In that instant, I thought about all of my touchdown runs for the PAL North Firefighters. I thought about my AAU basketball team, the Tim Thomas Playaz, and breaking free for a layup in the open court. I thought about the game in high school when

I scored five touchdowns in the first half versus Elmwood Park.

As Cro came at me, I sidestepped him and pivoted hard to the inside. He lunged, but he was already on his knees. Too late, Cro.

I was gone.

Down the twenty. Down the thirty. Only one man to beat—Eric Smith, number 33. He was off to my left. The sideline was a few yards to my right. If he shoved me, he could limit the damage.

But I was on fire. I was blazing.

Down the forty.

At the forty-five yard line, I looked into Smith's eyes. Defenders always have a look in their eyes. Sometimes it's one of hunger. Other times it's one of desperation. At that moment, me looking at Smith's eyes as he chased me down, we both knew he had only one option—to dive and try to grab my legs.

Smith dove like Superman, his arms outstretched.

I did a little skip move. A hop step, really. I timed it perfectly—*whoop*—like I'd just pressed the "B" button on a video game controller in a game of *Madden*.

As I leaped, Smith got an armful of air.

Daylight.

I was the teenage kid running home from Montgomery Park after hearing gunshots. I was the guy practicing curl routes on an empty football field up in Bridgton, Maine. I was the dude doing a forty-yard dash on a Pro Day with scouts watching from afar.

I was a blur down the sideline. The fifty. The forty. The thirty.

At around the twenty yard line, I looked up above the end zone and into the crowd. I saw my mother and Elaina, eight months pregnant at the time, going wild in that sea of green.

The ten.

Touchdown.

Salsa time.

For the first time all afternoon, MetLife Stadium was silent. Nothing.

Then I heard boos. The Jets fans were booing me.

But then I realized, those weren't boos, at all. They were saying, "Cruuuuuz."

They were saying *my* name.

Not bad for a guy named Victor Cruz.

HOMEGROWN

AS A KID, I saw the New York City skyline every single day of my life. The Big Apple was just a ten-minute car ride away from my childhood home in Paterson, New Jersey. It was an easy commute. Take the first left off Twentieth Street onto Madison Avenue, drive past the Banana King, hop on Route 3, cruise past Giants Stadium on the New Jersey Turnpike, and merge into the Holland Tunnel traffic. Get in one of the E-ZPass lanes, roll up your windows, and take the tunnel right into the heart of Manhattan. It was a straight shot. Wall Street, Times Square, all that action—it was always there, in the distance, seemingly within arm's reach.

But New York City might as well have been the Land of Oz, some magical world of mystery with streets paved with gold. In the first fifteen years of my life, despite its close proximity, I probably made that trip into New York a total of three times. And each one of those times was for a basketball or tennis tournament. I'd come in, play a game or a match, and get right out. There were no Broadway shows, no trips to the Disney Store, no Ack Coupes with twenty-two-inch rims.

New York City was fiction, a universe that existed in mobster movies and rap lyrics. It represented money, fame, and fortune. In Paterson, we didn't have money, fame, or fortune.

We had Italian combo heroes, soaked in oil and vinegar, at Skuffy's Subs on Goffle Road. We had the guy with the fluorescent neon green nylon pants who was always posting up outside the bodega on Crooks Avenue. We had street fairs where they'd sell funnel cakes for a dollar and cannolis for two. We had the barely paved parking lot with no backboards or rims that we turned into our own imaginary Madison Square Garden in front of School 21.

We had each other.

My entire childhood, that Manhattan skyline was always in the distance, always looming. It was my North Star.

But it represented more than fancy cars or jewelry. It represented making it. It represented success. And even at a very young age, I remember wanting it so badly. I knew it'd be hard work, but I was certain I would make something special out of my life.

I GREW UP in my grandparents' home on 44 East Twentieth Street. It was a three-bedroom apartment on the third floor of a red, brick walk-up building. I had my own room, my mother had hers, and my *abuela* and her husband had one, too. On the first floor of the building was a Spanish bodega, El Aguila Supermarket. A man named Teddy was the owner and one of the great characters of my childhood. Anytime I'd pop in for a juice box or a pack of basketball cards, Teddy would have a knock-knock joke or a noogie to give me in return. We lived on the third floor, two stories above Teddy's store. In between us on the second floor was Manny Quiles's Martial Arts Studio.

My grandmother arrived in Paterson from Puerto Rico in 1965 with no job, no home, no money, and my nine-year-old mother in tow. In the 1940s and 1950s, Paterson was a booming, industrious post–World War II town. There were factories, department stores lining the streets downtown, and the promise of new jobs for immigrants coming to the country. There was a big Puerto Rican presence, and my grandmother wanted to make a life in America for my mother and her.

She struggled. Life was hard. Her English wasn't very good, she was a single mother in a new land, and those jobs that were supposed to be so easy to find were, in fact, very hard to come by. There was a race riot in Paterson in 1964 after an incident where a group of African-American teenagers in the Fourth Ward pelted a police car with rocks. The cops responded with brutality and thousands of Paterson's African-American residents took to the streets in protest. In the late 1960s, Paterson transformed from a city comprised mostly of Irish- and Italian-Americans into a melting pot of different minorities. Peruvians, Dominicans, Colombians, and Puerto Ricans like my grandmother came to Paterson in pursuit of the American Dream.

Job opportunities came and went, but my grandmother eventually found herself a steady situation at a sewing factory, met my grandfather, and settled into that home on East Twentieth. My *abuela* was my everything, but my grandfather—my mother's stepfather—was my best friend. His full name was Fernando DeJesus, but he was always *"Papí"* to me.

Papí retired from his job of twenty years as a factory worker right before my mother had me in 1986, and we were attached at the hip for the first eight years of my life.

He was as old school as they came. I'm sure *Papí* wore clothes at some point in his life, but he was always shirtless in my memories of him. He'd wear the nicest, crispest brown slacks, a leather belt, beautiful polished shoes, and fancy argyle socks—but never a shirt. He was missing a finger from a factory accident he suffered in his twenties and had a huge scar down his back. My mother would later tell me that the scar was because he had his lung removed, the result of smoking too many cigarettes as a young man. I never knew him as a smoker, though, and I never got the gory details of the missing finger—I only knew him as *Papí*, the greatest man in the world.

When I say we were best friends, I mean it. We did everything together. Because he was retired, he was able to spend all day with me, and I don't remember many moments of my early years being spent without him by my side. Every morning, he would wake up at the exact same time—six thirty. He'd go to the breakfast table and my grandmother would serve him his coffee—always black, no cream or sugar—in the same white mug. He'd then head over to his rocking chair, lay out his newspaper, put on an old vinyl record, and hum to the music.

"HE LETS THE MUSIC BREATHE," MY GRAND-FATHER WOULD SAY, "AND THAT'S HOW ONE SHOULD LIVE HIS LIFE."

That music, if I hear it now, still gives me goose bumps. It wasn't the salsa or anything upbeat. It was old Spanish guitars and a man serenading a woman. The singer's name was José Feliciano, and his voice was like silk. It was beautiful. My grandfather would rock on that chair of his, put me on his lap, and just sing the same ten or eleven tunes in Spanish in my ear. When the album was finished, he'd play it again. I remember him telling me to listen not so much to the singer's words, but the *way* he sang them. José Feliciano never rushed, he never screamed—he was always even keeled and well paced. "He lets the music breathe," my grandfather would say, "and that's how one should live his life."

We'd then hit Eastside Park and do laps around the greens all morning. I'd climb the trees, run on the fields, and play in the dirt. He'd be with me, always one step behind, humming his songs in Spanish and watching me explore.

Some days, he'd take me to the old Hispanic barbershop on Market Street. The men in there loved having me around and I desperately wanted to be viewed as "one of the guys." They were straight out of a movie. They'd be speaking in Spanish about local Paterson issues or discussing the latest Knicks or Yankees game, and I'd nod along, a little five-year-old kid hanging with the adults. My grandfather would get a shave and a haircut in one chair, and I'd sit in a smaller brown one, shaped like a tiny horse, getting my hair cut right next to him.

My grandfather had his life in order. He would always tell me, "If your life is stable, the rest will fall into place." He kept things uncomplicated, but he was very strict in adhering to his daily routine. He ate three meals a day, at the same exact time each day, and he never strayed from that schedule. At five o'clock every night, it was dinnertime. No matter what was going on in the park or on the street, whether it was "game point" in a basketball game or the bottom of the ninth in a stickball battle, I had to be at that dinner table at five p.m. No ifs, ands, or buts. I'd kick and scream about how unfair it was that all my friends were able to stay out playing sports until all hours of the night, but he and my *abuela* had the best intentions in mind.

They knew that if I was in the house by five, at that dinner table, I couldn't be somewhere else getting into trouble. If I didn't make it back for dinner by five p.m., I wasn't eating that night. Plain and simple. And I liked to eat. My *abuela*'s food was incredible. You'd smell her cooking her pork chops from a block away, and the thought of her arepas still makes my mouth water.

I'd play sports with all the other kids in the neighborhood on the street right beneath my *abuela*'s kitchen window. At four fifty-five every day, she would scream from three stories up, "Victorrrrr!" and I'd shudder in embarrassment. All the other kids would make fun of me, and yell in their best sixty-year-old Puerto Rican woman voices, "Victorrrrr!" I'd just blush and shake it off.

One time, I ignored her screams for dinner and opted to just keep playing a game called "wallball" in the street. After a few minutes of silence, my friend Corey looked like he saw a ghost hanging over my shoulder. He said, "Um . . . Victor, I think your grandmother's coming," and when I turned around—there she was, storming down the street in her floral nightgown with my grandfather's black leather belt in her hand. She had curlers in her hair and fuzzy white slippers on, but she was out on the street with the crazed look of a woman scorned.

The other kids were all dying of laughter, and because we lived on a one-way street, I had no other option than to run past her. She came after me like Ray Lewis. I managed to elude her, shaking and baking throughout, and darted up three flights of stairs to the dinner table. Those moves you see on the football field on Sundays? Those weren't perfected at some fancy football summer camp. They were honed avoiding my grandmother's swinging belt on East Twentieth Street.

A lot of great games of *Knockout* and *Manhunt* were ended prematurely because of that five p.m. dinner rule.

Papi and I always managed to have fun, though, even inside the house.

I was a WWF freak. And guess what? So was he! My grandfather—who must have been in his early sixties at the time—was obsessed with professional wrestling. Of all the amazing WWF characters, he loved the Undertaker the most. The Undertaker was this towering, pale, half-dead character who was supposed to be from the underworld. He had this really slow gait and a persona that was full of doom and dread. *Papi* would pretend that he was the Undertaker and chase me around the house. When I say "chase," I mean he'd walk with these big, slow strides, just like the Undertaker did, and I'd run around the house like a madman trying to avoid his grasp.

My grandfather and I would always watch wrestling on TV and I collected all the WWF toys. Randy "Macho Man" Savage, Hulk Hogan, The Rock, Mr. Perfect, the Ultimate Warrior—I loved them all. I remember jumping off the top of my *abuela*'s favorite couch like I was "Superfly" Jimmy Snuka flying off the top rope, and getting an earful (and probably a spanking) afterward. *Papi* would always pretend he was disappointed in me for climbing up on the nice furniture. Then, when my *abuela* turned her back, he would slap me five for the great technique.

Football wasn't really on my radar when I was little. With all the wrestling that was on TV, how was I supposed to care about what Warren Moon and Jim Kelly were doing on Sundays? If the other kids my age were watching *Monday Night Football* in their living rooms, I had no idea. I was watching *Monday Night Raw*. I loved the signature moves, the drama, and most of all—the huge personalities that made it so fun.

One thing that was carried over from my living room wrestling career into my life in the elementary school classroom was all the acting. Just as the couch was my top rope and the carpet was my ring, the classroom at School 21 was my stage. I know, I'm probably supposed to tell you that I was a bookworm who could recite Shakespeare and the periodic table as a kid, but that just wasn't the case.

I liked social studies class and I remember memorizing all the presidents in fifth grade U.S. history, but the classroom *setting* was what I really thrived on. Every day, there'd be thirty-five people in the audience, including the teacher, and I'd be given the opportunity to perform. I wouldn't say I was the class clown, but I sure had fun.

I'd watch shows like *Martin* and *Family Matters* on TV, and come into class and reenact my favorite scenes the next day. My teachers, of course, didn't find my comedy routines quite as inspirational as I did. I'd be lying if I didn't say I spent quite a lot of valuable learning time sitting in the front of the classroom, the result of poor classroom behavior.

I had a natural curiosity to dive into things and explore. My mother would always encourage me to try new things, even if it was out of my comfort zone. Maybe my darkest secret that absolutely nobody knows about me is that I played the flute.

Yes, I played the flute.

I was in the fourth grade and for music class we needed to choose an instrument to play for the entire school year. My friends all picked the more "manly" ones, like the trombone or the trumpet. But all the cute girls in my class were playing the flute. That seemed as good a reason as any to give it a shot.

I was actually pretty good at it. I brought that little silver flute, tucked away in its brown case, everywhere I went. I'd practice in *Abuela*'s living room, learning the different notes from the sheet music and making a ton of noise until I got it right. I got made fun of by the older kids on the block, but I didn't really care about what they thought. I was the only boy who played the flute that year and I was the center of attention. What more could a ten-year-old kid ask for?

My flute days eventually came to an end when I wasn't interested in spending the next summer indoors mastering Beethoven's *Für Elise*. I never ended up performing at Lincoln Center, but the fact that I gave it a shot always made my mother proud. She wanted me to try anything and everything. In her mind, if I was busy with hobbies and after-school activities, I was challenging my mind and body in ways that'd be instrumental down the road. It'd also keep me off the streets.

MY MOTHER WOULD ALWAYS ENCOURAGE ME TO TRY NEW THINGS, EVEN IF IT WAS OUT OF MY COMFORT ZONE.

My mother worked very hard to provide for me. She was always on the move, often pulling double shifts and working overtime to pay the bills. Throughout my childhood, she managed multiple jobs at a time. Once I started getting a little bit older, she made sure I got into the YMCA after-school program on Ward Street. Every day after class, I'd catch a bus and head over to the Y. We did it all there. We swam in the pool, we played tag, and we did gymnastics. I was always competitive. If we were doing cartwheels, I'd make sure my form was the best. If we were holding our breaths under water, I'd come close to passing out just trying to be the one who could hold his breath the longest. I loved all the activities at the Y, but they were just hobbies, things to do.

My first *real* passion? The ancient art of tae kwon do.

THE SECOND FLOOR of 44 East Twentieth Street was the home of Manny Quiles's tae kwon do studio. I didn't know Manny Quiles's real name until much later in my life, though. To me, he was always "The Sir."

The Sir's studio was one story below my *abuela* and grandfather's home, and at all hours of the day, I'd watch as older kids shuffled up and down the stairwell in their white robes. I was always curious about what went on down there on the second floor, but my mother would tell me I was far too young for martial arts. By the time I was seven years old, my curiosity in the action downstairs was just too much for her to withstand. It was boiling over. She finally relented and I was enrolled in classes.

The Sir was probably in his late thirties or early forties, but he could have run a marathon or fought a tiger on a day's notice if asked to. He was in impeccable physical shape. He was Colombian with a grayish crew cut, and was always in his white robe, barefoot. In all my years of knowing The Sir, I can't remember him ever once wearing shoes. I'm sure he owned a pair, but the visual of him anything but barefoot just isn't in my memory bank.

I dove right into tae kwon do and excelled immediately. I loved the discipline and focus that was necessary to thrive in the sport. There were also clearly defined, tangible goals. The Sir's dojo was covered in floor-to-ceiling mirrors and had an unforgettable smell of sweat and socks. It was all business in there, and I liked that. We'd have classes three days a week, and when you arrived, you were in his world for that entire hour. No talking, no goofing off, and no horsing around. The Sir was Tom Coughlin before I ever met Tom Coughlin.

One time, we were getting ready to start class and one of the other boys, a real wise guy, said to The Sir, "Hey, Manny, I'm just not feeling it right now. Can we take a break?"

No one referred to The Sir as "Manny." You didn't call him anything but "The Sir." All of our jaws dropped to the floor at once. I thought, No, he did not just do that. That did not just happen.

The Sir calmly walked up to the boy and asked him, "What did you just call me?"

The kid casually replied, "Manny. Your name. My mother told me your name is Manny, so I'm calling you Manny."

The Sir just put his hand on the boy's shoulder and, in the softest voice, said, "Go get your stuff. Don't come back until you're ready to be serious about tae kwon do." The boy pleaded to stay, but The Sir wasn't having it. We never saw that kid in class again. I guess he didn't want it enough.

I did.

We had tests every three or four months and I'd study for them for hours. I refused to fail. It wasn't just going out there and sparring with opponents and winning matches. We had five-page paper packets that we had to memorize, too. There was a ton of information on those sheets—the history of tae kwon do, the great masters, all the different moves and positions. To pass The Sir's tests, you had to have all the information down. We would do sparring, we would do our pattern, and then we had to line up in front of a panel of judges who'd pepper us with questions.

The panel was made up of The Sir, a guy named Garfield who was one of the senior black belts, and an old Asian man that we all just referred to as "The O.G." This guy was no joke. He was probably sixty-five years old, but he was a ninth-degree black belt and could still do a spinning hook kick that'd knock your butt on the canvas. We *never* saw The O.G. all year, and then on test day, he'd appear out of nowhere.

He was like a mythical figure in all of our lives, and I knew a lot of my friends in those classes would choke and blow it on test days solely because of his haunting presence. They'd spend months memorizing the sheets and all their moves, but when he was in the room, they'd fumble their words and forget everything in an instant.

I always looked forward to my opportunities in front of The O.G. I'm not sure how he knew all of us, but he had the 411 on everyone. And he'd come prepared with questions that were personally altered to each and every one of our lives. My mother was so meticulous about my studying habits for those tests, and I never cared more about anything in my life. I'd sit in my bedroom, with no TV or music on, and study for hours. I'd know all the stuff inside and out, so by the time I was standing up in front of the panel, I'd be as cool as a fan. The O.G. would ask me a question and I'd just answer it. That was the best feeling in the world. To just know that anything he asked, I would be able to handle it. Test after test, I would be standing there like, "Anything you ask me, I'm going to know it." And I did.

Every year, I'd earn a new belt. I went from a yellow belt to a green belt, then to a blue, and to a red. The red belt is the belt before the ultimate honor—the black belt. I never wanted anything more than that black belt. I'd walk around the house in my robe, just practicing moves and reciting the tenets of tae kwon do. By the time I was up in front of the panel and the black belt was on the line, I was a Martial Arts Encyclopedia. I was ready for any question the panel could possibly ask me. When I got to test day, I stood up there, my head spinning with information.

"Victor, congratulations," said The Sir.

"What? There's no test?" I had prepared for months. I was ready for the toughest test of my life.

"There's no test. With your commitment and determination over the past few years, you've already proved to us that you're worthy," he said.

It was an incredible moment and an incredible honor. According to The Sir, at twelve years old, I was the youngest tae kwon do black belt in New Jersey State history. That was nothing to shake a stick at. I wore that honor proudly and cherished the feeling of achievement. I set my sights on a long-term goal and I had accomplished it.

Tae kwon do opened up new doors and opportunities for me. I got to travel across the country and perform in showcases. I even competed in international tournaments. The Sir took me under his wing and showed me a world I probably would never have seen without his tutelage. We took three different trips to Quebec City, Canada, and I competed with some of the world's best young martial artists. He'd rent a charter bus and we'd head up there on these weeklong trips that were full of great memories. I took tae kwon do very seriously, but I always remembered that regardless of how heated the competition got, it was supposed to be fun. From The Sir, I learned the importance of preparedness. If you came prepared, no matter what the situation, you could never be caught off guard.

I would never have met The Sir had we not lived one floor above his dojo. That's how life works, sometimes. You're just in the right place at the right time. You're put in situations where you have the opportunity to better yourself. In my case, a tae kwon do studio was downstairs.

After I earned my black belt, I decided to quit tae kwon do. It was time to try something new.

Two years later, The Sir's daughter earned her black belt at the age of ten.

I wasn't too upset. After all, records are made to be broken.

■　■　■

ONE DAY WHEN I was seven years old, I was eating a bowl of Waffle Crisps in my *abuela*'s kitchen when I heard a bit of a commotion outside our front door. I poked my head out into the hallway to see what was going on and saw my mother speaking with a tall African-American man in a T-shirt and blue jeans. As my mom spoke to this stranger, I remember thinking, Who is this guy? I'd never seen him in my life.

His name was Mike Walker.

He was my father.

Mike Walker met my mother at a bus stop in Paterson in 1982. He threw some pickup lines at her, and though she thought he was handsome, she deflected his compliments at first. She was on her way to work and wasn't interested in being hit on at seven a.m. But he, like me, was relentless with the woman he had his eyes on and wouldn't give up without a fight. When he offered her a ride to work in his car, instead of taking the bus, she finally said yes. When they discovered that they both shared the same birthday—March 1—just one year apart, a connection was made.

They hit it off immediately and began seeing each other soon thereafter. A firefighter in Paterson, my father had hours that were always changing and he was constantly on the move. But he'd find times to drop by my *abuela*'s house with chocolates for my mother or come by the bank she was working at with a bouquet of flowers. They'd go out here and there over the next few months and enjoy each other's company.

After four years of this on-again, off-again courtship, my mother discovered that she was pregnant. When she told him the news, he wasn't thrilled.

His reaction wasn't a shock to my mother.

She was aware that he already had a wife and two kids of his own, living in nearby Passaic, New Jersey.

He told her from the outset that with another family that he was providing for, he wasn't sure how large of a role he'd be able to play in this new child's life. Things got rocky. When she told him she was keeping her baby, he turned his back on the situation completely. On November 11, 1986, Victor Cruz—all nine pounds, three ounces of him—was born at Barnert Hospital in Paterson.

My mother was fortunate to have her mother and stepfather around, and the three of them are responsible for raising me.

As a little kid, I don't remember ever asking who my father was or feeling bad about not having him around. None of my friends on the block really had fathers, either. That's just the way it was. We all had strong single mothers who cared, loved, and provided for us. Maybe it was because I was so young or maybe it was because I was just loving life so much at the time, but there were no sleepless nights over having no dad in my life, no questions on Father's Day as to what had happened to mine.

Then, in 1993, he showed up. I'll never know exactly why, but something inside him, seven years after the fact, spurred him to take responsibility for his actions and become a part of his son's life.

I initially resisted. My life was good, and I remember thinking, Who does this guy think he is?

But that didn't last too long. It was cool having a dad.

I never resented him. I'm sure my mother could have used his help, and I know the pain he must have caused her when he turned his back on her, but I also know he wasn't proud of the way he handled the situation. He was ashamed. It takes a real man to recognize his wrongs and try to make good later on in life.

My mother and father never got back together, but they were always amicable. He lived one town over in Passaic and made a point to come around often. Dad had two other children—Ebony and Malik—and he brought me into their lives. He'd refer to Malik as my brother and Ebony as my sister, and they never denied me their affection. Though we didn't have the same mothers, the three of us were family right from the start.

My dad wanted to have a role in my life; he wanted to love me as a son. My mother could have denied him that opportunity, but she didn't. My mom's an incredible woman, and of all her great virtues, the fact that she was able to embrace Mike Walker entering my life at seven years old is one of the things I'm most thankful for. If it took a courageous man to knock on that door and say he wanted to meet me seven years after turning his back on my existence, it took an even stronger woman to say yes and grant him that honor.

IT WAS COOL HAVING A DAD. I NEVER RESENTED HIM.

Dad would come by three or four times a week and we gradually developed a real father-and-son relationship. He'd always be around and even came along with us to Canada for one of the international tae kwon do competitions. I was in awe of his career as a firefighter and of the courage that required him to do his job. I'd get scared when I'd hear the fire truck sirens at night, imagining the very worst and thinking that he'd be forced into a dangerous situation. When I'd see him the next day, I'd always be relieved that he was okay. He took interest in my studies, made sure I was staying out of trouble, and introduced me to a new sport.

When I was about ten years old, he plopped me in front of the television set and told me to watch something I'd never really seen before. It was an NFL game and the San Francisco 49ers were playing the Detroit Lions. Football was a little tricky to follow at first, but I remember the cameras always focusing on one guy—number 80 in white and red. His name was Jerry Rice.

Despite not knowing the rules of the game, I could tell that this guy must have been very special because he was the only player any of the announcers were talking about. Catch after catch, he'd make these great moves and have this look of determination in his eyes. I've since gone back and looked up the box score of that game, and it turns out that Rice did, in fact, have a monster night against the Lions. On September 25, 1995, he caught eleven passes for 181 yards.

Giants Stadium was just fifteen miles away from Paterson, but I had no allegiance to either the Giants or the Jets growing up. I never went to a game there as a kid; it wasn't even really an option. And though Jerry Rice was the first player to really catch my eye, I quickly became a fan of the 49ers' and the Giants' shared rivals—the Dallas Cowboys.

If playing the flute is my darkest secret from childhood, the fact that I was a die-hard Cowboys fan growing up is probably a close second.

Those mid-1990s Cowboys teams had it all. I loved everything about them. The big personalities, the cheerleaders, the winning tradition—it all really resonated with me. Michael Irvin, a wide receiver nicknamed "The Playmaker," would make tremendous one-handed grabs that I'd mimic when playing touch football in the street with friends. His teammate, Emmitt Smith, was the ultimate running back. My father would tell me to watch how Smith used his blockers and handled himself on the field. You never saw Emmitt Smith lose his cool or turn the ball over. I'd get anxious and ask my dad, "Why does he run it up the middle all the time? Why doesn't he just run to the outside away from all the defenders?" My father would explain the importance of the offensive line and how just because a running back had the ball in his hands, it was an eleven-man effort.

And then there was Deion.

Oh, man.

Deion Sanders was something else! More than being the best cornerback and punt return man in the game, Deion had personality and a unique style. He was a true showman. He had flash and jumped out of the TV screen. He wore these great bandannas and would do this signature high step move every time he had the ball in the open field. When it came to football, most of the players in the NFL were unrecognizable. Hidden by helmets with thick face masks, it was difficult to tell one player from the next. But everyone knew Deion. There was no mistaking him for anyone else on the field.

That 1995 Dallas Cowboys team was the first NFL squad I followed on a weekly basis. Fortunately, they were on national TV all the time. They went 12-4, breezed through the NFC playoffs, and beat the Pittsburgh Steelers in the Super Bowl. I remember watching that game and cheering so hard for "America's Team." Even at that age, the Super Bowl felt like a monumental event. On the grandest of stages, the Cowboys took care of business. My mother bought me a Deion Sanders number 21 jersey, the one with the stars on the shoulders, and I wore that thing *every day*. My father's daughter, Ebony, was six years older than me. For my birthday that year, she bought me a children's book about a little boy who aspired to someday play in the NFL. It had my name in it, and drawings of a boy overcoming all sorts of obstacles to make it to the big leagues. I loved that book and read it every night. I still have it today.

Two years after I'd watched my first football game on TV, my father came to the door one afternoon and asked me if I wanted to actually *play* football. I'd been "playing" football in the street with my friends for the past few years, but this was entirely different. This would be real, full-impact, tackle football on a team.

My mother wasn't so keen on me playing because of the physicality of the sport, but she left it up to me. When my father asked, "Are you going to play on the PAL North Firefighters or what?" I looked at her for guidance. She just shrugged and told me, "You're a big boy. It's up to you."

I'd be suiting up for the PAL North Firefighters a couple of weeks later. One of my teammates was Malik, my father's other son. Dad couldn't have been happier.

My father's life was finally coming together and falling into place.

FINDING
STABILITY

MY MOTHER WOULD later tell me that one of the reasons she even allowed me to play football was that it would keep me occupied five days a week after school.

I rep Paterson with a tremendous amount of pride, but it's not all roses and rainbows. As a kid, it's pretty easy to fall into the wrong crowds if you don't make an active effort not to.

When I was eleven years old, I missed the bus one day and had to walk home from School 21. It's a short, three-block walk from the school to my *abuela*'s house, and my mother told me to walk straight down Madison Avenue to East Twentieth Street. For whatever reason, I took a left down Broadway, instead.

I'd been told throughout my childhood not to walk down Broadway alone. Broadway was once a bustling street with department stores and popular restaurants, but by the late nineties, it had become dangerous. Broadway was always off-limits, but in this instance, I just thought it'd make for the quicker route. Once I started walking, I realized I'd made a mistake. There were older men lining the streets and an overall feeling of hopelessness. I was scared, but I kept on walking, thinking I'd be home soon enough.

Out of the darkness and off one of the stoops came a man who grabbed me by the collar of my shirt. He was older and stank of cheap liquor. I initially panicked, but he told me to calm down and that it was okay. "Chill out, little man. It's all good. Where are you headed?"

I told him I was going to my grandmother's house and that I was lost, thinking he'd be able to help me find my way. I was young and naïve. He was drunk.

He mumbled something incoherently and handed me a half-smoked joint. I'd never gotten high before, let alone smelled marijuana. "Take a hit, little man. Breathe in, and then blow it out."

He was persistent and when I refused, he started to get aggressive. "You've got to take a hit or you're never getting home," he said, grabbing my collar with a tighter grasp than he had earlier.

It was a terrible situation. I had to think and act pretty quickly, and in one motion, I grabbed the joint, threw it to the ground, turned around, and ran back to Madison Avenue as fast as I could. I sprinted to a nearby pay phone. My mother was working in the customer service department at Benjamin Moore paints, and I had the 800 number memorized. She told me to only dial it in case of emergency, and I thought this situation was no doubt an emergency. When I got a hold of her, I was crying, and she had my grandfather come and get me and take me back to their home.

That moment was symbolic of life in Paterson as a whole. One bad turn—on a street, or in life—and you could enter a dark and dangerous world.

My grandfather always said, "If your life is stable, the rest will fall into place," but life in Paterson wasn't stable. You had to work hard to *make* it stable. If you didn't walk down the right streets, you were going to find trouble. Instead of playing with coloring books or watching cartoons, you could be smoking weed with ex-cons on the corner.

Danger was always lurking and fights were just a part of everyday life. I don't think there was a day that went by in elementary and middle school when there wasn't a fistfight or a brawl of some sort during recess or lunch.

I was no angel. I remember one boy had a pass to wear his hat all day in school because he had gotten a terrible haircut the day before. The second we got out of first period, I went right up to him and ripped that hat off his head. His haircut really was awful. I wasn't a bully or anything, but I liked to entertain the other kids in school. I was always in pursuit of the next joke. And because I liked to entertain, I'd get into scrapes with the "subjects" of my attempts at comedy. I got in a fight with that boy, and if I recall, I think he won that one. (Rightly so.)

DANGER WAS ALWAYS LURKING AND FIGHTS WERE JUST A PART OF EVERYDAY LIFE.

Another time, there was a kid a few years older who took it upon himself to take my seat in homeroom. He was twice my size, but I wasn't just about to let some goon steal my chair. The right thing to do, of course, would have been telling the teacher, having her remove him, and going on with the rest of my day. But if I had snitched on him, I would have heard about it the rest of the week. So I took a different route in handling the situation. When he got up for the Pledge of Allegiance, I snuck up behind him and moved his chair five feet to the left. When he went to sit down, he fell flat on his butt. The entire class was in hysterics, but he didn't find it too funny. He got mad and wanted to fight me after school. I'm pretty sure we did.

Those fights were basically just kids being kids, but some weren't. Some were actually very real. One time, my friends and I were playing pickup basketball at Montgomery Park on Rosa Parks Boulevard. Five on five. I was never a big talker on the court, as I tried to let my game speak for itself. But my boy Pelli was a different story. He was the rapper in our crew of friends and he was always running his mouth, talking trash. We were going up against five Dominican kids, and I was just lighting it up. I couldn't miss a shot. After every basket our team scored, Pelli would get in the face of the kid covering me and taunt him. He was spewing all sorts of trash talk, "You can't hold my boy! You're terrible! We're eating you alive!" It started out as nothing much, but then it began to get serious. The boy got more and more physical with me on defense, and whenever Pelli would start shouting in his face, he'd answer with a shove or a stare.

After we beat them in a game to 21, the kid who was covering me came up to Pelli and told us to meet him in the parking lot.

Pelli and I shrugged it off. We figured whatever happened on the court stayed on the court. We were just having fun, and though Pelli probably took the trash talk too far, we weren't looking for any trouble.

But the kid wouldn't let it go.

After the game, my mom was supposed to pick us up in her van. When we got to the parking lot, though, the kid was waiting for us. Only, he wasn't alone. Twenty of his friends were there with him. Some were our age, but others were well into their teens. They all wore matching bandannas and some had baseball bats and bottles in their hands.

Pelli and I looked at each other. I remember asking him, "Pelli, what the hell's about to go down here?"

And Pelli, always the talker, looked back at me and said, "Vic, shit's about to go down."

I was, like, "Vic?! You were the one talking all that smack, not me!" But Pelli was my boy, and if "shit" was about to go down, I wasn't letting him go at it alone.

We both took our backpacks and jackets off and put up our fists. The first wave of kids came at us and we threw punches, doing our best to stay on our feet. It was six on one for both of us and we took our licks. When we escaped the first wave, we both tried bolting from the scene. We started running as fast as we could down the block, and they were throwing bottles at us and swinging wild punches. I was scared to death but knew I could outrun any of them. As I was running, though, I noticed one kid getting closer to me. I slowed down and, without even thinking about it, broke out a move that The Sir must have taught me. I leaped and spun in the air, simultaneously punching the boy square in the nose.

I'd never punched another person in the face like that. There was blood everywhere. The boy, probably two or three years older than me, let out this giant cry and screamed, "You broke my nose!"

I kept running but remembered that I had left my new North Face jacket behind in the parking lot. I was devastated, because I loved that North Face jacket. I knew how hard my mother had worked to buy me it, and to lose it over a silly fight was terribly irresponsible. I'd be grounded and have to explain to my mother the reason why her

> **I'D NEVER PUNCHED ANOTHER PERSON IN THE FACE LIKE THAT.**

hard-earned money had been wasted. At that instant, her blue minivan came flying by. Pelli was already inside the car and he swung the door open. I hopped in, out of breath, and looked at him. His face was all bruised up and he was bleeding. He'd gotten beaten up pretty badly. But he had my jacket in his hands. Pelli!

A week later, I was downtown walking up Market Street, and of course, I saw the kid I punched in the nose posting up on the corner. He had a huge white bandage on his face. I really had broken his nose. I tried keeping my head down, but he recognized me right away. "Yo, man, what are you doing on this block? You shouldn't be on this block. This is our block. I don't wanna see you around here ever again," he said as he got in my face.

I told him I was just trying to get home and didn't want any trouble. He stared me down for a bit, then let me go home safely without an altercation. I'd soon learn that those Dominican boys with the custom-made bandannas were in a gang known as the Market Street Dominicans, or "MSD" for short. They were one of several different gangs in town. That incident occurred when I was in eighth grade, but I avoided walking up Market Street alone for the next several years.

There were certain streets you just didn't walk in Paterson.

There was no blueprint on which ones those were, no guidebook. You learned from living.

MY MOTHER AND I moved out of my *abuela* and *Papí*'s apartment on East Twentieth street after my sister Andrea was born. Our new spot, on the corner of East Eighteenth Street, was slightly bigger than our old digs. I still had my own room, but we also had a front yard that I could play in and a big basement downstairs.

The washer and dryer unit was in the corner of the basement and there was a clothesline off to the side, but the entire middle was wide open. My friends would come over for sleepovers and we'd play hide-and-seek and capture the flag. There was wood paneling that lined the basement ceiling about nine feet off the floor and I'd spend endless hours pretending that I was Michael Jordan, Penny Hardaway, or J. R. Rider, slam-dunking a miniature NERF basketball off those panels. Eventually, the panels were completely chipped off and had to be replaced. Too many dunks from "Air Victor," I suppose.

Being a big brother took some getting adjusting to at first. I was always my mother's little angel, her one and only, and when Andrea was born—that all changed. I no longer was the most adorable kid in the family. I'd be off to the corner, doing a crazy back flip or showing off my latest tae kwon do moves, and Mom would be busy with Andrea, pinching her cheeks or fussing over something cute she said. It was all good, though, and after I saw how much my little sister looked up to me, I enjoyed having her around.

The basement, the front lawn, and the new addition to our family in the next room over were all the positive parts of living on East Eighteenth.

The negative was the street itself. Though just two streets over from my *abuela* and *Papí*'s place, East Eighteenth was a significantly more dangerous part of town. It was also much lonelier.

On East Twentieth, all of my friends lived in the houses next door. I was on the third story of our place, number 44, and my friend Franky lived ten feet away in number 42. Alex and Danny, two brothers, lived in 40. Domingo, a Puerto Rican boy we always just called 'Mingo, lived in 36. The Parkers—Corey, Justin, and Derrick—were in 34. We were all boys and within three or four years of each other. Birthday parties, holidays, Communions— we'd always celebrate them together. Those guys all knew about *Papi*'s missing finger and each one of us could rattle off all of 'Mingo's mother's favorite afternoon telenovelas. We were more than just neighbors and friends. All those guys were family.

We lived on a one-way street, so we played outside all the time without cars ever really bothering us. There was a peach tree next to the Parkers' place and we'd throw peaches as far as we could down the street. Sometimes we'd throw them at cars. We were this large, mischievous pack of boys and we did everything as one.

There was an old run-down house at the end of East Twentieth that we all said was haunted. The windows were boarded up and you could smell it from the street. I'll never forget that stench; it was like a rotting corpse. Rancid.

None of us ever dared step foot in that house.

One year on Halloween, though, we all agreed that we'd walk through the front door and into the haunted house together. It was our rite of passage, the night the boys of East Twentieth Street would all become men.

Alex was first and there was a line of us about six deep behind him. We'd talked about doing this for two months, each one of us reassuring the others that we wouldn't chicken out when Judgment Day arrived. When the moment of truth finally came, Alex took one step inside the house.

Silence.

We waited two or three seconds, but it felt like hours.

Then, with the shrillest scream you could ever imagine, he let out a primal noise, "Ghost! I see a ghost!"

We all screamed!

Alex lost it and ran out the front door faster than any of us had ever seen him run before. We followed him, tripping all over each other, laughing and shouting at the same time. We rolled over in laughter in the middle of the street. Maybe we weren't ready to be the "men" of East Twentieth Street just yet. To this day, the haunted house is still there at the end of East Twentieth Street. To this day, none of us have ever walked in.

I loved living on East Twentieth Street.

Living on East Eighteenth was very different.

Our new house was on one of the busiest corners in Paterson and there was always noise. Sometimes the noise was great. The guys on the corner blasting the latest Biggie or Jay-Z song from their boom boxes before the album even dropped was cool. I'd always be the first to hear the newest beats. The sound of the ice cream man's truck on a hot summer day always brought a smile to my face, too.

But the noise of gunshots didn't.

And on many nights living at 498 East Eighteenth, I'd be in my bedroom, trying my hardest to get to sleep, and I'd hear that sound of gunshots right outside my door. Sometimes they were far off in the distance, a few streets away. Other times they were much closer. Once I was playing video games alone when I heard gunshots so loud that they felt like they were going off right inside my house.

They weren't, but that fear of seeing something horrible—or God forbid, having something horrible happen to Andrea, my mother, or me—was always present. Without *Papi* or my father living with us, I was the man of the house. For a young kid in Paterson, that's an incredible burden to carry.

Sirens, shouting, and the occasional *wap-wap-wap!* of a Glock going off replaced the soothing sounds of José Feliciano's Spanish guitar from our place on East Twentieth.

A FEW YEARS after we moved, I got to see the homeland of José Feliciano and the extended Cruz family when we took a vacation to Puerto Rico. After a few days in Old San Juan, we took a trip to Arecibo, the small Puerto Rican town that my *abuela* grew up in. It was an incredible experience for all of us, and I was finally able to place faces to the names of family members I'd heard about my entire life. We stayed with my uncle Victor, my mother's sister's husband, at his place in Aguadilla. It was beautiful.

We'd be sitting having lunch on his porch and little wild horses would be running below us on the sand. I'd been to the Jersey Shore a few times as a little kid, but the beaches in Jersey don't hold a candle to the ones in Puerto Rico.

Every morning, we were woken up at six o'clock.

Not by an alarm clock, but by roosters. No lie, *roosters.*

"Cock-a-Doodle-Doo!" I thought they only made that noise in the cartoons, but it was real. And you didn't just roll over and ignore a rooster. Once they got started at six a.m., you were up for the rest of the day. No pillow in the world could block out that noise.

I learned a lot about my Puerto Rican heritage on that trip.

My *abuela* was always cooking the most amazing arroz con pollo and empanadas in her kitchen, and the sounds of the Spanish guitar, the merengue, and the salsa were the soundtrack of my youth. But until I actually went to Puerto Rico and saw its beauty with my very own eyes, I didn't feel truly connected to the native land of my mother and my *abuela.*

I LEARNED A LOT ABOUT MY PUERTO RICAN HERITAGE ON THAT TRIP.

There were very few Puerto Ricans in the NBA or the NFL when I was little. I always noticed that. You never saw players with Hispanic last names dunking basketballs or hauling in touchdown passes. I wanted to change that someday.

I didn't know what sport I'd end up playing, but I couldn't wait to have a team's name on the front of my jersey and the word *Cruz* written on the back.

A FIREFIGHTER'S SON

READ A BOOK about Larry Bird, the great Boston Celtics forward, when I was in seventh or eighth grade. Bird grew up in a small town in Indiana called French Lick. I always loved the name of that town—French Lick. He was something of a basketball prodigy, and though Bird didn't quite make it at the University of Indiana playing for Bobby Knight, he ended up taking a tiny school called Indiana State to the finals of the 1979 NCAA Tournament. Larry Bird was the pride of French Lick, Indiana. There was a picture in that book of a giant green sign, shaped like a basketball, on a main road in French Lick that read Larry Bird Blvd. He had a street named after him.

Tim Thomas was Paterson's version of Larry Bird. There were hundreds of great athletes that came from Paterson, but for one reason or another, none of them seemed to ever make it. You'd hear about a football star who was recruited by a Big 10 school, only to fall into the wrong crowd or break a leg and not make it to the pros. There'd be basketball players from the early nineties that we'd hear about at the park, "This guy was the best. He could dunk two balls at once from the free throw line," but there'd always be a "but" attached to the end of the statement. "But he ended up getting shot" or "But he ended up in jail." There was no "but" attached to Tim Thomas's name.

He was the rare big man who played like a guard, a Magic Johnson–type for our generation. In 1995, his senior year at Paterson Catholic, he averaged twenty-five points and fifteen rebounds per game and was a national superstar. Everyone in Paterson knew about Tim Thomas. Everyone in Paterson *loved* Tim Thomas.

My father once took my brother, Malik, and me to see him play in high school, and it was unlike anything I'd ever witnessed before. There were fans sitting on top of each other in the bleachers. Little kids, even younger than me, had homemade signs made up with Tim Thomas's face on them. Adults, guys my father was friends with, would just go on and on about him. He was a seventeen-year-old kid and he was the most popular athlete in all of New Jersey, let alone Paterson.

Thomas was the rare athlete from our city to not screw up and blow it. He had the world at his fingertips and he *didn't* piss it away. There were no criminal charges, no unfortunate incidents, and no devastating injuries. He was a McDonald's All-American, the ultimate honor for a high school basketball player, and got recruited by just about every big school in the country. When he chose to go to Villanova in Philadelphia, we all became Villanova fans overnight. The entire town went out and bought Villanova Wildcats T-shirts and supported that team. And when he was drafted by the New Jersey Nets and traded to the Philadelphia 76ers in the 1997 NBA Draft, the Philadelphia 76ers became the unofficial NBA team of Paterson, New Jersey.

He was smooth in the NBA, a six-ten big man who passed the rock and shot the three. He played fourteen seasons in the pros, bouncing around from city to city, always starting or coming off the bench for good squads. Tim Thomas made it. In a town where so many guys didn't, Tim Thomas defied the odds. My father would tell me, "Keep it up. Keep studying, keep playing, and keep surrounding yourself with the right people. You can make it. Just look at Tim Thomas."

Thomas's high school coach at Paterson Catholic was a man named Jim Salmon. My father and Mr. Salmon were very friendly. Working for the city as a firefighter and involved in all of the town's Little Leagues and sports programs, my dad was one of those guys who everybody just kind of knew. He always had a connection or a hookup of some sort. If I needed something—any-thing—I'd ask my dad and there'd be some guy from Paterson, or the next town over, available. A lawyer, a tutor, a recommenda-tion letter—my father always "knew a guy."

Dad introduced me to Jim Salmon at a young age, and he took a liking to me. I played basketball the right way. Though I could shoot well and jump high, I always got a thrill out of bringing the ball up the court, making the right pass, and doing the little things that helped my teams win. I'd be the kid taking offen-sive charges in pickup basketball games—where fouls are never called—for the sake of taking a charge. I was always diving for loose balls, scraping my knees, and fighting to give my teams another possession.

As a point guard, I always had the ball in my hands, dictating the tempo of the game. I got more of a kick out of making the right pass that led to the game-winning bucket than being the guy scoring it. For the most part, my basketball education was learned on the street, playing pickup at the park, and on TV, watching my heroes. I'd go into my basement on East Eighteenth with my Spalding basketball and just practice moves for hours at a time down there. Penny Hardaway had a no-look pass in Game One of the 1995 NBA Finals that I'd mimic, by myself, facial expressions and all. Tim Hardaway, no relation to Penny, had a move called "The Killer Crossover"—a quick crossover dribble at the top of the key—that I mastered. I loved Michael Jordan, of course, but it was the point guards, the table setters, that I really admired. Penny Hardaway, Tim Hardaway, Kenny Anderson, Isiah Thomas, and John Stockton—the guys who made the rest of their team-mates better—were the players I wanted to emulate on the court. I'd spend many afternoons at the park and at the Y, just playing pickup basketball. I didn't care how old or how big the other guys on the court were, I was going to be the point guard making things happen. I loved to compete and I loved to win.

Jim Salmon saw something in me and with some needling from my father, he asked if I wanted to play for his Amateur Athletic Union—also known as "AAU"—team. After Tim Thomas made it to the NBA, he and Mr. Salmon teamed up to start a traveling basketball team made up of the best kids from our area. Though Thomas didn't have much to do with the day-to-day operations of the squad during the season, his influence would be all over everything we did. Our team's name? The Tim Thomas Playaz.

Every kid in Paterson wanted to be on the Playaz. Every kid in the *state of New Jersey* wanted to be on the Playaz. I was one of the youngest guys on the squad but got some serious playing time. Jim Salmon would toss me the ball and have me play point guard with guys who were three or four years older than me. My job wasn't to score thirty points or stick my tongue out like I was Michael Jordan. My job was to put my teammates in the best positions possible for success.

Those Playaz teams were loaded with future college and NBA stars. I played with J. R. Smith, currently a shooting guard for the New York Knicks, and guys like Sean Singletary, Brandon Costner, Earl Clark, Gerald Henderson, and Wayne Ellington.

For me, a kid from the streets of Paterson, being able to wear the name Tim Thomas on my jersey was the ultimate thrill. Jim Salmon had a garage full of great Tim Thomas Playaz shirts, jerseys, and shoes. I'd always be in that garage, checking out the latest jersey designs or sneakers. Sometimes, when Jim wasn't looking, I'd take an extra T-shirt or headband. The older guys on the team would tease me because I was always over at Jim's place, helping him organize the garage or giving him a hand with some odd task or household chore. But that was by design. My mother and father knew that, just like when I was at the Y or with The Sir in his dojo as a little kid, if I was at Jim's working or helping him out—I couldn't be on the street, getting into trouble. Jim Salmon always watched out for me. I wasn't the best basketball player in all of Paterson, but he took me under his wing like a young apprentice.

When I finished the eighth grade and graduated from School 21, I was supposed to attend Eastside High School. One of the two big public high schools in Paterson, Eastside was made famous by the 1989 movie *Lean on Me*. In that film, principal Joe Clark, played by Morgan Freeman, shapes up a violent, out-of-control student body and gets things in order. He uses radical methods of discipline, like locking the children into the classroom and dangling them over rooftops, but eventually Principal Clark gets Eastside back on track. At the end of the movie, the student body comes to love Joe Clark and they all pass the requirements on their final exams to keep Eastside from being overtaken by the state authorities.

It's a great film and a true story, but it's not like Eastside became some perfect school, free of violence, after that movie came out. It was located on Park Avenue, and Park Avenue was tough. On that street corner, right outside the school, there were always drug dealers and gang members posting up. The school was massive, too. There must have been twenty-five hundred kids at Eastside.

Though many of my friends were going there, my mother suggested I attend Passaic County Technical Institute, one town over, instead. Academically, Tech had a better reputation than Eastside, and athletically, they were far superior. Though it was never explicitly said, my mother also knew there was a lot less of a chance of me finding trouble at Tech. It certainly wasn't a country club, but there were no gangs hanging outside the school's front entrance, no violence in the hallways. To get in, I had to write a thousand-word essay on why I wanted to go there. I took a lot of pride in that essay, explaining how I could make a better life for myself with the courses offered at Tech. I was accepted and was on my way.

OUT OF THE BLUE

But when I first got there, it was overwhelming. My freshman year at Tech was the first time I was in a big school setting. Though it didn't have as many kids as Eastside, there were still three hundred students in each grade. The school was physically enormous, too. There were floors, floors, and more floors.

And I took advantage.

Instead of raising my hand or taking a leadership role in the classroom, I'd ask if I could use the bathroom. And then I'd go on walks. Like, really long walks. I'd just stroll the halls for ten minutes, twenty minutes, thirty minutes. I'd do laps around the school, like some wandering soul, popping my head into random classrooms and causing trouble. I was one of the twenty or thirty kids in the school to have a Motorola Talkabout. They're long extinct now, but at the time they were as hot as iPhones. If you had a Talkabout, you could talk to the other people who had Talkabouts, as if it were a walkie-talkie. So I'd press the button at all hours of the day and just ask, "Where you guys at?" And sure enough, fifteen or twenty kids would respond, and we'd all just decide to meet outside the cafeteria or the gym and hang out. We'd goof off all day long.

Academics just weren't a priority. I was doing well enough where no eyebrows were raised, but I wasn't learning anything. I'd get Bs and Cs, and my mother would say, "You should be doing better than this, Victor," and I'd just shrug it off. "Bs and Cs are fine," I'd tell her, completely satisfied with mediocrity. I figured if I wasn't failing out of school, I was in the clear. But that was the wrong attitude, and it'd be that same attitude that'd end up costing me later in life.

Athletically, things were great, as they always seemed to be. I played on the freshman football team and had a good season. It was the first year Tech had a freshman football squad and we only played four games. I enjoyed it, but basketball was my true love, and that's where I excelled.

Tech wasn't a traditional basketball powerhouse, but there were a pair of kids a year older than me who brought the school's hoops program some national recognition. Darryl Watkins was seven feet tall when he was thirteen years old. By the time he was a sophomore in high school, he was considered one of the top thirty high school basketball players in the entire country. His nickname was "Mookie" and he was unstoppable in the paint. One of Mookie's best friends on the varsity team was a boy named Colin Bailey. Colin wasn't quite the dominant player that Mookie was, but he had a silky-smooth jump shot and could run the court. Though I started the season on the junior varsity team, I befriended both Mookie and Colin and we had a real chemistry on the court during practice. We were the future of the basketball program at Tech. I'd play point guard, Colin would play forward, and Mookie would be the center. The varsity coach, a nice man named Ron Austin, would tell me to just bide my time on the JV for a season, and the next three years, I'd be the man bringing up the ball for the varsity team.

Paterson Catholic and Tech were archrivals. They were Giants-Eagles before I even knew what Giants-Eagles meant. Paterson Catholic, because it was a private school and was known for sending Tim Thomas to Villanova and the pros, was considered a powerhouse in New Jersey sports. But Tech, a public vocational high school, had the better team and the brighter future. That season, we traveled to Paterson Catholic's gym to play them in a highly anticipated battle. The JV games were always before the varsity ones, and when our game got started, there was already a gym packed full of fans.

It was the first time I'd played in front of a large crowd and I thrived on the energy in the gym. They weren't there to see me—they were there to watch Mookie and Colin go at it versus Paterson Catholic—but I did my best to make them notice the kid excelling in the JV game.

Sometimes on the basketball court or on the football field, you enter this place called "The Zone." You're not supposed to acknowledge when you're in "The Zone," but when you are, you simply cannot be stopped. That day, I was in "The Zone." I scored twenty-seven points, had ten assists, and we upset Paterson Catholic. It was just the JV game, but there were a lot of important basketball people in the crowd. College scouts were there to watch Mookie and Colin, but so was Tommy Patterson, the head coach of Paterson Catholic at the time. After the game, he patted me on the head and said he was very impressed with the way I played the point guard position. As I was leaving Paterson Catholic that night, I walked by the trophy cases in the hallway. There were pictures of Tim Thomas and his teammates, giant state and county championship trophies, and decades of history and rich tradition encased on glass shelves.

I'd later feel the same way walking around the Giants' facilities, staring at framed photos of Bill Parcells and images of Frank Gifford, Phil Simms, and Michael Strahan.

SOMETIMES ON THE BASKETBALL COURT OR ON THE FOOTBALL FIELD, YOU ENTER THIS PLACE CALLED "THE ZONE."

Mookie, Colin, and the rest of the varsity guys got the best of Paterson Catholic's varsity team that evening. After the final buzzer, we all piled on to the bus in our uniforms, cheering like we'd just won a national championship. It was a great day for Tech, but I left that gym knowing I wanted to someday be a part of the Paterson Catholic tradition.

I finished the season averaging twenty points per game for the JV team and suited up for the varsity squad in a few games down the stretch. But just as things were going great on the court, they started to get worse in the classroom. I'd be up all night, shooting hoops or on the phone with friends, and I'd forget to study or do my homework. Those Bs and Cs were becoming Cs and Ds and my behavior in the classroom wasn't much better. I was always rather respectful to my teachers as a kid, but at Tech I started slacking off. I was still the same entertainer I was in the fourth grade, but I didn't have a flute or an A+ on a book report to bail me out. I spent countless afternoons in detention, writing on a chalkboard until six p.m. I was screwing up and my mother and father knew it.

That's when Jim Salmon stepped in.

I got home from school one day in late February of 2001 and Jim was seated on the living room couch with my mother and father. I don't remember Jim ever being in my house prior to that moment. Something was up. As I think back on it now, it must have looked like a scene right out of that *Intervention* show on A&E. My mother and father had let Jim know how much I was struggling in school and they were all concerned that I was starting to develop the same tendencies that had sidetracked so many promising athletes from Paterson in the past. I was cocky, girls were starting to notice me, and people I'd never even met—adults—were telling me how good I was at basketball. It was all starting to go to my head, and as a result, my effort in the classroom had hit rock bottom. Who am I kidding? There was no effort at all.

"I'm taking you on a trip. Just the two of us," Jim said with a stern voice. Where were we going? I had no idea.

"Pack a bag for two days and two nights, and grab a snack for the road. We're taking a flight," he said as my parents nodded in agreement. There was this awkward moment where I kind of looked to them for refuge, for a clue as to what was going on. They stared right back at me. Jim then said, "Now."

Now?

So I packed a duffel bag and hopped in Jim's car. When we got on the road, I started to ask him a million questions. He told me to just relax.

At the airport, I was handed a plane ticket. Destination: Raleigh, North Carolina.

Raleigh, North Carolina? Where the hell was Raleigh, North Carolina?

"You're coming with me on a trip that could change your life. I want to introduce you to some people and show you some things."

A life-changing trip, huh? I buckled my seat belt on the plane and imagined the very worst.

When we landed, we rented a car and drove from the airport in Raleigh to a town called Durham. It was the last week in February, but the weather was perfect. And everything was so . . . green. There was green grass, green trees, and green ivy on all the buildings. That car ride must have lasted thirty minutes, but it felt like I was going through some sort of time machine to a different world. Where was I? I felt like Dorothy, only I was telling Jim Salmon, my AAU basketball coach, that I didn't think we were in Paterson anymore.

We took a right turn on to a long, willowy road and saw beautiful buildings and students dressed in all blue.

"Welcome to Duke." Jim smiled.

Duke? Like Christian Laettner, Grant Hill, Coach K Duke? I was pinching myself. My whole life, Duke basketball was right up there on my Mount Rushmore of sports with the Dallas Cowboys, Chicago Bulls, and, well, Tim Thomas. And here I was, a fourteen-year-old kid from Paterson, New Jersey, driving through Duke's beautiful campus.

We pulled up to an apartment complex and out of one of the apartment's front doors came a familiar face I'd known from watching high school and college basketball games on the TV in my living room on East Eighteenth Street.

"Jim! What took you so long, man?" asked Dahntay Jones, a six-foot-six small forward from Trenton, New Jersey. Dahntay Jones had been a star in high school and was the best player on the Rutgers basketball team his first two years in college. He transferred to Duke at the end of his sophomore season. He was sitting the 2000–2001 season out, one of the NCAA's rules for transferring from one school to another.

"Dahntay, I want you to meet Victor Cruz. He's a young, up-and-coming point guard from Paterson," said Jim as he introduced me to a New Jersey sports legend. Jim had known Dahntay from Dahntay's AAU basketball days and was one of the positive male role models in *his* life.

"If this guy says you're good," Dahntay said, smiling as he put his arm around Jim's shoulder, "you must be pretty good."

That night, Coach Salmon, Dahntay, and I went to dinner at one of the fancier restaurants in Durham. I was pinching myself the entire time. Students and parents would come over and stop at the table to welcome Dahntay to Duke and tell him how excited they were for to have him to suit up next season for the Blue Devils. Dahntay would then introduce them to me! "This guy could be the next great Duke point guard, like Bobby Hurley or Jay Williams." It was surreal.

Midway through our dinner, another familiar-looking person came walking over and sat down at our table. "Jim Salmon, in the flesh! When I heard you were in town, I had to come by." This guy was unmistakable. It was North Carolina's star shooting guard, Joe Forte, the reigning ACC Men's Basketball Rookie of the Year. I never realized how close the University of North Carolina's campus in Chapel Hill was to Duke's in Durham, but they were just a short drive away. North Carolina State's campus, in Raleigh, was nearby, too. I was in basketball heaven.

At dinner that night, Dahntay and Joe spoke to me like big brothers. They told me how important it was for me to treat the classroom as seriously as I treated the basketball court. They were both enrolled at two of the finest universities in the country, but they didn't just show up and enroll in classes. They earned it.

"There were guys who were just as good as me during my freshman year of high school," said Forte, a high school hoops legend from the College Park, Maryland, area. "But a lot of those kids didn't make it. They ran into trouble or their grades kept them from making it to the next level. Don't be one of those guys."

Dahntay was a Jersey guy, like me, and took particular interest in my studies. "What are you doing after practice? Are you going home and studying? Or are you meeting up with your friends and screwing around? Get your schoolwork in order and the rest will follow, man. College coaches won't even look at you if you're flunking out of high school."

It was a sobering dinner, but one that I sorely needed. I was a point guard on the junior varsity team. I wasn't Darryl Watkins and I certainly wasn't Dahntay Jones or Joe Forte. Having those two guys—two college basketball legends—talk to me about algebra and social studies was invaluable.

The next day, Jim and I sat in the parents' section at Cameron Indoor Stadium. It was like the Paterson Catholic gym on steroids. What an incredible atmosphere. It wasn't as big as I'd imagined it would be, but it was twice as loud. The students had their faces painted blue and there were clever chants for every player on the visiting Virginia Cavaliers.

When the game started, I recognized another familiar face on the court. Donald Hand was Virginia's captain and a guy I'd seen play point guard on the Eastside Park courts most of my life. He was a Paterson Catholic graduate and starting for the Cavaliers. Jim pointed to Donald and said, "Everyone talks about Tim Thomas in Paterson, but I'm almost just as proud of Donald's accomplishments. He's going to graduate from the University of Virginia with a degree in anthropology."

Duke blew out Virginia that night, and I remember making eye contact with Dahntay Jones at one point toward the end of the game. He had this huge smile on his face. He, like me, was a kid from a tough part of New Jersey. And here he was, just a few years out of high school, playing at Duke.

After the game, Donald Hand came running over to give Jim a huge hug. He'd known Coach Salmon his entire life. Hand wasn't quite the same type of national star as Jones or Forte—no one had any posters of Donald Hand hanging in their bedrooms—but he was one of the most respected point guards in all of college basketball. He was smart, tough, and selfless. Jim told Donald that I was a young player from Paterson and Hand looked me right in the eye. He got very serious and said, "Always be proud of where you came from. Paterson sticks together. Always be sure to represent Paterson with class and dignity. You're next in line, man. Do Paterson proud."

It was all such an incredible experience. The smile couldn't be wiped off my face for weeks. My friends, some of whom were already getting involved with gangs and drugs at Eastside High, couldn't believe me when I told them about my weekend.

But the basketball wasn't what stuck with me. The life lessons were. Donald Hand, Joe Forte, and Dahntay Jones weren't lucky. They weren't blessed with superhuman skills and hadn't just dropped on to three of the more prestigious college campuses in America. They worked hard to get where they were, both on the basketball court and off. Donald Hand grew up in the same neighborhood that I did and ended up with a degree from Virginia. Sure, Tim Thomas was in Milwaukee playing with Ray Allen and Glenn Robinson on the Bucks. But Donald Hand was graduating from one of the best schools in the country that spring. These things were all possible. I was seeing it with my very own eyes.

The trip to North Carolina motivated me to get my act together. In the last two quarters of my freshman year, I got all As and Bs.

I also started to look into transferring to Paterson Catholic.

■ ■ ■

AFTER MY FRESHMAN season, Mookie, Colin, and I started talking about our futures at Tech. They were both big-time high school basketball stars at the time, but I was just a part-time role player. They told me that they'd been thinking long and hard about it and though they liked Tech, they wanted to transfer to Paterson Catholic.

It was a tricky situation.

There was a lot of excitement at Tech about the basketball program after that 2000–2001 season. For the first time since I was old enough to follow it, Tech actually had a better squad than Paterson Catholic. If all three of us left, we'd cripple the team. We'd be called traitors. We'd be downright hated at Tech.

I'd made some friends at school, but I had always wanted to play for the Paterson Catholic Cougars. I'd wanted to go where Tim Thomas went as a little kid, and now, having met him during my weekend in Durham, I really wanted to go where Donald Hand went. I craved that sense of tradition and I wanted to write my own chapter in Paterson Catholic history.

More important, PC suited me in the classroom better than Tech. The classes at Tech were enormous and there wasn't much keeping me from roaming the halls all day. At Paterson Catholic, it was much smaller and every student was accounted for. When Darryl and Colin said they were considering the move, I said I was in. After my mother agreed (and came up with the money to pay for private school), it was a done deal. I was going to be a Paterson Catholic Cougar.

But it wasn't that easy.

If it were just me—five-foot-eight Victor Cruz, the point guard on the Passaic County Technical Institute's junior varsity basketball squad—transferring from Tech to Paterson Catholic, nobody would have blinked an eye. But Darryl Watkins was a seven-foot basketball prodigy. Colin Bailey had college scouts watching his every game. When all three of us filed our transfer forms at the same time, a maelstrom of controversy erupted.

The New Jersey State Interscholastic Athletic Association, a nonprofit organization sanctioned by the state to oversee high school athletics, cried foul. In what came as a major surprise to all three of us and our families, the NJSIAA blocked and denied our transfer requests, ruling Darryl, Colin, and me ineligible for the upcoming basketball season. Why? They said it was because our transfers were illegitimate and that we were only going to Paterson Catholic for "athletic reasons."

So we took the organization to court.

The three of us each hired our own lawyers and on a balmy day in late August 2001, I made the trip to the Bergen County Courthouse in nearby Hackensack. The whole thing was crazy.

Because of how high profile an athlete Darryl was, there was media coverage in all the newspapers for weeks leading up to each of our days in court. I'd be hanging out at the Y, minding my own business, and kids I'd never met before would say, "You're Victor Cruz, right? You're in the papers, man."

My dad found me a lawyer through a friend of his—he always knew someone—and I put on my best slacks, a button-down, and a blazer. I'd never been in a courtroom before. The ones in the movies were far more glamorous.

I didn't expect to actually have to speak, but at some point in the middle of the proceedings, the judge pointed to me and asked, "Victor Cruz, why do you want to attend Paterson Catholic?"

I had never been so nervous in my life. I told the judge the truth and in my pubescent, cracking voice, said something along the lines of "The classroom environment suits me far better at Paterson Catholic than at Tech. I also am a good Catholic. I go to church every Sunday morning and I am interested in learning more about my faith. I want to attend Paterson Catholic and I always have since I was a very little boy, sir."

The judge nodded in approval and I looked behind me to my mother and father. They were in the courtroom and both gave me a thumbs-up.

The NJSIAA ruled with an iron fist and their decisions were rarely ever challenged. But Darryl, Colin, and I felt as though we had strong cases. It turns out we did. The judge only needed a few hours, and at the end of the proceedings, declared that association's rules were "vague and ambiguous" and its penalties "arbitrary, capricious, and unreasonable." Mookie, Colin, and I were going to be Paterson Catholic Cougars after all.

It was a strange few weeks and it was a great relief when the judge ultimately sided with us, but I remember asking my father why a group of adults would care *so* much about which high school my two friends and I went to. "Nothing's ever going to be handed to you, son," he said.

The irony of the whole situation was that the grown men at the NJSIAA and Tech didn't care about the kind of educations that Mookie, Colin, and I were receiving. *They* were the ones who were only concerned with basketball. If Darryl wasn't seven feet tall and Colin didn't average thirteen points per game, those old men in the suits wouldn't have cared about where we studied biology and chemistry. We were just basketball players to them, not students. Cogs in a system. "Nothing will ever be handed to you, son." I'd remind myself of that statement numerous more times throughout my life.

Once everything was cleared and official, life was good. I was fifteen, I was going to the same school that Tim Thomas and Donald Hand once attended, and I was excited to enter the next stage of my life.

Because of the court case, I missed summer practices for the football team. I'd wanted to play on the squad, but it'd have to wait another year. Who needed football, though? I was looking forward to becoming the next great point guard at Paterson Catholic.

That first week of my sophomore year was pure bliss. I was the new kid in school, and by that time, I was beginning to fill into my body a bit. I wasn't the same awkward Victor Cruz who wore glasses and extra-baggy Enyce jeans in the seventh grade. I felt good about myself and loved wearing that Paterson Catholic maroon sweater every day to school. I dove into my studies and actually found myself enjoying the subjects we were learning. With just twenty kids in each class, I felt like the

I WAS EXCITED TO ENTER THE NEXT STAGE OF MY LIFE.

teachers cared about us. The second week started off great, too, and I remember coming home from school that Monday, recording DJ Clue's *Monday Night Mixtape* session on Hot 97 FM that evening, and playing it on my Sony Walkman on the way to school the next morning.

At Paterson Catholic, every school day starts with homeroom. At eight a.m., you come in, you put your books in your locker, and you get settled in an assigned classroom. The homeroom teacher, who in my case was Father Murphy, takes attendance and you say the Pledge of Allegiance as a class. There's a TV in every classroom turned to channel 1, an educational station that only airs in schools. No one really ever paid attention to what was on channel 1, but sometimes you'd check it out and they'd be telling you about the latest current events in the Middle East or what the president was up to. That Tuesday morning, we were going through our normal homeroom routine when a few of the students noticed some weird images being shown on channel 1.

Father Murphy was unaware of what was going on, so he turned the volume up on the TV. Over and over again, we watched the same visuals on loop. Two planes had crashed into the World

Trade Center. I was convinced we were watching a sneak preview or a trailer to some new disaster movie, an *Armageddon*-like film that'd be coming out over the holidays. But the more we watched, the more it became evident that this was no fictional film.

New York City had been attacked by terrorists.

If you were to ask me about any other day of my sophomore year of high school, I couldn't tell you too many details. But I remember every minute of 9/11 as if it were yesterday.

Instead of everyone going to first period, Sister Gloria, the principal at Paterson Catholic, called everyone to the auditorium. She told us that there had been an attack on New York City and that we'd be having an early dismissal. She advised us to go directly home and to connect with our parents and loved ones as soon as we left the school grounds.

I was young, though, and when I tell you that New York City felt like it was a million miles away, I mean it. I'd been there just a handful of times in my life and it just didn't seem like what I saw on TV had any *real* impact on my life. So, what did I do on 9/11? I didn't go right home. I went and played basketball at the park with my friends.

We figured, "Well, it's New York City, not Paterson," and did what we did on every other half day. We played H.O.R.S.E for hours and basked in the bright September sun.

At around two p.m., I checked my cell phone, one of those old Verizon flip phones, and saw twenty-five missed calls from my mother.

Twenty-five.

I called her immediately and she was out of breath, simultaneously screaming and crying, "Victor, where have you been?"

I told her that I'd been at the park, just playing basketball, and asked why she was so upset.

When I got home, the gravity of the situation became a lot clearer. I watched the coverage on the television and saw the faces of those New Yorkers running in the clouds of smoke. I discovered that it wasn't just a freak accident on a random Tuesday in September, but, rather, a calculated attack on not only New York but Washington, D.C., too. Thousands of Americans went to work that Tuesday like they would have on any other day, only to never return to their families.

Many of those individuals were firefighters.

I thought of my father, a Paterson firefighter of more than two decades.

Then I thought of all of the children of all the innocent people killed in the attacks.

I got a hold of my father on the phone and he let me know that he was safe and sound, but that there were some good men and women lost that day. I didn't sleep that night, thinking about him, thinking about life, and thinking of that New York City skyline. The first fifteen years of my life, that skyline had been a symbol of invincibility. Things could be tough in Paterson, but there was always New York City. No one could touch that skyline and what it stood for.

But New York City wasn't invincible. Nothing was.

The next morning we were woken by the sound of a phone ringing before the sun came up. It was my father. My mother handed me the phone and he told me that he was heading down to Ground Zero. He explained that he felt it was his duty as a firefighter to volunteer and help those in need.

I was scared.

Was it safe? What if there was another attack? What if parts of the buildings fell on his head while he was volunteering his services down below? His other son, Malik, two years older than me and a high school senior at the time, came over to our house and sat with me the entire day. Malik was always a bit more sensitive than me and questioned why our father had to go.

"This is what Daddy wants to do," I told him. "He's been doing this his entire life. He wants to help. He'll be there for a few days and he'll come back soon. It'll be straight."

My father spent the next five days at Ground Zero, volunteering his services. He'd call home after each one of those days, but he'd never give us any details on what he saw.

In the years that followed, I would ask him about that week of his life, but he would never offer up much.

After 9/11, I had a new appreciation for my father and his life's work. He was an American hero. I always think of that iconic image of the firemen putting up the American flag amidst the rubble of Ground Zero, and I get goose bumps. My father was one of those brave men.

I also had a new sense of connection to New York City.

The entire country bonded together during that time, but New Jersey and New York got even closer. New York was no longer this distant, far-off dreamworld. New York and New Jersey were one.

TRYING SOMETHING NEW

PATERSON CATHOLIC HAD everything I was looking for in a high school. My grades immediately improved because I found the classes interesting. The teachers cared about us, too. Sister Gloria, the principal, was always concerned with my well-being. She loved the school's football and basketball teams, but she also cared about our efforts in the classroom. A short, older Spanish-speaking woman, she was a tough cookie with a heart of gold. I saw a lot of my mother's best qualities in Sister Gloria.

There was a strict dress code at PC and I wore the standard-issue maroon sweaters with pride. I was truly part of the Paterson Catholic family, and whether it was the long-sleeve cardigan or the sleeveless sweater vest, I treated those tops like they were prized possessions. I still have many of them, crisply ironed and perfectly folded, in my bedroom dresser on East Eighteenth Street.

I played point guard for the varsity basketball team and we had a phenomenal season. Our squad was loaded with tremendously talented players. Mookie and Colin got even better in their junior years, but we also had an electric shooting guard named Marquis Webb. Marquis and I made for a dynamic backcourt duo. He was one of the best defenders I'd ever seen step on a basketball court.

We won the county championship that year, beating Passaic High School in the championship game. People from Passaic and Paterson don't really get along as it is, but this game was especially tense, because there was lingering bad blood over Mookie, Colin, and me transferring from Tech the previous year. We beat them handily and I got to hoist my first Paterson Catholic championship trophy. I was officially a part of the PC tradition. That team photo was framed and encased in the hallway.

The real highlight of that sophomore season for me, though, was a game we played against Don Bosco Tech. They weren't a very good team, but their starting point guard was none other than Malik Walker.

Yes, my older brother, Malik.

My father did his very best to attend all of our games, regardless of the sport, and you always *knew* when Mike Walker was in the stands.

That father whose voice can always be heard above all the others in a gym full of people? That was my dad. He'd be the one screaming at the referee from the bleachers about a bad call or razzing an opposing coach for a bad decision. One time he got so heated over an officiating mistake that he was physically removed from the premises. I probably should have been embarrassed, but I remember laughing the entire time as he was taken outside by a group of security guards. But he was right! The call was terrible. (Or at least I'd like to think so.)

Malik was a solid player. He had a nice jump shot and a good court sense. We played one-on-one a lot as kids and he'd always beat me. Physically, he was just stronger and he'd bully me inside. When I turned thirteen, that all changed. He hadn't beaten me in years. This would be the first and only time we went head-to-head in a high school basketball game.

My father showed up an hour early for the game, as nervous as I'd ever seen him. His stomach was in knots. He had his video camera in his hand and told both Malik and me that he wouldn't be "choosing sides." This was my father's Super Bowl. Malik and I both got a kick out of how much the game meant to him.

We blew Don Bosco Tech out of the building that afternoon. Coach Patterson drew up all sorts of isolation plays for me and I had a blast, scoring a few buckets right over Malik. Our whole team was cheering me on from the bench and even Malik had a good laugh at the "Victor vs. Malik" strategy that Coach Patterson employed.

Dad, meanwhile, was silent.

He didn't say a word the entire game. He told us both afterward that he promised himself he'd be quiet. My mother laughed at that one, saying, "That was the only game where I didn't hear your dad's voice in the background from start to finish."

I still have the videotape of that game. When I know Malik's coming over to my place, I'll not so subtly have it playing on the TV as he walks through the door. "Oh, hey, I'm just watching some basketball game from a few years ago," I'll say with a sly grin on my face. That one never gets old.

That following summer, I traveled the country with the Tim Thomas Playaz. Jim took us to some of the top AAU tournaments and we got to face off against elite basketball players from all over America. I got to go to Las Vegas, Hawaii, and Minnesota, places I'd never been before but had wanted to visit my entire life.

Meanwhile, back in Paterson, things weren't going as well for some of my friends from childhood. Basketball and my mother's hard work provided me opportunities that were very rare for a kid from East Twentieth Street. As I was practicing crossover dribbles and studying for Father Murphy's Scriptures tests, many of my friends were getting into trouble.

During my sophomore year, alone, four of my best friends from School 21 became fathers. Several of the girls I'd been innocently flirting with in the cafeteria just two years earlier were now young, single mothers. Kids I'd been friendly with would stop showing up to Montgomery Park to play basketball. I'd find out that they were in jail or, worse, no longer with us.

It was very easy to fall into bad situations in Paterson. You didn't find them. They found you.

IT WAS VERY EASY TO FALL INTO BAD SITUATIONS IN PATERSON. YOU DIDN'T FIND THEM. THEY FOUND YOU.

I took a bus to Paterson Catholic every day. It picked me up two blocks from my house, I had a five-minute ride through town, and I reported to homeroom. Once I was within those walls, I was in a bubble. I was safe from outside influences. Many of my friends weren't as fortunate.

There would be fights every day at Eastside. I would ask about old friends from School 21, and say, "Yo, how's so-and-so doing?" only to find out that "so-and-so" had been jumped, stabbed, or shot a few weeks earlier. It was always something. I never heard, "Oh, he's got a new job," or "He just got an A- in social studies."

A lot of my friends stopped playing sports or bothering with video games after school. They'd spend their free time just hanging out on Park Avenue. My *abuela* used to tell me, in Spanish, "Nothing good happens after five p.m." By the time I was in high school, I was starting to understand what she meant.

When Paterson Catholic had half days and the Eastside kids didn't, I'd go over to Park Avenue and see all my Eastside friends coming out of school. Every time I was there, there'd be something crazy going on. Someone was in a fight, someone was getting robbed, or there were different gangs squaring off. Guns, knives, drugs—you name it. Eventually, I just stopped going. What was the point?

The gangs got larger and more involved with everyday Paterson life as I got older. Pelli and I had our run-in with the MSD and they never fully went away. Pelli was Dominican himself, and for whatever reason, they had problems with him. The two of us would hang out just about every weekend. Most of those times, we were looking over our shoulders.

The gangs weren't how they're depicted in the movies. Sure, we had the Bloods, the guys dressed in all red, but Paterson gangs are dictated more by the streets you live on than the color of your shirt.

You didn't mess with the Kean Street guys. They were predominantly Latin dudes who ran that part of town. The cats on Rosa Parks Boulevard were mostly black guys, and for whatever reason, they had years and years of beef with the MSD guys over on Market Street. You'd rarely see a Rosa Parks guy on Market Street, or vice versa. If you did, it meant something was up. The Rosa Parks guys also didn't get along with the dudes on North Main Street. And then there were the gangs on the other side of town in North Paterson. They had their own gangs over there and an entirely different lay of the land.

There were all kinds of dynamics, and if you didn't know them, you'd find yourself in trouble.

I avoided that trouble and that's a testament to my mother. She always made sure that I stayed on the straight and narrow. Throughout high school, my mother worked full days and overtime hours and would still be there in her beaten-up blue minivan, waiting for me outside the YMCA or the Willowbrook Mall at nine thirty at night. She tried her best to be at every game, every team dinner, and every trophy presentation. There'd be times when she'd pick me up at a friend's house after school and she'd ask where his mother was. I'd shrug. The mother either wasn't around or was in her bedroom, with the door closed. My mother would be so upset when she'd hear that and I never understood why she cared about what my friends' moms were up to.

A lot of my friends whose mothers didn't take active roles in their teenage years ended up dropping out of school, in gangs, or in jail. I didn't realize it at the time, but my mother knew the effect of her being in that van waiting for me or in those bleachers cheering me on. She used to tell me, "Be present." She always was.

My mom was meddlesome when she felt she had to be—I'm sure my high school girlfriends didn't always appreciate that—and she always needed to know exactly where I was. I'd get annoyed when she'd yell at me for not calling her *the second* I got home from school, but it all makes a lot more sense now. She was raising both Andrea and me on her own and wanted to give us every opportunity to succeed in life. She was tough because she had to be.

I'm forever grateful for that.

Mom couldn't be everywhere, though, and some of the best times I had in high school were Friday nights spent at a place called Skaters World.

Yes, Skaters World.

It was a roller-skating rink up in Wayne, New Jersey, a suburban town about fifteen minutes north of Paterson. It's also where I learned how to talk to a female without completely fumbling my words.

On those Friday nights, Pelli, my friend Kyon, and I would get dressed in our best clothes, drench ourselves in Versace Blue Jeans cologne, and get a ride to Wayne from one of our mothers or one of the older kids with a car.

We'd get to Skaters World around eight thirty and skating was never even an option. I don't recall ever actually renting a pair of roller skates. We'd set up shop in a corner and just hang out. I'd be sporting my leather Paterson Catholic varsity basketball jacket, the one with "County Champions" embroidered in fur on the back, and "Vic" in cursive on the front, and puff my chest out like the coolest guy in the building. There were packs of girls from all the neighboring schools, just milling around. We'd get slices of pizza, drink soda, and do our best to look like we knew what the hell we were doing.

At eleven, the nights took off.

The DJ, a charismatic dude named Big L, would take the microphone and urge everyone to "Get on the rink."

Big L played the hottest music. This was around 2001 and 2002, and Cash Money was *it*. Juvenile, Young Buck, Mannie Fresh, Lil Wayne, the Big Tymers, BG—Big L played it all. We'd dance our faces off. I'd sweat more on that dance floor than I ever did in a basketball game, just grinding to Juvenile and Soulja Slim's "Slow Motion" or Cam'ron's "Oh Boy." There was always a Notorious B.I.G. and Puffy set that drove the girls wild, too.

During the first few hours of a night at Skaters World, you'd meet a group of girls from another school outside the rink and make small talk. Then, when you got on the dance floor, you'd find that crew of girls, link eyes with the one you were talking to, and pair off. I was no professional dancer, but I had some moves. Pelli was an absolute clown, but he did, too. We'd have a blast out there, getting girls' numbers and acting like big shots.

If I was spending the majority of my high school Friday nights at a place called Skaters World, I probably wasn't getting into too much trouble. My mom wasn't crazy about me coming in at one in the morning, but she slept better knowing that there were worse places I could be than a roller-skating rink in Wayne, New Jersey.

Skaters World closed its doors in 2010. It's a shame. We had some great nights at that place in high school. More than anything, it was an alternative to hanging out on the streets of Paterson.

Malik graduated from Don Bosco Tech in June of 2002. He was an honor roll student and cracked 1100 on his SATs. We went to his graduation ceremony and it was one of the first times I ever saw my dad show real, raw emotion. He would scream at basketball games and spank me when I got out of line, but my father never really let his guard down. Even after 9/11, he was a rock. That afternoon, I saw him well up with tears.

Malik was headed to Delaware State to study business. We went out for a nice dinner after the graduation ceremony and my father was glowing throughout the entire meal. I was excelling on the basketball court, but Malik was a star in the classroom. Both of my father's sons were on paths to better lives than the one that he had. His American Dream was being fulfilled.

He pulled us both together that night and put his massive two arms around our shoulders. "I just want to tell you both how proud I am of you." It wasn't often that my father showed that kind of sensitivity. I'll never forget that moment.

ONE AFTERNOON DURING the summer between my sophomore and junior years of high school, my father asked me if I was going to play football for Paterson Catholic the following fall.

I shrugged indifferently. I liked football and still followed my Dallas Cowboys on Sundays, but I hadn't really considered playing for Paterson Catholic. Basketball was my sport, and after winning the county championship in 2002, playing a larger role on the hoops team in 2003 was my primary focus.

"You should play football, Vic. You're pretty good," he told me.

Dad was always the biggest fan of my skills on the gridiron, dating back to the days when he was Coach Bulldog's assistant coach on the PAL North Firefighters, so I knew his opinions came through a pair of rose-tinted glasses. But I was intrigued by the idea. At the very least, I figured, it'd keep me physically active until basketball season. I liked football and hell, it was something to do. It beat playing video games and practicing no-look passes in the basement on September afternoons.

"YOU SHOULD PLAY FOOTBALL, VIC. YOU'RE PRETTY GOOD," HE TOLD ME.

When I spoke to the football coach, Mr. Wimberly, he was open to me joining the squad.

"I'll tell you now, though, Victor," Coach Wimberly said, "football's a whole lot different than basketball."

Truer words had never been spoken.

In basketball, there are five guys on a court. For the most part, the best five players on the team emerge and a chemistry is built around their strengths and weaknesses. Within five minutes of playing with those four other guys, you can usually assess each individual's role on the squad. I'd never had to really "try out" for a basketball team. Once I got on the court, I stepped into the role of point guard and ran the show. It always came easily to me. Dribble, pass, shoot, and defend. There were in-bounds plays and a couple of offensive sets we'd run, but for the most part, it was just playing basketball. I'd been doing it since I was five.

When I showed up for my first Paterson Catholic football practice that August, there were about eighty-five kids on the football field. They all had their own football vocabulary and set positions. Having not played real, organized team football in three years, I was overwhelmed.

I once read that when Drew Brees got to Purdue his freshman season, he was the sixth quarterback on the team's depth chart. When I arrived at that first football practice of my junior year of high school, I wasn't even *on* the depth chart.

I knew a lot of the kids on the team from classes and they all asked me the same question, "Aren't you a basketball player, Vic?"

And I answered them all the same exact way, "Yep."

It didn't take long for me to get on that depth chart and start climbing it. I played wide receiver and cornerback, new positions for me, and had some immediate success during those late August practices.

My second cousin on my father's side, Lorenzo Crawford, was a former Paterson Catholic football star. He played wide receiver for the Cougars in the 1990s and held just about every school receiving record.

After my first week of practice, Lorenzo was standing on the sideline watching from afar and Coach Wimberly screamed over to him, "Hey, Lorenzo, your cousin Cruz here is going to break all of your records!"

Without a pause, Lorenzo yelled back, "Records were made to be broken, Coach!"

Talk about high expectations.

The reality was that I had good speed and the right mind-set for the wide receiver position. I was about five-foot-nine with long arms and above average hand-eye coordination. From my experience playing point guard in basketball, I had good instincts and the ability to see a play developing before it unfolded. That worked to my advantage on the football field. A cornerback would be lined up on the inside of me and I'd take the right angle to burn by him on the outside. I had a knack for watching the defenders' eyes and knowing their every move, before even they did. Sometimes I'd gamble and be wrong. Most times, though, I'd gamble and be right.

But I was raw. And when the season started, I still was the third-string receiver. I'd have to prove myself.

The football team was loaded with characters. T. J. Tillman, our quarterback, was a big personality. He also had a cannon for an arm. One of our best defensive players was our starting linebacker, Chenry Lewis. Chenry was a hilarious Jamaican kid who never gave up his "Rasta" roots. When the coach asked him what position he wanted to play, Chenry said he wanted to be the kicker. He was six-foot-four and 220 pounds, and he wanted to play kicker! He loved just kicking that football and when the coach finally relented and told him to give a field goal a try in practice, he booted one straight through the uprights from forty-five yards away. From that point on, he kicked all of our extra points and field goals. Chenry Lewis was the only defensive end/kicker I'd ever heard of.

The best player on our team was our senior running back, a boy named Jordan Cleaves.

Jordan was our leader in every sense of the word. He was the first guy at practice every day and would be the one already taping up his ankles when you got into the locker room. "You ready to dominate today, Cruz?" he'd ask me. I was a basketball player, giving football a shot and just trying my best to get on the field at receiver, but he always saw great potential in my skills. "You can be great, Vic," he'd tell me.

Jordan's story was similar to mine. His father, Mr. Thompson, was a security guard in town, and Jordan's mother, Ms. Cleaves-Thompson, was a schoolteacher at one of the elementary schools. They, like my mother and father, both made great sacrifices to pay for Jordan's Paterson Catholic tuition and put him through private school. In turn, Jordan stayed out of trouble and always did them proud. Everyone loved Jordan, and not just because of his warmth and his infectious smile. Everyone loved Jordan because of how he made you feel about yourself. Here I was, a kid from the basketball team, stepping into his football locker room. Instead of rejecting my attempts at a new sport or keeping me from the team's inner circle, he embraced me as one of the guys immediately.

Jordan and I quickly became very close friends. He'd drive me home from football practices in his old Dodge Stratus and make me laugh. When petty things like playing time or an issue with a girl would get me down, he'd flash a giant smile and say, "Enjoy life, Vic. We're blessed, man."

Jordan was a star running back on the football field, with a running style that reminded me of Ricky Watters, the old San Francisco 49ers legend. He wasn't the biggest guy, but he was as strong as an ox. Jordan stayed low to the ground and always found openings through the seams created by the offensive line.

Jordan's best friend was a boy named Rashawn Ricks, another kid from a tough part of Paterson. Rashawn went by the nickname "Rocky" and played linebacker. Those two were inseparable and because of them, there were always big-time college scouts at our games. Throughout that season, we'd hear in the locker room before the games, "Hey, Notre Dame is here to see Rocky" or "The defensive coordinator from Clemson is in the stands." But it never fazed Jordan and Rocky. They were always the coolest, calmest guys in the locker room and in the huddle.

I remember in one game, Rocky went down with what appeared to be a really bad leg injury. "Hey, I'm fine, Coach," he told Coach Wimberly despite obvious pain.

He went back in the game and had ten tackles and two sacks in the second half. Afterward, doctors told Rocky that he had played that entire half on a partially torn anterior cruciate ligament in his knee, the type of injury that would end most professional players' seasons. Rocky laughed at the prognosis. "Yeah? Wow, that's crazy," he said.

He wouldn't miss a snap the remainder of the season.

I learned the value of being a good leader in the locker room from Jordan Cleaves and what toughness was—both mental and physical—from Rashawn Ricks.

COACH WIMBERLY WAS a screamer. I don't think he ever whispered anything in this life. We would joke that when he spoke to his wife at night, he'd shout in her face, *"Good night, honey! I love you!"*

He was always chewing and spitting sunflower seeds. He'd be yelling something on the sideline, and as he did it, there'd be this spray of sunflower seed shells that came with whatever he was saying. Everyone who ever suited up for Coach Wimberly knows about those sunflower seed showers. Sometimes you'd get caught in the line of fire and take one directly in the face. Talk about Call of Duty.

Though I was picking up the game, I hadn't really made much of an impact as the third wide receiver in the offense. The truth of the matter was that I had no idea what I was doing at the position. The other starting receivers, a boy named Marcus Robinson and a tall, rangy kid named Adrian Rodriguez, knew all the routes and had a good rhythm with T.J., our quarterback. I'd just run as far as I could and hope T.J. would throw me a long pass. It wasn't cutting it.

So I decided to change the situation.

I knocked on Coach Wimberly's office door one day after practice and asked him to teach me how to play wide receiver. He smiled, and in one of the instances in his life where he wasn't screaming, said, "I was wondering when this day would come, Victor."

He sat me down and taught me something called the "Route Tree." The Route Tree is a basic diagram that outlines all of the possible different routes a receiver could make on a given play. Coach Wimberly took to the chalkboard in his office, a place we called "The Dungeon," and listed out all the different routes—Flat, Slant, Curl, Hook, Comeback, Dig, Out, Corner, Fade, Post, and Go. All season, I'd just been running Go routes, where our center would snap T.J. the ball and I'd run as fast as I could past the cornerback covering me. It was a dead sprint, every single time. Sometimes T.J. would heave one my way. Most of the time he wouldn't.

Marcus and Adrian, the two starting receivers, had been playing football their entire lives. Two seniors, they were well versed in the Route Tree. While I was just "going deep" every play, Marcus and Adrian were working the middle of the field, picking up valuable first downs and getting more of T.J's passes thrown to them.

Coach Wimberly drew the Route Tree on a piece of paper and told me to study it. "Once you get these routes down, you'll be a difficult guy to cover," he told me.

I studied that Route Tree like I used to study the five-page packets before The Sir's tae kwon do tests. Every night, I'd quiz myself on the Five-Yard Out and the Skinny Post. My mother would sit down with me at the kitchen table and show me flash cards with routes drawn out. I'd have to tell her which ones they were.

Jordan Cleaves would stay late after practice, helping me nail the intricacies of the Curl and Dig routes, too. I was quickly realizing what Coach Wimberly meant when he told me that football is a whole lot different than basketball. Whereas basketball is mostly rooted in instincts and one's natural ability, football is a thinking man's game. It's cerebral. You can't just walk onto the football field and be a star. You'd get your head knocked off. You have to work at it and that means doing some of the less glamorous things of the sport—like studying the Route Tree or running the same pattern twenty times in a row until it's mastered.

A few weeks later, Coach Wimberly lined me up at the number two wideout position. I was replacing Marcus in the starting lineup.

Marcus could have taken the news of his "demotion" poorly or spited me for it, but he never did. He handled it just about as well as any seventeen-year-old high school kid could have, and before that next game, said something along the lines of "You earned it. You made this happen. Congratulations."

I scored two touchdowns that game. Marcus had one from my old third wideout position, too.

As the season progressed, more and more college coaches would be in those stands. After one of our final games, Coach Wimberly pulled me into "the Dungeon" and handed me a glossy pamphlet. In big, bold letters, the cover read UNIVERSITY OF VIRGINIA 7-ON-7 FOOTBALL CAMP.

I'd always been interested in UVA, dating back to my weekend in Durham when I met Donald Hand. Apparently, Al Golden, Virginia's defensive coordinator at the time, was in the stands scouting Rocky and had liked the way I played.

"Coach Golden asked that I pass this pamphlet along to you," Coach Wimberly told me. "He thinks you should attend their camp this summer."

I went home that night and immediately studied up on UVA

football. Al Groh, the former coach of the New York Jets, was in his second year in Charlottesville. Al Golden, the guy who asked Coach Wimberly about me, was the youngest defensive co-ordinator in college football. Their roster was full of big-time college football players. Matt Schaub, the eventual starting quarterback of the Houston Texans, was their team captain, and Wali Lundy—another New Jersey kid—was their star running back. In the nineties, some big-time players, like Tiki and Ronde Barber, had gone there.

Up until that moment when Coach Wimberly handed me the UVA football camp pamphlet, I always just kind of assumed that basketball would be my ticket out of Paterson and into college. Never did it once cross my mind that maybe it'd be football that took me to new and exciting places.

I signed up for that camp and spent the rest of the school year looking forward to the opportunity.

Football, huh?

Why not?

LIFE IS A TEST

IMMEDIATELY AFTER THE football season ended, I was out of my pads and into my Nike high-tops. We had a county championship in basketball to defend. I assured the rest of the guys on the team that although I had enjoyed some success on the gridiron, I was still their point guard and still committed to putting Darryl and Marquis in position to score as many points as possible. And trust me, score points they did.

Both of those guys had huge years and we were one of the best teams in the entire state. Colin had moved back to Canada, where he was born, but our team got great production from some other guys.

We lost the title game to St. Patrick's, but it wasn't so bad. Mookie got a full scholarship to play center at Syracuse, and Marquis was headed to Rutgers. Jim Salmon told me that the coaches at Creighton, a Division I school in Nebraska, had asked him about me, but I wasn't even sure I wanted to play basketball in college anymore.

After the season, a kid at a house party from another town came up to me and asked, "Hey, aren't you a football player, Vic?"

I answered him the same way I did when all the football players used to ask me a similar question about basketball: "Yep."

ON A SATURDAY morning in June of my junior year, I popped my head into Teddy's bodega below my *abuela*'s house and grabbed a banana and a Capri Sun juice box out of the refrigerator in the back.

"What's up, Vic? Why are you up so early on a Saturday morning?" Teddy asked in his usual inquisitive tone.

"I'm taking the SATs today, Teddy. They say I need a banana and some vitamin C."

Little did I know then that the SATs required a whole lot more than a piece of fruit and some juice.

When I got to the testing center, a high school in nearby Lodi, New Jersey, I looked around the class and saw a bunch of strange faces. I was distracted by the foreign environment and once the test began, my brain went completely blank. For whatever reason, I couldn't focus. I was always good at English class in school, but when I looked at those analogies on the SATs, they just didn't make much sense. Math wasn't my best subject, but I was having trouble answering even the easiest questions. The SATs were just two and a half hours long, but it felt like they went on forever. By the time I was on the final section, I had completely spaced out. It was too nice outside. I wanted to play basketball or run routes with Jordan.

I finished the test and didn't think twice about it. I was just happy to be done.

I got my score in the mail a few weeks later and it was abysmal. A 720.

You get two hundred points for just filling your name in correctly.

Though I wasn't overly concerned with my performance, my mother was alarmed. I'd worked so hard my entire life to get good grades in school. To blow my chances at a college education because of a bad SAT score would be foolish.

"Victor, you can't get into any good colleges with a 720," she explained to me. But I didn't want to hear it. I knew I'd be able to take them again the following year. It was my first time even seeing the SATs.

Coach Wimberly was a bit concerned about the scores, too. He called me into his office and explained that I'd never play college football if I couldn't get high enough SAT scores to qualify academically. It didn't make sense to me. All these guys playing major college football did well on the SATs? How could that be?

But it was true. To be academically eligible for Division I-A or Division I-AA football, you had to maintain a certain GPA and break a specific score on your standardized test. "No matter how many touchdowns you score on the football field or how many assists you record on the basketball court, you won't go to college with a 720," he told me.

NO OBSTACLE WOULD END UP BEING GREATER THAN THAT TEST.

I'd gone up against some of the best defenders in the country, both in basketball and in football. No obstacle would end up being greater than that test.

One of the best days of that summer was attending Paterson Catholic's Class of 2003 graduation ceremony. Mookie, Marquis, Jordan, and Rocky were some of my best friends, and seeing them all in those maroon-and-gold caps and gowns really made me happy.

Jordan graduated near the top of the class and was headed to Virginia State, a historically black college in Virginia, where he'd play running back for the Trojans in the fall. Rocky got a full scholarship to Rutgers, the state school of New Jersey. He was a highly recruited player and could have gone almost anywhere in the country, but he chose to stay close to home. Close to Paterson.

The University of Virginia football camp would be the first week I spent away from my friends, family, Jim, and everyone else I knew my entire life. I had been to some cool places and seen some really great things, but I was never really ever alone. At UVA, I showed up with a backpack of clothes and an open mind.

The University of Virginia, like Duke, was another absolutely gorgeous college campus. There was a lot of history in Charlottesville, and on the first day that we arrived, the coaches told us that Thomas Jefferson, James Madison, and James Monroe—three former U.S. presidents—were among the school's original board of advisers. They paired us off into groups of two and put us in dorm rooms.

But every player there was dwarfed by a guy from a town called New Iberia, Louisiana.

Early Doucet looked like a grown man at the age of seventeen. He was six feet tall and two hundred pounds and ran like the wind. I'd never heard of him, but he was unlike any wide receiver I'd ever seen before.

The Route Tree that I obsessed over? Early knew it inside and out and probably twenty other patterns that Coach Wimberly had never even seen. He had this thick Southern drawl and muscles that looked sculpted out of clay.

When we got on the field that first morning, I lined up at cornerback against him, and it was as if I wasn't even on the field. He lit me up. I couldn't stop him. A pass was thrown above my head and I figured it was headed out of bounds. With one hand, Early reached out over my shoulder and hauled it in. He went eighty yards untouched for a touchdown.

We had some really good football players in New Jersey, and I would have put guys like Jordan and Rocky up against anyone, but Early Doucet was a whole other type of player. He was elite.

All day at those practices, we'd hear the coaches compliment him. "Early" this, "Early" that.

Deservedly so. He was that good.

I got burned by that kid from Louisiana a few dozen times that week, but I made a few good plays myself. The last night, one of the assistant coaches knocked on my dorm room door and told me that everyone was thrilled with the way I had played.

I left that camp feeling good about my performance and my chances at becoming a college football player, but also wondering how I'd ever make it to the NFL with specimens like Early Doucet roaming the planet.

Though I played well during my week in Charlottesville, UVA never offered me a scholarship. They were very selective with the guys they recruited from outside the state, and their New Jersey scholarship offer ended up going to another wide receiver from New Jersey—a boy named Marquise Liverpool. He was a star at Don Bosco Prep, a football powerhouse.

Marquise never went to Virginia, though, and when the Seattle Mariners selected him in the thirty-third round of the 2004 Amateur baseball draft, he chose the baseball diamond over the gridiron.

Life works in funny ways.

After three years of struggling in baseball's minor leagues, Marquise was released by the Seattle Mariners organization in 2006. When he was twenty-three years old, he enrolled at Temple University in Philadelphia, becoming one of the oldest freshmen in all of Division I-A football. His head coach at Temple was the same guy who encouraged me to attend the UVA summer camp in 2003, Al Golden.

Marquise had an outstanding career at Temple and was eventually signed by the Detroit Lions as an undrafted rookie free agent in 2011.

Some guys—the Early Doucets of the world—have traditional paths to the NFL. They dominate at summer camps in high school, win Sugar Bowl titles playing for Les Miles at LSU, and get drafted by the Arizona Cardinals.

Other guys are forced to take unconventional journeys like Marquise Liverpool.

Everyone's story is unique.

THERE WAS A ton of buzz surrounding our football team heading into my senior year. We'd had a great 2002 season and though we were losing important players like Jordan, Adrian, and Rocky, T.J.,

Chenry and I were all ready to step into the leadership roles they'd left behind. We had some great younger guys on the team who took their games to the next level that season, too. Kit Pommels was our Devin Hester. He'd return kicks, play running back, work that second receiver role, and give opposing teams nightmares. Our new starting running back, a junior named Tymier Wells, was a worthy replacement for Jordan. He ran the ball hard and he never fumbled.

The summer before that season, there were newspaper articles about our team in both the *Newark Star-Ledger* and the *Bergen Record*. Every major New Jersey news outlet predicted us to win the state championship.

When we got to practice that August, Coach Wimberly introduced a new play to the offense: Twins Right Tarzan.

I loved Twins Right Tarzan.

The play lined both Kit and me to the right of T.J., and when the ball was snapped, we'd both run ten yards and crisscross. Kit would make a cut toward the middle of the field and I'd go deep on a post pattern.

We must have run Twins Right Tarzan ten times a game, and it worked just about every time Coach called it in from the sideline.

That 2003 season was just plain silly. We blew all of our opponents out, and each one of us put up huge individual statistics. In half of our games, we'd be winning by so many points at halftime that T.J., Kit, and I would be taken out of the game after the second quarter. The Paterson Catholic field was called "The Swamp" because it didn't have a proper drainage system. We used the elements to our advantage. We were familiar with "The Swamp," and if visiting teams needed a quarter to adjust, they were already playing from behind.

We played Elmwood Park in a game that was supposed to be very competitive. They'd had a few big wins early on in the season and there were articles in all of the newspapers that week suggesting they'd give us a good fight.

I ended up scoring five touchdowns in the first half of that game, in five different ways: a kick return, an interception return, a punt return, a rushing touchdown on a reverse play, and a receiving touchdown on Twins Right Tarzan. There was a kid at St. Mary High School that season scoring eight and nine touchdowns a game. I had five in the first half and wanted to score ten or eleven. But Coach Wimberly kept me on the sidelines in the second half, like he often did. "We don't do that at Paterson Catholic," he told me. "We always win with class."

We won by more than forty points and I didn't touch the field during the third or fourth quarters.

I had over eight hundred receiving yards and caught nineteen touchdown passes my senior year. As Coach Wimberly had predicted sixteen months earlier, I broke most of my cousin Lorenzo's school receiving records.

But the college scouts weren't impressed.

Every game, I'd put up eye-popping numbers and make dazzling plays, but the college coaches in the stands never bothered speaking with me afterward. They were there to watch Chenry and Kit, not me.

It was devastating.

I'd ask Coach Wimberly why none of the big schools were interested in me, and he'd tell me that he was as confused as I was. "You'll get your shot, Victor," he'd say. "I'm not sure where, but you'll get your shot. And you'll prove them all wrong."

I remember countless Saturdays that season spent on my computer at home, going on recruiting sites like Rivals.com, and looking up the other wide receivers that these colleges were courting. There'd be a wide receiver from Atlanta with the exact same height and weight as me, listed as a "four-star" recruit.

Rivals.com listed me as a "one-star" recruit.

It burned me up inside and I played most of that season with a giant chip on my shoulder. I was constantly trying to prove myself to those scouts, to show that I, Victor Cruz, was the playmaker they needed on their teams in the Big East and the SEC.

But ten games came and ten games went that season and no Division I-A schools came calling. I visited Rutgers toward the end of the year, but I always felt that trip was just a favor to Coach Wimberly or a clever recruiting tactic by the Rutgers coaching staff. Chenry was debating between Rutgers and a few other schools at the time and the Rutgers coaches knew that the two of us were close buddies. Perhaps they thought bringing me to campus for a day would give them the edge on landing Chenry.

Once we got to Piscataway to meet with the coaches, my mother and I were excited. Going to Rutgers would have been a tremendous honor.

But when I met with Greg Schiano, the head coach at the time (and now the head coach of the Tampa Bay Buccaneers in the NFL), he didn't exactly roll out the red carpet for Victor Cruz.

He said that he liked what he'd seen of me, but with just two years of real high school football experience, I was probably still too raw to play in the Big East. There were several other scholarship offers already out, he explained, and his staff had to wait and see who was accepting them before being able to offer me anything.

Coach Schiano told me he'd be in touch, but that call never came.

Other college coaches would tell Coach Wimberly that I was just too small to play the wide receiver position for a big-time college football program. At five foot nine, I was by no means a tiny guy, but I certainly wasn't the same type of physical specimen as an Early Doucet or a Calvin Johnson, a six-foot-five man-child from Sandy Creek High School in Georgia.

I'd spend endless hours on those recruiting Web sites reading about guys like Ted Ginn Jr., a five-star recruit from Cleveland, Ohio, and Adrian Peterson, a big running back from Palestine,

Texas, wondering if I'd ever get the chance to line up against them. They might have been bigger, stronger, and faster than I was, but I knew nobody wanted it more than me.

We went undefeated during the regular season, setting up a state championship game against Bayley-Ellard High School. Malik's old school, Don Bosco Tech, had closed its doors the year before and the Bayley-Ellard squad was basically an all-star team made up of the best players from the two schools.

THEY MIGHT HAVE BEEN BIGGER, STRONGER, AND FASTER THAN I WAS, BUT I KNEW NOBODY WANTED IT MORE THAN ME.

Since a lot of the Bayley-Ellard players were Paterson kids and the town had just invested a lot of money into a new field house on the corner of Market Street and Madison Avenue, the coaches asked the NJSIAA if we could play our game in Paterson instead of at Giants Stadium where the other championship games were being held. When my good pals at the organization said yes, we were all very excited to play for the state title in our hometown.

Every person in Paterson attended that game. There were grown men watching the game on the roofs of their cars and little kids sitting on the shoulders of their friends. We came out and had our best effort of the season, beating them with ease. After the game, I posed for a photograph with my mother and my father that I still have in a frame right by my bed. We were state champions and we'd won the title in the town we'd always called home. My mother and father were there, together, cheering me on.

We were treated like kings around town for the next few weeks. I'd walk into Teddy's bodega and he'd say, "Take whatever you want, Vic! You're a champion!" It felt great, but when people would ask me where I was playing in the fall, I'd answer with a shrug. I wasn't sure.

Though I had my heart set on playing for a major Division I-A college program, Coach Wimberly suggested that I meet with a few of the Division I-AA coaches who were asking about me. I initially resisted, before speaking with my old teammate Jordan Cleaves. He, too, was a star at the high school level. But because of his size, Jordan wasn't recruited by any teams in Division I-A.

He ended up going to Virginia State University, a Division II school. I called him up on the phone to discuss my future and Jordan said, "Victor, you don't need to be a small fish in a big pond. You're better than that. If you were to go to Rutgers or West Virginia, you'd just be another guy from New Jersey fighting for playing time. Go visit those Division I-AA schools and become a star."

After a pause, he added, "We'll be teammates in the NFL someday, man. We'll buy our mothers mansions and wear Super Bowl rings around Paterson. Go to a smaller school and prove everyone wrong."

Jordan Cleaves always had the right thing to say. He may have been slightly crazy with all of his talk about the NFL and our mothers' mansions, but he was a believer. He saw something special in me when a lot of others didn't.

My mother and I visited Hofstra University, a Division I-AA school up in Long Island, and it was a totally different experience than when I'd met with Coach Schiano at Rutgers. Two juniors on the team gave me a tour of the school, and the coach, a kind man named Joe Gardi, told me they'd be thrilled to have me on their squad.

I also visited the University of Delaware, another Division I-AA school. Though I didn't end up joining the Fighting Blue Hens football team, I sometimes wonder what it would have been like if I had. A year after my recruiting trip to Newark, a quarterback from South Jersey named Joe Flacco decided to transfer from the

University of Pittsburgh, where he'd lost the starting job, to Delaware. Flacco to Cruz? I can only imagine the kind of numbers we would have put up together in college.

I was sold on the University of Massachusetts Amherst the second I stepped foot on campus. Located in a woodsy town about ninety miles west of Boston, it reminded me of the beautiful green campuses in Durham and Charlottesville. The football team's head coach, a guy named Mark Whipple, said that they'd had their eyes on me all season. He even mentioned my performance against Elmwood Park.

On my official visit, I got to hang out with some of the older guys on the squad. We hit it off right away. Shannon James, the team's top defensive back, told me about his recruiting experience. James Ihedigbo, a starting safety from western Massachusetts, told me about his. Our stories were all so similar. They, too, had outstanding high school football careers. But when the time came to decide where they'd play in college, the big-time Division I-A programs never came knocking. "So we came here," Ihedigbo told me. "And guess what? We got playing time right away and we love it. I'd probably still be stuck on the bench if I was playing somewhere else."

My mother loved UMass, too, and Coach Whipple told me, "Victor, a full scholarship is yours. You just need to get those SAT scores up."

I gave my verbal commitment to Coach Whipple and came back to Paterson with a Minutemen Football sweatshirt that I wore everywhere around town. I was going to college and I was going to play football.

I just needed to conquer the SATs.

AS MY SENIOR season on the basketball team began, my mind wasn't focused on pick-and-rolls and offensive rebounds. All I could think about were my SAT scores.

I took the test, again, in December and got an 840. It still was not a high enough score to play football at the next level.

I was in constant contact with Coach Whipple and he kept telling me, "You just need to get a few more of those questions right. Just a few."

In January of my senior year, I got a text message from an unknown 413 number. The text read "You around?"

I called the number and it was Shannon James, the star defensive back from the UMass football team. "Hey, Victor. I didn't want you to hear this from someone else first. Coach Whipple just announced he was leaving us to take the job as the quarterbacks coach of the Pittsburgh Steelers," Shannon said.

I panicked. Who was the new coach going to be? Would he know my name? Would I fit into his offensive system? More importantly, did I still have my scholarship? Shannon didn't have any answers.

A few days after my conversation with Shannon, I heard from the new coach at UMass, a man named Don Brown. He was coming from Northeastern, another Division I-AA school, where he had spent the last several years building the team into a contender. When I spoke with Coach Brown, he said that his staff was very excited about having a guy like me joining the program. He put my fears to rest when he said that my scholarship was still intact. At the end of the phone call, though, he said something along the lines of "Now, just go ace those SATs."

The basketball season went well. We played some of the best teams in the country and did more than just hold our own. The whole season was building up toward a big game versus St. Patrick's, a rival Catholic school, from a few towns over. St. Pat's had always been good, but that season—they were fantastic.

It'd be a televised game and all of Paterson was abuzz. All eyes would be on us. One day during practice that week, someone special paid us a visit.

Right through the gym doors, dressed in more bling than you'd find in the Tiffany's store in Manhattan, came Tim Thomas.

"Coach Patterson, can I talk to these kids?" he asked.

Thomas, the hero of so many of our childhoods, brought us into a tight huddle and told us to be proud of our school, to be proud of where we were from. At the time, he'd banked close to $80 million in basketball contracts and had his own shoe deal. But when he heard Paterson Catholic was playing St. Patrick's, he made it his business to be there.

"I've been following you guys all season," he said. He then pointed to each of our team's starting five, one by one, telling us about what we were doing right and wrong. Tim Thomas was averaging thirty-two minutes a night and scoring fourteen points per game in the NBA, but he had time to check in on the Paterson Catholic basketball team.

"Paterson's a part of me. It always has been and it always will. Someday you will all understand. Always be proud of being from Paterson. Always."

It was the same message Donald Hand had given me in Durham.

Paterson wasn't just some town in New Jersey. Paterson was more. It molded boys into men. We went out and won the game versus St. Patrick's, and Tim Thomas cheered from the stands.

So, if we could beat St. Pat's with one of my childhood idols watching, why couldn't I beat the SATs? I'd ask myself that question time and time again.

I took the test a third time in February. Back then, you could dial an 800 number and get your scores over the phone instead of waiting the extra few days to get them in the mail. I figured a change of routine couldn't hurt. When the automated voice revealed my score, my heart sank to new lows. An 820, even lower than the last time I'd taken it.

After basketball season was finished, I took the test again. I prepared long and hard, taking out every "Princeton Review" SAT prep book in the school library and doing practice exams at home. My mother would serve as the proctor and sit with an egg timer as I ripped through sections one by one. I'd do well on those practice tests, building up my confidence.

But on the day of that April exam date, my head was just somewhere else. I don't remember exactly why, but I was drifting in and out. I couldn't focus. I blamed the weather outside. I blamed the pressure.

But those weren't good excuses. I'd done just fine in the classroom my entire life and I'd always thrived in high-pressure situations. For whatever reason, though, this test was just getting the best of me. When I got the score of that fourth attempt at the SATs back in the mail, I was beside myself. An 820. Again.

0 for 4.

I'd never gone 0 for 4 from the free throw line. I'd never gone 0 for 4 in Little League baseball. I'd never gone 0 for 4 in anything in my life. I was 0-4 in taking the SATs.

I got on the phone with the UMass admissions office, and a woman there told me the minimum score that I needed to be deemed academically eligible for the following season. I'd have one more chance to take the test in June, and I had to get at least a 920 to qualify for the 2004 college football campaign.

If I didn't get that 920? Coach Brown told my mother and me that if I couldn't get the necessary score, "we'd have to explore other options."

I didn't know what that meant and I didn't want to find out. So I hit the books. Hard. The test prep books, my old trigonometry books from my sophomore year, my thesaurus—I had them all in a stack on the nightstand by my bed. I went cold turkey from all of my vices. I stopped playing video games, I wasn't going to the park to play basketball after school, and I didn't spend late nights on the phone with the girls Pelli and I had met at Skaters World.

I was an SAT studying machine.

Everyone else at Paterson Catholic was enjoying cases of "senioritis" and slacking off, but I was working harder than ever.

I took the test on another sunny morning in June, exactly one year after the first time I took it, and had a good feeling walking out of the room. I didn't zone out, I finished all five sections, and I didn't leave many questions blank.

No one had ever gone to college on the Cruz side of my family. My mother, my *abuela*, and *Papí* took so much pride in telling everyone back in Puerto Rico that I'd be attending the University of Massachusetts Amherst in the fall. For all of my athletic achievements and fancy newspaper clippings, nothing made them happier than the fact that I was college-bound. I just had to get that 920.

When the envelope came in the mail a month later, I stared at it for an hour before opening it up.

Then, like quickly ripping off a Band-Aid, I decided to just dive into the envelope and find out my score. When I opened it, my greatest fears were realized.

I'd gotten a 900.

I'd fallen twenty points short.

Twenty points was the equivalent of three questions. If I'd skipped five questions, instead of answering them wrong, I would have gotten the score I needed. I was stunned and I was embarrassed. Worst of all, I'd felt like a total failure. For the first time in my life, I had set a goal and I didn't achieve it.

My father came over to the house that night and told me not to let the news defeat me. He said the same thing he told me when Mookie, Colin, and I were fighting the NJSIAA's ruling four years earlier, "Nothing's going to be given to you in this life, son."

When my mother and I spoke with Coach Brown and the folks in the UMass admissions office, they explained that my scholarship wasn't being pulled. It'd just be put on hold until I got the necessary SAT scores to be deemed academically eligible.

At the time, I couldn't imagine taking the test again. I'd taken it five times in twelve months and never wanted to see another analogy or reading comprehension passage for the rest of my life. To even consider sitting in one of those rooms again, with that number 2 pencil in my hand and a banana at my side, made my stomach turn.

"So, when's the next test?" my mother asked, thinking the answer would be July or August.

"October," the admissions woman responded.

October? That was still five months away.

"What am I supposed to do until then?" I asked, hoping there'd be a way I could at least still be on campus for orientation in August with the other freshmen.

Coach Brown then explained the process that he had in mind. I'd go to something called a "prep school" for the fall semester. At this prep school, I'd take a few courses, play football, and focus solely on raising my SAT scores. There'd be no distractions there. No girls, no Pelli, no Skaters World, and a regimented schedule that'd guarantee I was zeroed in on raising those scores.

It sounded like prison.

The worst part? It was in Maine, eight hours away from home.

It was a lot to digest at once, but Coach Brown said that this was a common path to college for a lot of young men in my situation.

I had no other choice. I was headed to Maine.

My mother took out a small loan from the bank to pay the tuition and I registered for the SATs in October. I'd never been to Maine. Hell, I didn't even know where it was on the map. But come September, that was where I'd be spending my every waking hour.

■ ■ ■

IF YOU WERE a teenager living in northern New Jersey during the 1990s and 2000s, you built your summers around the July Fourth fair at the Meadowlands. Each year on Independence Day, they'd turn the parking lot in between Giants Stadium and the IZOD Center in East Rutherford into a giant carnival with rides, games, and concession stands. For a teenage kid, the July Fourth fair was like the dance floor at Skaters World times a million. There were just packs and packs of teenagers everywhere you looked. When the sun went down, there was a fireworks show that I'd put up against any other July Fourth celebration in the country.

I was so upset about my SAT situation that I didn't really enjoy senior week or my high school graduation. I moped around everywhere with a "Woe Is Me" grimace on my face. It took until the July Fourth fair for me to really even come out of my funk.

Jordan and Rocky were both back from college and I was excited to see them. They'd finished their freshman years at school and had some incredible stories to share. Jordan had heard all about my situation and told me to quit pitying myself and to smile, instead. "We're blessed, Vic," he said. "Don't stress out, man. Someday, when we're both in the NFL in our mothers' mansions, we'll laugh about this. Just relax, dude."

He was right. So I'd have to wait a semester before I got to college? Big deal. I, unlike most of the kids I grew up with, still had the opportunity to go to college. I had a great group of friends, a mother and father who loved me, and a bright future ahead. Things weren't so terrible in my life. Walking around the fair that night with Jordan helped put things in perspective for me. What was I so bummed out about? Life was good.

After the fireworks display and about three cotton candies too many, I gave Jordan a hug and told him I'd call him the next day. It was great seeing him.

I caught up with some of the kids in my grade and we hung out at the fair well past midnight. When we finally called it a night, it must have been three in the morning. It was one of those great high school evenings that you'll always remember. We were all going our separate ways in the fall—some to college, some to the military, some back to Paterson, and one to a prep school in Bridgton, Maine—and on that July Fourth, we just got to enjoy one another's company one last time.

On the car ride back to Paterson from the Meadowlands, my friend Julissa got a phone call on her cell phone. As she answered it, she leaned forward and turned the car radio's volume down.

"What?!" she asked the person on the other end in a horrified tone.

Julissa then started sobbing uncontrollably. She was hyperventilating in the backseat.

"What is it?" I asked, knowing something bad must have happened.

She couldn't breathe. She started screaming, "No! No!"

We pulled the car over and I took her outside.

"Julissa, what is it? What happened?" I asked, fearing the absolute worst.

Then, through her tears, she looked me straight in the eye and told me the news: "Jordan Cleaves died in a car accident tonight."

That wasn't possible. I'd been with Jordan the entire day and just said good-bye to him a few hours earlier. We'd just discussed the types of mansions we'd be buying our mothers when we got to the NFL.

I told her she was wrong.

"Vic, he's dead. Jordan's dead," she said, through a stream of tears. "He was driving home in the rain from the fair and his car flipped over on Route Twenty."

I couldn't feel my knees. I fell to the ground and immediately started crying.

As Julissa got more details on the accident, the news only got worse. Jordan wasn't driving home alone in his Dodge Stratus that night. Rocky, Rocky's brother Marquette, and Marquette's friend Donald were all in the car, too.

Jordan, Marquette, and Donald all died instantly from the sudden impact of the crash, and Rocky was in critical condition.

"They don't think Rocky's going to make it," she said. "And if he does, he'll never walk again."

It was three thirty in the morning and I was on the side of the road, in the fetal position, weeping.

How? Why? I didn't understand.

Jordan was one of my dearest friends, and of all the teammates I've ever known, he was the one I felt most comfortable opening up to. He never wasted his words and when he spoke, people listened. Whenever I was feeling down, he'd put things into context and remind me how blessed I was.

His integrity was unmatched, and when I began thinking about his mother and father, I started to break down.

Rocky, meanwhile, was invincible. He was a 240-pound tackling machine. I saw him record ten tackles on a torn ACL. Now he was never going to walk again?

I attended Jordan's funeral and the wake, but it still never felt real. To this day, I feel the urge to pick up the phone and call him. Jordan's death made me realize the fragility of life.

The crazy part was that he was always trying to make me realize it while he was alive.

I knew I'd never see Jordan Cleaves again. We'd never hop in his Dodge Stratus and go get a slice of pizza at Frank and Joe's and we'd never have another opportunity to run through Coach Wimberly's Route Tree together. But I promised myself I'd someday fulfill our dreams.

I'd make it to the NFL and buy my mother that mansion. Not just for myself, but for Jordan, too.

Rocky survived the crash and made a miraculous recovery. When he woke up from the accident a few days later, he didn't

I'D MAKE IT TO THE NFL AND BUY MY MOTHER THAT MANSION. NOT JUST FOR MYSELF, BUT FOR JORDAN, TOO.

remember a thing. The doctor told him that he'd lost not only his best friend in Jordan, but his older brother, Marquette, too. He couldn't move his neck. The doctors told him he'd be fortunate to walk again.

Not only did Rashawn "Rocky" Ricks walk again, but he was back on his feet and training for football season a few months later. He'd never get a chance to play, though, as the medical professionals all told him he'd risk paralysis if he took a bad hit to the neck.

Rocky could have let the news crush him and ruin his spirit. But he was a fighter. He did his nickname justice.

Nine months after being the lone survivor in a fatal car crash that took both his best friend and his brother, Rocky Ricks walked into Rutgers coach Greg Schiano's office and told him he'd never play a down for the Scarlet Knights. He then asked Coach Schiano what he *could* do, instead.

For the next four years, Rocky was a student assistant, serving as a part-time coach for all the defensive ends and linebackers on the Rutgers football team. He lugged equipment to and from practices, watched game tape late into the evening hours, and scouted all the opposing teams. He'd never make another tackle, but he was still making a tremendous impact. I had some initial resentment toward Coach Schiano because of the way my recruiting visit went, but I saw the kind of man he was when he let Rocky keep his full athletic scholarship and join the coaching staff.

Rocky told Coach Schiano, "I can't play the game anymore. But I can't get away from it, either." Coach Schiano wouldn't let him.

Rashawn Ricks graduated from Rutgers in four years and still checks in on me today. He has a tattoo that reads "I wish I could hold you now." Jordan and Rashawn were the captains of the Paterson Catholic football team, but they were so much more than just teammates to me.

I think about them all the time.

AS I WAS getting mentally prepared for my version of *The Odyssey* to an all-boys prep school in Bridgton, Maine, Pelli called me up in late August of that summer with a harebrained scheme. He was seeing a girl named Tara from Passaic, New Jersey, at the time and she had some friends he thought I should meet.

"Tara's friends are hot, man," he said. "And you're not going to be seeing any women for the next six months. It might be good to talk to some girls while you can."

I felt like a sailor being sent out to sea.

His idea was great, in theory, except for the fact that we were meeting these girls at The Wild Bull, a twenty-one-and-over bar, in Clifton. We were just seventeen.

We didn't have fake IDs, we weren't big drinkers, and we certainly didn't look like we were twenty-one years old. Fortunately, we were with Pelli's girl, and girls seem to play by different rules when it comes to getting into bars underage.

When we got past the bouncers and inside, Pelli ordered a few shots of Hennessy. We chugged them with no chasers. The shot tasted like flaming liquid detergent. We ordered another round. I guess we were gluttons for punishment.

Pelli's girl was cute and friendly, but her friends hadn't arrived yet. As we waited, Pelli and I just posted up at the bar, trying to fit in. Thinking back on it now, we must have looked like complete fools, taking shots of Hennessy and leaning up against the jukebox like we were tough guys.

After a few hours of waiting for Tara's friends to arrive, I got restless and told Pelli that I was going to head home.

"You've got to stay, man. Stay for me."

If the seventeen-year-old Victor Cruz was anything, he was a good wingman.

I'm forever grateful that I stayed that night.

When her friends arrived, one stood out from the pack. She looked like Russell Simmons's wife at the time, Kimora Lee, and was an absolute knockout. She was drop-dead gorgeous.

I was always pretty smooth with the opposite sex—or at least I thought I was—but when I saw this girl, I was tongue-tied. I didn't know what the hell to say.

She strutted over to our table like she owned the place.

The way that every guy in there was staring at her, she damn well could have owned it.

"I'm Elaina." She smiled, extending her hand out in my direction.

"Uh, I'm Vic," I stammered out.

Barely.

We made small talk for a few minutes and went our separate ways. I left The Wild Bull that night thinking I might have been drunk. I left also *knowing* that I was in love.

The next morning, I woke up at seven and called Pelli. He wasn't used to seven a.m. phone calls. "What's wrong, dude?" he asked, still half sleeping.

"When are we hanging out with those girls again?"

Pelli laughed out loud. "You think you've got a chance with Elaina, don't you?"

It turns out that Elaina was more than just a pretty face. She had graduated from high school at the age of fifteen, and though I was just getting ready to attend prep school, she was already heading into her junior year at Florida International University.

"Elaina's not some girl," Pelli said. "Elaina's a grown-ass woman."

It was as if he was challenging me, or questioning my ability to win her affection. If Elaina's beautiful eyes weren't enough motivation, Pelli's complete lack of confidence in my game only added fuel to my fire.

A few nights later, we snuck into another twenty-one-and-over bar, a club in Lodi called Swizzle. When Elaina walked in, she took my breath away, yet again.

Instead of standing there and staring at her from a distance, drooling like a dog, I decided to play it somewhat cooler this time. There were other girls in the club, so I started dancing with them. Every so often, I'd look in her direction and catch her glancing back at me.

As I was talking with one of the other girls, someone bumped me hard in the back. I turned around, thinking it was a drunk guy losing control.

It was Elaina.

"Oh, I'm sorry. I didn't see you there." She smiled.

It was no accident.

I smiled back, said it was okay, and kept on with my half-baked "hard-to-get" routine. Thinking I was cool, I backed away and walked to the other end of the bar. She shrugged and started dancing with another guy.

Had I blown it? Was she going to end up with the other dude for the rest of the night? I realized that my plan had backfired and called Pelli over to discuss it. I was like Eli in the huddle, ready to draw up some game-saving Hail Mary play. But there was no need. Pelli told me that after we'd hung out with their crew the other night, Elaina couldn't stop talking about me to her friends.

"Just play it cool," he said. "And stop running away from her."

A few minutes later, Elaina left the dance floor and walked right over to me. "What's up with you?" she asked. "Are you shy or something?"

"I'm not shy." I smiled back. "I'm not shy at all."

From that moment on, we were inseparable for the rest of the summer. We started dating, almost immediately, and realized that we had a lot in common. Elaina, like me, was half black, half Puerto Rican. She, too, had big dreams and was on the path to achieving them. We introduced each other to our families and spoke all day and night on the phone.

"That girl's going to be the mother of my baby someday," I told my mom.

I wasn't kidding.

THE REAL WORLD

THE DRIVE UP to Bridgton was straight out of a bad movie. My mother and father were in the two front seats of my mom's Ford Explorer and I was in the back. Every thirty minutes, I'd ask "Are we there yet?"

The answer was always "Not even close."

We stopped in Amherst, Massachusetts, for a quick bite to eat and I said, "Okay, we've got to be almost there now."

"We've still got another five hours, Victor," my mother responded.

For a kid from Paterson, Bridgton was no different than the planet Mars. It was way up in the woods of Maine in its own little world. Add in the fact that I was now madly in love with Elaina and eighteen hundred miles away from her, and that first week on campus made for anything but a smooth transition to life at prep school.

But I wasn't at Bridgton Academy to make friends or explore the wonders of the Pine Tree State. I was there to raise my SAT scores.

During my first day on campus, I met another football player named Courtney Greene.

"Where the hell are we, man?" Courtney asked me on line in the cafeteria.

We started talking and it turned out that Courtney was in a situation very similar to mine. He'd been a football star at New Rochelle High School in New York, but didn't have the grades to play college football coming out of high school. He committed to Rutgers and they shipped him up to Bridgton for the semester to get his academics in order.

Courtney and I were two city kids in a strange, strange world. The only thing in the entire town of Bridgton other than the school was a post office. There's a Laundromat on every corner in Paterson. The closest Laundromat to Bridgton Academy was thirty-five miles away. The closest mall was in the city of Portland, and getting there required a two-hour drive.

The few times we actually left campus were for trips to Wally World, or as most Americans call it—Walmart. "Wally World" was paradise to a bunch of cooped-up seventeen-year-old kids. It was ninety minutes away, but we all giddily piled into vans to walk the aisles and buy bags of Skittles and Doritos.

Courtney and I kept each other entertained, but my days at Bridgton were spent focusing on two things: the SATs and Elaina. She and I would write cheesy love letters and e-mails, encouraging each other to chase our dreams. I was madly in love.

Sports took a backseat for the first time in my life as I circled the October SAT test date and Thanksgiving weekend as my new first down markers.

The week before I took the SATs in October, I had a long talk with my mother on the telephone. She told me to just relax and to walk into the room with a clear head.

"Everyone's so proud of you, regardless of what score you get on your SATs, Victor."

I'd viewed the April and June SATs as make-or-break situations. Though I usually stepped up under pressure, I let the test psych me out on both occasions. I knew I was smart enough to score a 920, and after a few months of isolated preparation in the woods of Maine, I was confident I could get the score that I needed to move on to the next phase of my life.

I WAS MADLY IN LOVE.

Courtney and I walked into the testing center and wished each other the best of luck. I didn't bring a banana or a juice box.

I didn't need 'em.

Four weeks later, I got my score in the mail.

A 1040.

I had knocked it out of the park. I was going to college, baby! I called everyone I knew, starting with Elaina. She was thrilled. To this day, I have no idea how I would have gotten through that semester at Bridgton without her keeping me sane.

My mother, *abuela*, and *Papí* were all overjoyed. I'd be the first Cruz to go to college.

My father was excited, too, asking me when the first game of the following college football season was. "I'll be there, screaming from the stands," he assured me.

I'D BE THE FIRST CRUZ TO GO TO COLLEGE.

I finished out the semester in Maine and bid farewell to Courtney. He got the SAT scores he needed that day, too, and started four years at safety for Rutgers.

I made a trip out to New Rochelle to visit him the following fall and he took me to his former high school's Friday night football game. One of the littlest guys on the field stole the show that evening.

"Who's *that* kid?" I asked Courtney, amazed by what I was seeing.

"Oh, that's Ray Rice. He's got a chance to be really good. He's probably too small to play in the NFL, but he'll be a nice college football player. I'm trying to get him to come to Rutgers."

Everyone's story is unique.

I GOT TO UMass in the spring of 2005 and was blown away.

Everyone was nice. Everyone was cool. Everyone was beautiful. Girls I'd never met before were waving to me across the Student Union. Dudes I'd never met before were offering to help carry my bags. The faculty and alumni were welcoming me to campus and wishing me a great semester.

The older guys on the team who took me around campus fourteen months earlier were all excited about my arrival. They initiated me into their group the only way they knew how.

We partied.

And we partied hard.

I'd been to house parties in Paterson before, but nothing like the bashes they threw at UMass. Every other night, there was a fraternity, sports team, or off-campus apartment throwing a kegger. You know that scene in *Old School* where Snoop comes onstage and Will Ferrell goes into "Frank the Tank" mode? Well, during those first few months up at school, my nickname could have been "Vic the Tank."

I'd worked so hard just to get into college that once I finally got there, I wanted to celebrate. Every day was another opportunity to enjoy the brisk Massachusetts air and all the perks that went along with being a football player on a full scholarship.

I forgot all about studying, schoolwork, or even attending class. Who cared about any of that? I was a big-time college football player now.

My roommate freshman year was a great kid named Shawnn Gyles. Shawnn was a safety on the team, which made our pairing as roommates awfully interesting on the football field. We'd get up at five thirty in the morning every day that spring, sleepwalk together to practices, and then go at it one-on-one for three hours straight. The second practice ended and the final whistle blew, we'd leave it on the field and return to being the best of friends.

Shawnn and I had some good times together, to say the least.

One night, we were with a bunch of guys from the team at a bar called The Pub. Being a football or basketball player at UMass is a lot like being a celebrity in a small town. If you're an athlete, you never have to pay for a drink or wait in a line. We were having a great night and decided to bring the party back to our dorm room.

It seemed like a brilliant idea.

Yet there was no way the older guys on the squad would dare walk into a freshman dormitory. They had their own apartments off-campus. A senior strolling around Washington Hall wasn't exactly the epitome of cool.

Shawnn and I didn't realize that the older guys weren't joining us on the voyage back from the bar, and when we got to our room, we noticed that it was the two of us . . . and five girls.

I was still dating Elaina and had a collage of photographs of the two of us hanging directly over my desk. Shawn had a girlfriend back home in Ayer, Massachusetts, whom he worshipped, too.

This was trouble.

We looked at each other with devilish smirks. We were confused. We were flattered, sure, but still confused. How'd this even happen?

Before I could even think of what to do, Shawnn got a text message on his cell phone. His face went blank.

He pulled me into the bathroom in the hallway, "Vic," he said without blinking, "My girlfriend is downstairs."

In the two months that we'd been living together, Shawnn's girlfriend never once surprised him by just showing up unannounced. Of all the nights for her to hop in her car and drive ninety minutes to surprise her boyfriend, she chose the one where we had five girls hanging out in our dorm room.

I acted fast.

"Girls, you've got to go. I don't feel well. I think I drank too much," I said, putting on an Oscar-worthy performance.

"I thought you said you guys wanted to hang out. Is it something we said? Something we did?" one of the girls asked.

"No, no. I just have to be up really early and must have eaten something bad tonight," I answered as I ushered them out the door. "I also think I've got the flu." I rattled off every possible illness or excuse in the book. We needed to get these girls out of our room, and we needed to get them out of there fast.

I thought we were in the clear and timed the whole thing perfectly. As I was guiding the girls into the elevator, Shawnn's girlfriend was just pulling up to the dorm in her car. We were going to make it!

He went down to meet her in the lobby and I pumped my fist like I'd just caught a fifty-yard pass over my shoulder for a touchdown. Success!

But I celebrated too soon.

Apparently, on her walk through the front lobby of the dorm, one of the girls we kicked out of our room was speaking very loudly.

"Vic and Shawnn always flirt with girls and lead them on, but they never do anything. They're players," she said in a voice so loud that most of Amherst, Massachusetts, could hear.

Naturally, Shawnn's girlfriend was sitting right there in the lobby, listening to the girl's entire rant. By the time Shawnn got down there, his girlfriend was already halfway back to her car.

Flag on the play.

He'd spend the next twelve hours on the phone, apologizing profusely.

Just a random Saturday night in the lives of Victor Cruz and Shawnn Gyles.

I finished that first semester with hundreds of new friends. I might have been the coolest guy on campus.

But my grade point average was an appalling 1.6.

The dean of admissions called me into her office and told me that I'd need to raise my GPA above a 2.0 not only to stay on the football team, but to remain at UMass.

I said I understood and headed home to Paterson.

School was out for summer.

■ ■ ■

IN LATE JULY, I called up Shawnn to see if he'd be my roommate in the dorms, but he had some disheartening news to report. To remain academically eligible for the 2005 season, he needed to pass an English course over the summer up in Amherst. He went to class every day and wrote a twenty-page final paper.

A month later, he still hadn't received an e-mail with his final grade for the course.

When he called up his guidance counselor at school, the unthinkable was revealed. Though he was certain he did everything right in registering for the class, there was a clerical error. His name wasn't in the system and there was no record of him ever signing up for the class.

Because the course was just based on that one final paper at the end of the semester, the mistake was never caught by Shawnn, the school, or the professor. He'd spent the entire summer in Amherst, working his butt off, for a class that he was never enrolled in.

Shawnn did all he could to object, but the rules were the rules. He wasn't allowed back into school and he wasn't on the squad that fall.

He'd never make it back to UMass.

THOUGH I WAS upset to learn that Shawnn wouldn't be joining me back at school, I was excited when I found who'd be replacing him as my new roommate that semester.

Liam Coen was a six-foot-two skinny white kid with strawberry blond hair from a small town in Rhode Island.

He was also a hell of a quarterback.

We lived on the seventh floor of the Kennedy dormitory and hit it off right away. Liam and I came from *completely* different backgrounds, but we actually had a lot in common. Our birthdays were just two days apart, we both loved playing the *Madden* video game, and we each valued family and friends above all else.

He didn't have the strongest arm, but he was an incredibly accurate passer. Liam could hit any receiver, in any situation, right in the numbers on the front of his jersey. His father had been his coach in high school and his grandfather had been the captain of the Boston College football team in the 1940s. Football was in Liam's blood. We took our official recruiting visits to UMass on the same day in the winter of '04 and became fast friends when I got to campus the following spring.

I was redshirted that year, meaning I'd sit the entire 2005 college football season out and watch games from the sidelines. It wasn't a punishment. Coach Brown didn't think I was ready to make an impact yet, and instead of throwing me to the wolves before I was ready, he felt that a year of observing and learning would do me some good. Except for the really rare talents that play right away, most college football players are redshirted during their first season on a team.

Though I couldn't suit up for the games, I could still practice. I was on the scout team, which meant that I had to learn the other team's offense and play the position of the opposing number one receiver against our starting defense each week in practice. Scout team guys aren't supposed to give the starters trouble, but I was giving our top cornerbacks and safeties headaches every practice.

"Cruz, we're lucky we don't have to play against you on Saturdays," James Ihedigbo, our top safety, would tell me after practices.

Things on the football field were going great, and though I wasn't playing on Saturdays, I was making an impression on Coach Brown and the rest of the guys on the squad. I was working my tail off and learning our offense inside and out.

"You're still raw, Victor, but you could end up being one of our starting receivers next year. Just keep up the hard work," Coach

Brown told me one day after a particularly strong practice. "And get your academics in order, son."

I wish I'd listened to the second part of his statement. Unfortunately, I was too fixated on the first.

I was taking care of business on the practice field, but in the classroom, I was stinking it up.

Unlike Paterson Catholic, where the classes were small and the teachers knew the students by their first names, the UMass lecture halls were massive. The introductory courses that I was taking that year had fifteen hundred students in them.

I found excuses for everything and when I'd get an F on an assignment, I wouldn't let it bother me. I'd rationalize things by asking, "Why should I devote time to learning about the War of 1812 if I am torching Shannon James in practice every day? I'll never be asked to discuss the War of 1812 for a living."

I didn't attend many classes and when I did, I'd usually just put my head down on the desk in front of me and take a nap.

My behavior was shameful.

On exam days, I'd show up and just assume I'd copy off someone else in the class. If the other students didn't willfully *let* me cheat off them, I'd get angry. "Goody Two-shoes," I'd mutter, and they'd roll their eyes.

My head was in the clouds and I was living in a dreamworld where Victor Cruz was the only person that mattered. I had become the stereotypical dumb jock.

I had been blessed with the opportunity of a lifetime—a full-time college scholarship—and was too busy with video games and late nights at The Pub to realize that I was letting it all slip away. The success was getting to my head. In truth, it wasn't even any actual success at all. I wasn't even playing on Saturdays; I was just on the scout team. I was an above-average *practice* player.

My mother would call and ask about my grades and I'd blatantly lie to her, saying that they were fine.

Elaina and I were also beginning to grow more and more distant. Days would go by where I wouldn't hear from her and I'd barely notice. I was too busy having fun with the other guys. I'd go out until all hours of the night and wake up at noon.

I was loving college life and I was loving myself. To borrow a line from Terrell Owens, one of my favorite players growing up: "I loved me some me."

My inflated ego had gotten out of control and without Elaina, my mother, my father, Coach Wimberly, Jim Salmon, or Jordan Cleaves there to bring me back down to Earth, I lost sight of my goals.

I went home for the holidays that December thinking all was good in the world of Victor Cruz. When my grades arrived in an e-mail a few days before Christmas, the reality of the situation became clear.

My GPA was a 1.8 for the semester, and a 1.7 overall. Anything less than a 2.0 wouldn't cut it.

I was expelled.

I hadn't played in a single football game and I was already kicked out of college.

I figured there had to be some kind of mistake. There's no way they could just boot me out of UMass. Not when I was playing so well in those practices. Not when everyone on campus was telling me how great I was. Not when I hadn't paid for a drink at The Pub all semester.

But it was the truth.

All those hours studying alone in the library at Bridgton Academy, all those nights spent alone in my room with my SAT prep books, and all the talks about the NFL with Jordan were for naught.

I was now just another jobless college dropout living under his mother's roof.

■ ■ ■

ELAINA CAME OVER to the house the night I got my grades and we worked out a plan of attack. She'd help me write a letter to the dean of admissions as I broke the news to my mother. The former was a lot easier than the latter.

My mother was so proud of the fact that her son was in college. She told everyone she knew and wore her UMass shirts and hats everywhere she went in town. She wasn't just proud of the fact that I went to college, though. She loved that I had worked so hard to get there. She took pride in knowing just how much I'd overcome to get to Amherst.

In less than eight months, I'd squandered it all.

When I showed her my grades and explained what they meant, she didn't say a word. She just shook her head in disappointment. I'd let her down. My mother always had an answer for everything. An old saying, a joke, a quip—something. When she heard the news of my expulsion, she was left speechless.

I sent a detailed e-mail to the admissions office asking what I could do to get back into school. The response wasn't exactly what I had hoped.

No matter what, I'd have to miss the spring 2006 semester at UMass.

I could enroll in classes at a local community college, but there was no guarantee that I'd be readmitted into school. I called Coach Brown, but he told me there was really nothing he could do. Being an athlete, he explained, didn't mean a thing to the admissions office. There'd be no special treatment.

A few days after the New Year's holiday, I drove my mother's car to the County College of Morris. I walked in and signed up for a full slate of courses. I was back at stage one.

In late January, I got a call from one of my old teammates up at UMass with some terrible news.

Liam's mother had passed away.

She had been sick with Lyme disease for a very long time, and the weight of the illness had put a strain on her relationship with Liam's dad. Liam was an only child and he was their everything.

When Liam's mother got very ill, she fell into a deep depression. He'd mention things in passing to me, but we never got into too much detail in our dorm room. He'd often sneak into the hallway and have intense phone conversations with his father that lasted for hours, but I always just assumed those talks were about school or football.

In just his second year on campus, Liam was the football team's starting quarterback, he was an A student, and he had a stunning girlfriend who absolutely adored him. All seemed perfect in Liam Coen's life.

It wasn't.

He got a phone call from his mother a month after the football season. She was frantic. His father was in the hospital with what doctors described as heart congestion and she wasn't sounding like herself.

She called him in tears, repeatedly asking Liam if he loved her, if he thought she was a good mom. He told her that she was, and kept building her up, saying that she was a fantastic mother and that he loved her very much. They spoke for a few more minutes and Liam hung up the phone, but he was deeply concerned with her behavior.

Liam's mother was found dead in her home the next morning. She had taken her own life.

When I heard the news, I immediately got my phone and called Liam. I wanted him to know that his mother loved him very much and that her death wasn't his fault. I wanted him to know that I'd always admired his strength, and that he'd made an incredibly positive impact on my life. I wanted him to know that although I was no longer enrolled at UMass, I could be on the next bus up to Rhode Island if he needed me.

But when Liam answered the phone, my mind went completely blank. I strung a few sentences together, but didn't say any of the things I'd wanted to say.

About an hour after we hung up, he sent me a text message: "Hey, Dude, thanks for calling. It means a lot to me. It's great knowing I've got friends like you."

Little did I realize how much I'd come to lean on *him* in the coming years.

AS A YOUNG boy in our apartment on East Twentieth Street, I'd marvel at how *Papí* lived his life according to a strict schedule. He was a creature of habit. He'd eat his three meals at the same exact time every day and stick to his daily routine.

Those next six months, I did the same. Every weekday, I'd wake up at seven a.m. and drive my mother to her job at Benjamin Moore Paints. After dropping her off, I'd take the car to school and stay until six p.m. At six thirty, I'd pick her up from work and drive us home. We'd have dinner and I'd go to bed. Rinse and repeat. That was my life in the spring of '06.

It was a boring existence, but one I was fine with.

Occasionally during that period of my life, I'd drive down Park Avenue or stop at one of the other busy street corners in town. I'd see guys I grew up with, wearing new clothes and hanging out. They always seemed to be having so much fun and girls were always buzzing around them like bees on honey.

It would have been easy to blow off a class here or there and join them, but I resisted. I was back in Paterson for a reason and I needed to stay focused. My goal was to get back into UMass, and nothing was going to get in my way.

At the end of May, I sent my County College of Morris, spring 2006 semester transcript to the admissions office at UMass. Three Bs and an A.

In early June, I got a formal letter back in the mail. It started with "Congratulations!"

Though my grades didn't transfer over, I'd be back on campus and on the team in the fall.

I had yet another new lease on life and was excited to get back to school that August. I called up Liam to see if he'd be my roommate in the dorms. I couldn't imagine living with anyone else.

"I've got the *Madden* game cued up and ready to go," he laughed.

I was happy to be back on the squad. Whereas Liam was named our starting quarterback, Coach Brown still didn't think I was ready to get playing time on the field. Having missed the spring practices, he let me know that I likely wouldn't be playing much in 2006.

I was disappointed but understood Coach Brown's decision. The offense was running a complex offensive scheme and having missed months of practice in the spring, there was just no way he could put me into a game.

"Use this season and watch how the older guys go about their business," he told me.

I felt that I was one of the best athletes on the team, but being the best athlete doesn't necessarily mean you're the best player. The game of football is one of physical skills, but it's also one that's quite cerebral. My physical skills were always going to be there, but I needed to master the offense. That'd take hard work and a disciplined approach toward film sessions. It'd also take time.

I didn't get on the field once during that 2006 season.

I'D *THOUGHT* I'D done significantly better in school that fall, but when my grades came in an e-mail that December, the news was bleak.

I'd gotten a 2.2 for the semester, but my cumulative grade point average was still below a 2.0.

I was getting kicked out of school. Again.

This time, I didn't have Elaina to cry to. We'd been on a break. My mother thought I was kidding when I told her the news. My father didn't understand.

I called Coach Brown, but he'd had just enough conversations with me about my grades. "It's like a broken record, Victor. I don't know what to tell you this time," he said. "How many strikes do you want? How many strikes do you expect?"

My mother and I hopped in her Ford Explorer and drove four hours to Amherst. We arrived at the office of Ms. Pamela Marsh-Williams, the associate dean for undergraduate advising. She'd never seen or heard of me before. She certainly didn't care how many receptions I once had for the Paterson Catholic Cougars.

"Victor, I'll be honest, your options are quite limited," she told me as she thumbed through my transcript.

My mother was distraught. She explained to Ms. Marsh-Williams what I'd been through, what I'd overcome to make it to UMass.

But Ms. Marsh-Williams didn't budge. "I'm impressed with Victor's story, Ms. Cruz," she said. "But once he got here, he *stopped* working. We have an academic standard to uphold, and your son hasn't lived up to it. I hope you understand."

Though she was stern, Ms. Marsh-Williams had the decency to sit with us and discuss all of my possible options.

As it turned out, not only did I have awful grades, but I wasn't even enrolled in the right classes. There were several key core classes that I still hadn't taken.

"You have to go back home to Paterson and find an accredited institution," she explained. "When you do, you're going to have to take several classes—more than you've ever taken in a semester here—and you're going to have to earn very high marks in all of them."

I was scribbling notes in a spiral notebook, nodding, and not saying a word. Though she didn't have to, Ms. Marsh-Williams went online and listed out some of the different community colleges in northern New Jersey where my credits *and* grades would transfer. The three Bs and an A at the College County of Morris were nice, but those grades didn't count at UMass. Only the credits did.

"You're no longer a student here, Victor," she told me as we wrapped up the conversation. "I can't do much more for you. It's on you now."

My scholarship was revoked, all of my belongings were removed from the dorm, and I climbed into my mother's car with my tail between my legs.

We didn't speak the entire four-hour drive home.

MOM HAD PAID for my high school education at Paterson Catholic and taken out a loan for my semester in Bridgton. I couldn't ask her to pay the tuition at Passaic County Community College. I'd have to get a job.

I put on a nice pair of slacks and a button-down and took her car to the Garden State Plaza, an upscale shopping mall in Paramus, New Jersey.

I'd always liked men's fashion and figured if I was going to work in a mall smelling the Cinnabon store all day long, I might as well get a decent employee discount somewhere cool out of it. I walked into the GUESS store, visualizing myself as a suave salesman selling designer jeans.

"What's your story?" the manager, an attractive woman in her late twenties, asked me.

I told her that I was home from college and needed some extra cash. I'd work hard and show up every day with a smile.

"So, sell me some jeans," she responded.

"What?"

"What do you mean 'What?' If I were a customer walking into this store today, what would your sales pitch be? Sell me some GUESS jeans."

I was caught off guard. I'd never *sold* anything before. I certainly hadn't sold $120 designer jeans.

"Hey, I'm Victor," I started.

"Are you trying to pick me up?" she snapped back. "I'm here to buy jeans. I don't care what your name is."

"Yeah, so, uh, what style are you looking for, ma'am?" I mumbled, realizing this job interview wasn't going particularly as well as I had imagined it would.

"What style am I looking for? You're the salesman. Should I go online and come back and tell you what style I'm looking for? Or should I just go to another store where they'll tell me what style looks best on me?"

I shook the woman's hand and thanked her for her time.

I'd never be the top denim salesman at the GUESS store in the Garden State Plaza.

A bit discouraged, I stumbled into another men's clothing store called Image. The manager was a young guy named Jeff, who seemed a bit over his head. They sold some high-end brands— True Religion, 7 For All Mankind, Diesel—and played good music in the store. I told him I was interested in working there and that I liked the lines they carried.

Jeff looked at me and nodded. "Can you start tomorrow?" he asked.

"I can start today," I answered.

Jeff hired me on the spot and I got right to work. I'd use the money I made at Image to pay for my tuition and books at PCCC. Every other day, I alternated between going to classes and working eight-hour shifts at Image.

Jeff was a good dude and I'd often tell him about my dreams

of playing in the NFL. He'd usually say something encouraging and then tell me to go fold a pair of jeans in the back.

My days working at the mall were long and tedious. There were no chairs at Image, so I was always on my feet, standing upright. Jeff gave his employees a thirty-minute lunch break each day, but by the time I'd finally get to the food court across the mall, fifteen of those thirty minutes were already gone. I remember sneaking into the men's restroom on the second floor and locking myself behind a toilet stall door. I wouldn't use the facilities. I'd just sit. It felt so good to just sit.

But I liked the job. Jeff was always upbeat and his work ethic reminded me of my mother's. He had a family that he was providing for and was always the first one to arrive at the store in the morning and the last one to leave at night. I liked the employee discount, too. Nobody had better jeans at PCCC than me.

One day that January, I was unloading boxes in the back room when I heard a loud commotion coming from the front of the store. When I popped my head out to see what was going on, I saw fifty people walking into Image at once. We'd be lucky to get fifty shoppers over the course of an entire day. Something was up.

The crowd of people didn't consist of shoppers. They were Giants fans.

Michael Strahan, a defensive end on the Giants at the time, walked into Image and a mob of fans followed him. I watched as Strahan laughed, posed for photographs, and looked at everyone directly in the eye when he spoke to them. Strahan was one of the most recognizable faces in the NFL and he knew the responsibilities that came along with that. He was as comfortable and as polished as anyone I'd ever seen. With his smile and humility, Strahan made every one of those fans feel like he or she was the most important person in the store.

Jeff was helping Strahan pick out some new clothes. I kept my distance until he called me over. "Vic, you've got to meet Michael Strahan," he shouted from across the store.

I put the box cutter down and shuffled my feet over to greet the Giants All-Pro.

"Vic's a football player," Jeff told him as he put his arm around my shoulder. "He played wide receiver at UMass. He's back home getting his grades in order. He's one of the best employees I've got. This kid's a tremendously hard worker."

Strahan smiled and told me to keep on working hard.

"THE NFL WILL FIND YOU IF YOU'RE GOOD ENOUGH."

"I went to Texas Southern," he told me. "Texas Southern, man. The NFL will find you if you're good enough."

Strahan bought a pair of jeans, signed a few autographs, and was on his way. But his message that day was clear. For all the ups and downs I'd been through in the past few years, I was still just twenty years old. Sure, I was working at a second-tier men's clothing store in a shopping mall in the suburbs. And, yeah, I was no longer on a college football team.

But if the NFL could find Michael Strahan at tiny Texas Southern, they could certainly find me at UMass.

I just needed to get back there.

WHILE I WAS occupied with a full course load and spending long hours on my feet at the mall, things weren't going very well for other members of my family.

Papí was sick.

"Your grandfather has colon cancer," my mother told me one day when I was studying at the kitchen table.

Week after week, I'd visit *Papí* and see a shell of the guy I once wrestled with as a kid. He took so much pride in being a strong, youthful man. As the cancer spread, he began to age considerably and lose weight at a rapid pace. Watching the slow progression of the cancer take hold of his spirit was incredibly difficult on my mother and *abuela*. I had a hard time watching all three of them struggle with his illness so mightily.

My father was in a dark place, too.

In February of that year, I got a call from my older sister, Ebony. She had recently given birth to a beautiful baby boy and I was thrilled to be an uncle. Jordan Turner was Dad's first grandchild.

Ebony was fed up, though. Not with Jordan, her newborn son, but with our father.

They'd been fighting a lot and in their most recent conversation on the phone, he cursed her out and called her several nasty names.

Ebony was always the apple of my father's eye. She was crushed by his harsh words.

I couldn't understand how he could speak to his only daughter the way he did. I hung up the phone with Ebony and told her not to worry about it. She was a young, single mother and needed the emotional support of her father. I was disgusted by his behavior and called him to let him know.

We went at it. I said some mean things that I probably shouldn't have and he came back at me with fury. He was already mad at me for getting kicked out of school, and my phone call that night only enraged him more. We tore into each other, saying very hurtful things, for a heated five minutes.

Before hanging up, I told him that I never wanted to speak to him again.

I never did.

MAYBE I COULD have been more understanding.

My father worked twenty-five years for the Paterson Fire Department. In the winter of 2006, he was driving down the very same Route 20 that had taken Jordan Cleaves's life two years earlier, and got in a serious car accident. When he visited a doctor after the crash, he was told that he'd have to take some time away from work.

My father never used a sick day in all the years he fought fires. I don't recall him ever taking a vacation, either. Dad hated missing a day of work. He was a fireman's fireman. That's what everyone would always say. The job defined him.

Following the doctor's orders, he begrudgingly went on disability leave. Dad was in chronic pain from the injury but knew that he had to return to the job soon. He was restless doing nothing at home, and the idleness of being on leave was killing his morale.

He was also a few years from receiving his pension and couldn't run the risk of somehow losing his job before he hit that benchmark. When he spoke with his fire chief about coming back to work, he requested being put on light duty, something rather common for a firefighter returning to work after a bad accident.

His request was denied.

Though I'll never know all the details, I do know that he returned to work far sooner than he should have.

Things got worse.

Just as he was getting back into the flow of his normal routine, he began feeling a series of sharp pains in his stomach and chest. He was vomiting and suffering from nausea. He went back to the doctor's office and was told that he had liver disease.

My father, the unbreakable man, was crumbling.

He hit a new low in March of 2006, when, after twenty-five years on the job and just a few months after surviving a near-fatal car accident, he was fired. The reasons were never explained.

There'd been a long history of racial tension within the Paterson Fire Department. My father would hide the details of just how bad things were from me when I was a kid, but the stories I'd hear on the street and in school were awful. In 2004, a group of Paterson's African-American and Latino firefighters filed a civil complaint, alleging racial discrimination in the department's hiring practices. The case was highly publicized and settled when both groups agreed to achieve a 50 percent minority hiring goal and implement a new recruitment program committed to bringing in qualified minority candidates. My father was encouraged by the 2004 court ruling and thought it was a sign of better times on the horizon.

Less than two years later, he was fired from the only job he'd ever really known.

In May of 2006, he and four other African-American firefighters in Paterson filed another lawsuit against the fire department, alleging discrimination, harassment, and unruly retaliation from their supervisors. My father didn't think he was fired because of his performance, his illness, or a head-count issue. He believed it was a result of speaking out against his bosses during that 2004 trial.

As he awaited a ruling and his reinstatement to the department, his medical coverage ran out.

He, like *Papí*, began to rapidly lose weight. He stopped seeing his doctor.

The situation swallowed him whole. As one of the first African-Americans to have a leadership role within the Paterson Fire Department, he took a tremendous amount of pride in overcoming the challenges he'd faced in those early years on the job. For all he'd given to the city, he was repaid with walking papers just five years before he was set to get his pension.

He was angry, he was hurt, and he was very ill.

His personality changed over the course of those thirteen months. He was no longer the happy-go-lucky Mike Walker whom everyone in town knew and loved. He wasn't the bundle of joy that lit up any room he walked into. He wasn't the screaming dad in the basketball bleachers, yelling, "That's my son!" anytime I made a play.

He was someone else.

The loneliness might have affected him the most. I was up in Amherst, Malik was at Delaware State, and Ebony had her hands full, working a full-time job and raising a new son in Piscataway.

My father lived for his job as a firefighter and his kids.

Now he suddenly had neither.

I was upset with how he had spoken to Ebony and couldn't get over the things he had said to me. Sure, he was going through some rough times, but we all were. *Papí* was sick with colon cancer and I was sheepishly walking around Paterson, mortified to be back at home after flunking out of school twice. He was the one who always told me, "Nothing's going to be handed to you, son."

So, why was he letting a string of unfortunate events rob him of his livelihood? Why was he letting some crummy news defeat him? Why was he taking it out on Ebony?

I loved my father so much. I thought that if I gave him the silent treatment for a few months, he'd snap out of his funk and make a change.

That change never came.

ON MARCH 1, 2007, I was sitting at my computer when my older brother Malik's phone number flashed on my cell phone. We'd text each other all the time, but Malik and I rarely spoke on the phone. I answered with a bit of apprehension.

"It's Daddy, Vic," he said with a trembling voice. "They found Daddy, Vic. He's dead."

I told him to shut up and I hung up the phone. Malik was being dramatic. Malik was always dramatic.

He immediately called me back. "I don't have time for this,

Malik," I told him, not wanting to even acknowledge what he had said.

"Vic, he's dead. Daddy's dead."

I went silent.

I couldn't react. I didn't know *how* to react. I felt numb.

My mother then called me from her office at work. It was true, she said. She wept hysterically into the phone. "Your father's gone, Victor," she cried. "I'm so sorry. Your father's gone."

Malik's mother, Jackie, my father's ex-wife, spoke with Dad often. When she hadn't heard from him for a few days, she went over to his apartment to check in and make sure everything was okay.

The radio was blaring and the lights were on inside. She suspected that everything was fine, but when she opened the front door of his place, she smelled an awful odor.

Jackie took two steps inside his apartment, looked into my father's bedroom, and found him sprawled out on his stomach with a stream of blood coming from his mouth.

She rushed over to him. He wasn't breathing. She screamed in horror.

My father had committed suicide.

I wouldn't believe that he was gone until I saw his face, in the open casket, at his wake a few days later.

That whole week is still a complete blur.

Friends would call me, but I'd have nothing to say. People would stop by the house to offer their condolences and I'd close the door to my bedroom.

His wake was held at the New AME Zion Church in Paterson, and there were at least four hundred people in attendance, paying their respects.

It was an amazing melting pot of people, both young and old. There were firefighters whom he'd been friends with since the 1980s, teenage kids he taught how to swing a baseball bat in Little League, and elderly women whose lives he'd changed. They all came up to me and told me what a wonderful man he was.

I didn't cry at the funeral or the wake. Everyone was hysterical around me, but I didn't shed a tear. I couldn't.

I didn't think he'd want me to show emotion. He would have said, "Be strong, Vic. Be strong."

I said good-bye to Mike Walker that day, but assured him that he'd be with me for the rest of my life.

My father was my idol. He still is. He embodied everything that I find honorable in a man—strength, courage, selflessness, good humor, and responsibility. He was always honest and he was always ethical. He truly lived his life to the fullest. I think about him every time I step on the football field. I think about him every time I kiss my baby daughter good night.

I think about him all the time.

ELAINA AND I hadn't spoken for months, but she made the trip to Paterson to be by my side at my father's funeral. She was my rock during that confusing period of my life. We'd stay up late, just talking, and we'd work through some of the anger and sadness I had bottled up inside.

A few days after my father was laid down to rest, I was sitting on my computer when I got an instant message from Liam. He hadn't made the trip down for the funeral, but he'd sent me a series of text messages when he heard the news. I'm not sure if he felt awkward calling on the phone or just didn't know if he had it in him to say the things he wanted aloud, but he chose Instant Messenger as his way of reaching out to me. I'll never forget what he wrote.

"Hey, I'm here for you, Vic. Anything you need, I'm here. Anything."

I thanked him and tried changing the subject to football. He'd just finished a breakout season in which he'd thrown twenty-six touchdown passes.

He took a while to respond. He then responded: "You don't have to go through this alone. Please call if you need anything. Anything at all."

If there was one person in the world who could possibly relate to what I was going through at the time, it was Liam Coen.

I've never told him how much those instant messages meant to me. I have a feeling he already knows.

ONE NIGHT THAT April, I went out with a group of the Paterson guys to see our boy Cancun perform. He was an aspiring rapper and my friends thought I could use a night out on the town to unwind.

It felt good to blow off some steam. I'd done nothing but study, work, and mourn over the past several weeks. I was mentally and emotionally exhausted. I had a few drinks, a ton of laughs, and even hit the dance floor for a set. Just as Cancun took the stage, though, a brawl between two rival gangs broke out in the middle of the club.

The last thing I needed to be a part of was a stupid fight. I headed for the exits. As I bobbed and weaved my way through the frantic crowd, I heard the sound of gunshots.

Wap-wap-wap!

It was the same noise I'd heard all those nights in my bedroom on East Eighteenth Street. Everyone in the club screamed, scattered, and ran for cover under tables and chairs. I just kept walking. I never broke my stride.

When I got outside, I caught my breath and sat on the curb. I stared at the sky and took a deep breath.

Everything in my life was happening so fast. I needed a break. From school, from work, from all the thoughts I was having about how things had ended between my father and me, from the mayhem that was going on inside that club.

I just sat on the curb in silence, with cars whizzing by and commotion all around me.

At that moment, I had an epiphany. Something clicked.

I decided that I was going to ace my final exams, get back into school, and achieve all of my goals.

No more excuses. No more pitying myself. No more sleepless nights spent staring at the ceiling wondering how I had pissed it all away. No one was going to do it for me. No one was going to *give* me anything. I'd have to scrape and crawl and earn every grade, every yard, and every dollar.

It's the only way I'd make it happen.

I wanted it no other way. A rush of adrenaline came over me. I was excited to live the rest of my life. I had a moment of clarity on that curb and it all started to make sense: I could accomplish anything I set my mind to. I just had to go out there and *do* it.

My friends came running out of the club a few minutes later, all fired up and angry. Someone pushed someone, someone's girlfriend was shoved in the back, and someone said something about another guy's cousin. I loved all those guys, but I didn't care. At that point, I couldn't imagine caring less.

"I'm sorry, guys. I'm done. I'm going home."

I knew what I had to do.

My *abuela* was right. Nothing good happened after five p.m.

But that moment of clarity changed my life forever.

Things would never be the same.

CHAPTER 7

COURTESY OF LIAM COHEN

WAITING FOR A CHANCE

ENTHUSED AND NOW energized to hit the books, I approached the next few months at PCCC like I would a big football game. I circled all the dates of my final exams and created detailed work-back plans, identifying the days where I'd devote to studying weeks in advance.

Though I tried telling myself not to care how others viewed my situation, I hated the whispers. Everywhere I went in town, I'd catch people pointing and talking to their friends. They saw me as another Paterson failure, another local kid with a golden ticket for a better life who chose to give it all away, instead. I'd go to Frank and Joe's for a slice and the guys behind the counter would ask me how college was going. I'd smile and say things were great. I didn't want to tell anybody the truth.

Jarris Rogers was an old football teammate of mine at Paterson Catholic. A year younger than me in school, he was enrolled in a few of my classes at PCCC that spring.

One day, after a few weeks of exchanging hellos and small talk, he pulled me aside after class: "Yo, Cruz, why the hell are you *here*? Why aren't you up at school playing ball? You're one of the best football players I've ever seen, man. Why are you at PCCC?"

I was too ashamed to share with him my tale. How do you tell someone that you'd been given a full ride to college, kicked out of school twice, and were now being forced to start from scratch?

"I'm just home for a few months," I said, trying not to look at him directly in the eye. "UMass is letting me take some courses here while I take care of my family stuff. You know, with my dad and all."

Jarris nodded, but he knew it wasn't the truth. "Okay, man," he responded. "Well, we're all pulling for you, Vic. Make Paterson proud, man."

I'd take the city bus to PCCC and just walk around the campus, thinking. I'd think about my father, I'd think about *Papi*, I'd think about Elaina, and I'd think about my uncertain future. I was never a real introspective person, but during those few months, I didn't have very much to say. I just thought a lot.

I took five courses at PCCC that semester and each one of them fulfilled a core curriculum requirement at UMass. By the time I sat down to take my exams in May, I knew all five subjects inside and out. I didn't fear those finals. I embraced them.

When I got my grades back later that month, I smiled for the first time in what felt like an eternity.

Five courses—four As and one B. All the grades were transferable to University of Massachusetts Amherst.

I called the admissions office. If I could get the paperwork over in a few days, I'd be a candidate for readmission into school.

In early June, I got word. I was accepted.

It'd be the fourth time in three years that I celebrated getting into UMass. There'd be no fifth.

INSTEAD OF HANGING around Paterson the rest of the summer, I decided to head up to school and get a head start on things. I knew a bunch of the football guys were renting an off-campus house and wondered if they'd mind adding one more to list of tenants.

I just so happened to know the right guy to call.

"Absolutely!" Liam shouted when I asked if there was a spare couch to crash on. "Get up here. We need to get you back on the field and playing football."

He was right.

Though there were a million things going on inside my head when I was off the field, things felt normal when I was on it. Liam and I would wake up early, walk to the football stadium, and run routes for hours.

By the summer of 2007, Liam had already established himself as one of the best quarterbacks in all of Division I-AA football. He had sports reporters interviewing him and professional scouts dissecting his every pass. At that point in his career, he had twenty-four starts and thirty-six career touchdown passes under his belt. Me? I had zero games and zero pass receptions on my résumé.

But Liam had faith in me. He'd tell me how much he was looking forward to finally playing together.

One day after one of our throwing sessions, he asked me how I was doing. I kind of shrugged and said things were fine.

"People used to ask me, 'How can you even think about football?' or 'How do you just go on with your everyday life?'" Liam said as we walked from the field to the off-campus house. "It's because my mother knew how much I loved the sport. It would have been selfish of me to quit. She wouldn't have wanted it that way."

Just eight months after losing his mother in 2006, Liam threw on his helmet and pads and went to work on the football field. That next season, he started all fifteen games, threw twenty-six touchdown passes, and broke the UMass single-season passing efficiency record. In his first season as the full-time starting quarterback, he led UMass to the Division I-AA Championship Game against Appalachian State.

He also earned a 3.4 grade point average.

On that summer day in 2007, Liam reiterated that he was there for me. He didn't shed any tears or get overly philosophical. He just said that he was there.

It's all he had to say.

■ ■ ■

ON THE FOOTBALL field, I felt like I was ready to finally make an impact. But our receivers were good. Seniors like J. J. Moore, Michael Omar, and Rasheed Rencher had been key offensive players for several seasons. I was still considered raw, and though Liam helped me learn some of the nuances of Coach Brown's offensive scheme over the summer, I wasn't one of the top receivers coming out of camp.

> WITH *PAPÍ* AND MY FATHER NOW NO LONGER IN OUR LIVES, I WAS TRULY THE MAN OF THE HOUSE.

Because of my academic situation, I wasn't able to suit up for the first five games of the 2007 season, either. I'd watch from the sideline, taking mental notes. I was fine with that. It just felt good to be back on the squad.

On October 1, I got a phone call from my mother.

Papí had passed away.

I knew he'd been sick and was suffering for quite some time. I'd been coming to grips with his inevitable passing for months. He was in a better place now. He had lived a beautiful life.

I went home the next day and sat in my *abuela*'s apartment on East Twentieth. I looked around the room and saw my grandmother, my mother, and my little sister staring back at me. It hit me.

With *Papí* and my father now no longer in our lives, I was truly the man of the house.

I'd do my best to make those men proud.

NEARLY THREE YEARS after committing to play for Coach Mark Whipple in the winter of 2004, I suited up for my first college football game on October 13, 2007. We were playing Villanova at home. Before the game, I looked to the family section of the

McGuirk Alumni Stadium stands where my father would have been seated. I smiled knowing that he probably would already have lost his voice by kickoff.

I only caught one pass that entire 2007 season, but it felt great to be a real part of the team.

"You ready to have a breakout year next season, Vic?" Liam asked me after one of our last games.

"You have no idea," I answered.

That semester, I didn't do much on the football field, but I was a star in the classroom. I finally picked a major, African-American History, and found the courses to be fascinating. I genuinely liked the subject matter and scheduled office hours to further discuss topics with my professors after class. My father was a proud African-American man who knew all of the challenges and achievements of the civil rights movement's pioneers. I used his love and passion for the subject as motivation and dove into my schoolwork like never before. I recorded two As and two Bs, bumping my cumulative GPA up to a 2.75. That December was a lot different than the two Decembers before it. When my grades came in over e-mail, I didn't cower in fear. I ran into the kitchen to share them with my mother and sister.

The man of the house had turned things around.

Six months after being so ashamed with my life that I felt the need to lie about it to old friends, I was happy.

It'd been so long since I was just happy.

HEADING INTO THE 2008 season, everybody was wondering who'd fill in for all the senior receivers that we had lost to graduation the previous year. Though the media and assistant coaches expressed concern, Liam and Coach Brown knew who'd be filling in—a guy named Victor Cruz.

I'd trained all summer and by the time we got to campus in

the fall, I was already in midseason form. It became obvious in those first few weeks of training camp that Liam and I had something very special going on. I quickly emerged as his number one receiving target.

Our third game of the 2008 season was against James Madison University, a conference rival of ours. We were ranked third in the nation and they were ranked seventh, and neither team was particularly fond of the other. On our first drive of the game, Liam hit me for a five-yard pass. On our next drive, we connected on a nine-yard out. I was feeling good, but at the end of the first half, we were down 31-10.

Liam pulled me aside in the locker room during halftime. "Vic, you can beat that guy who's covering you out there, right?"

I nodded. I always felt like I could beat anybody.

"Then what are we waiting for? Let's get started with that breakout year of yours."

In the second half, I caught eleven passes for 238 yards and scored two touchdowns. I'd found myself in "The Zone" again. Everything Liam threw in my direction, I caught. Outs. Posts. Hooks. Everything. I couldn't be stopped.

The play everyone remembers from that game, though, is the one that still eats at me today. Liam threw me a ten-yard slant that I caught in stride. I beat my first man and had nothing but daylight in front of me. I ran sixty yards and was headed for the end zone when, for reasons I still don't understand, I started swerving inside and out instead of running in a straight line. Out of nowhere, I was tripped up from behind on the five yard line. I'd run sixty-seven yards and *didn't* score.

All of my teammates had a good time with that play after the game. "You thought you had a touchdown and you got caught from behind!" my fellow receiver, Jeremy Horne, laughed afterward.

I promised myself I'd never get caught from behind again.

We lost the game that afternoon, but I'd finally emerged onto the scene. My thirteen catches more than doubled my entire career reception total heading into the game, while my 262 receiving yards almost tripled my career yardage numbers. Both statistics broke UMass school records.

But I was just getting started.

The next week, we traveled to Lubbock, Texas, to play Division I-A power Texas Tech. The Red Raiders were one of best teams in the Big 12 and had the top receiver in the nation that year, a guy named Michael Crabtree. He was rumored to be the first pick in the upcoming NFL Draft and was listed as a preseason Heisman finalist. That day, in front of the biggest crowd to ever watch a UMass sporting event, I caught five balls for fifty-four yards. Crabtree caught just five for sixty-two.

WHAT CAN I SAY? I WAS ALWAYS A FAN OF CREATIVE END ZONE CELEBRATIONS.

I'd started to show a bit of personality on the field, too. After I scored a touchdown against Rhode Island, Scott Woodward, our backup quarterback, ran onto the field to hold the ensuing extra point. Before he got to the line of scrimmage, he found me, gave me a chest bump, and we both did a little spontaneous dance move. It was odd, but we loved it.

Sure enough, it became something we did after every one of my touchdown catches that season. I'd find Scott, we'd bump chests, and we'd shimmy.

What can I say? I was always a fan of creative end zone celebrations.

Liam and I were in a groove all year long, and by the end of the season, we'd both put up huge statistics. In 2008—my first real season playing college football—I led the team in receptions and receiving yards. Liam, meanwhile, shattered every UMass career passing record there ever was and finished his four-year stint as our starting quarterback with ninety career touchdown passes.

At the end of the season, there was a big football awards banquet that all of the players and their families were encouraged to attend. My mother and sister made the trip up from Paterson.

Not surprisingly, Liam won the Team MVP award. For four of his five years on campus, he *was* UMass football. I was thrilled to see his efforts recognized.

At the very end of the night, Coach Brown took to the stage and announced the winner of another award.

"This young man's overcome a lot of adversity in not only the past twelve months, but the past four years," he began. "A lot of kids would have given up on their dreams a long time ago. Others might have tried taking an easy way out. But this kid just kept on working. He kept on believing. Victor Cruz, please come up to the stage and accept the award for the Most Improved Player of 2008."

As I got up to walk to the podium, I noticed that the rest of the room started getting up out of their seats. Were they leaving?

Not quite.

It took a second to dawn on me, but I quickly realized that everyone was standing and clapping for *me*. It was the first and only standing ovation I've ever received.

I was incredibly touched. Coach Brown gave me a hug and I looked out into the crowd and saw my mother crying. She knew how much the award meant to me. She knew the path I'd taken to get to that podium at the front of the room.

A few weeks later, my grades came in the mail. I got a 3.0 that semester, bumping my cumulative grade point average to a 2.9.

My life was finally stable. Things were falling into place.

Papi would have been thrilled.

IN JANUARY 2009, Coach Brown announced that he was leaving UMass to take an assistant coaching position at the University of Maryland. Kevin Morris, our offensive coordinator, got promoted to the position of head coach. We all loved Coach Morris but knew there'd be a void without Don Brown leading us onto the field on Saturdays. With Liam graduating that June, it became increasingly clear that I'd have to step up and become one of the leaders of the team.

I relished the opportunity and, along with fellow seniors Jeromy Miles and Vladimir Ducasse, organized team workouts and weight-lifting sessions throughout the spring. I became more vocal and set an example by being the first one to the gym in the morning and the last one to leave the facilities at night. It wasn't enough to just be a good player anymore. I wanted to be the guy the younger players looked up to.

That March, I received an e-mail from the UMass admissions office with the subject line "Victor Cruz: Academic Standing."

My heart sank.

What now? Had I enrolled in the wrong classes? Was there something wrong with my credits from PCCC? Was I being accused of breaking the honor code?

I opened the e-mail and was pleasantly surprised by its contents. It turned out that because of all the college credits I had picked up at Bridgton Academy, College County of Morris, and PCCC—I already had enough credits to graduate.

I spoke with my academic adviser and learned that I'd only have to take one course my senior year. It was for my African-American history major and it required me to write a thirty-five-page senior thesis paper.

I'd never written a ten-page paper before. The thought of doing a thirty-five-page thesis paper was daunting. But as I'd done with everything else over the past few months, I decided to embrace the challenge and conquer it.

My senior thesis was titled "The African-American Male Athlete as Captured by the Media," and it required several months of hard work and dedication.

I spent hours in the library, researching the different ways men like Jackie Robinson, Muhammad Ali, and Jim Brown were portrayed by the media during their respective playing days. I took detailed notes, tracking how national outlets covered recent stories involving NFL stars Michael Vick and Adam "Pac-Man" Jones. I didn't wait until the last minute, scrambling to put something together in late April. I worked on that thirty-five-page paper throughout my senior year, fine-tuning my points and refreshing my words.

Writing my senior thesis, more than anything I accomplished on the football field, was easily my greatest achievement at UMass.

I always knew I could catch footballs and score touchdowns if given the opportunity. But writing that paper was something a seventeen-year-old Victor Cruz would never have dreamed of doing. It would have seemed unimaginable. To conquer the task took patience, dedication, and ingenuity. I spent two semesters working on that paper.

I got an A.

I graduated from the University of Massachusetts Amherst that December. My final GPA was a 3.2.

MY SENIOR SEASON was another strong one. Though Liam was no longer our quarterback, I still caught fifty-nine passes and scored five touchdowns. I had a big day against Albany, scoring twice, and in the final game of my college career, I had eleven receptions for 155 yards against Hofstra. I was named to the CAA All-Conference First Team, a tremendous honor, and finished fourth all-time on the UMass career receptions list. When we had our annual team banquet in January, I was chosen as the 2009 Team MVP.

I'd had a productive two years on the field, but I might not have been noticed by the NFL at all had it not been for my teammate Vladimir Ducasse.

A fellow senior in 2009, Vlad was a six-foot-five, 325-pound scientific anomaly. He was easily one of the biggest and strongest players on the team, but he also had incredibly quick foot speed. He was huge, but he was agile. NFL scouts were enamored with Vlad's physical build, and when he flat-out dominated opposing defensive ends during our junior and senior seasons, pro teams across the league began to take notice.

Each week during the 2009 season, coaches and front office personnel from all thirty-two NFL teams would flock to Amherst to watch Vlad practice. We'd seen guys from the pros come to UMass games to scout players like Liam and James Ihedigbo in previous years, but we'd never seen anything like the interest Vlad was generating.

On any random weekday afternoon, you'd see guys from the Cleveland Browns or the New Orleans Saints watching our practice from the sidelines. My teammate Jeremy Horne would always say, "Thank you, Vlad. I hope you don't mind if Vic and I steal the show."

Vlad would give a big smile and a laugh. "I don't mind at all," he'd say. "Let's *all* make it to the NFL."

Jeremy and I would go out of our way to work extra hard in front of the scouts at practice. One time, our new quarterback, Kyle Havens, threw a pass three yards behind me. In one motion, I stopped dead in my tracks, reached behind my back, and caught the ball with one hand. It was straight out of a Randy Moss highlight reel. I finished the play and immediately looked over to the mob of scouts watching from the sidelines, seeking their reactions. An older gentleman in an Indianapolis Colts baseball cap mouthed the word "Wow" and scribbled notes into his notepad.

I remember thinking to myself, The Colts? I could get used to having one of the Manning brothers as my quarterback.

While Vlad was clearly the main attraction, Jeremy and I were leaving the scouts with some additional things to think about on their trips back to their respective NFL cities.

After the season, a local sports agent named Jack Huntington offered to pay for my NFL Draft training down in Bradenton, Florida. I signed on the dotted line and was sent to Athletic Edge Training Center, a performance training facility where NFL Draft prospects prepare for tryouts.

In Bradenton, I trained with some of the best players in all of college football. Trindon Holliday was an electrifying kick return star out of LSU and one of the fastest people on the planet. Juice Williams was a quarterback from the University of Illinois and a guy I'd watched play in the Rose Bowl on TV the previous New Year's Day. Every morning in Bradenton, we'd wake up, hit the weights, and talk football.

"Cruz, you're pretty damn good," Juice once told me after a training session.

Trindon and Juice would always ask how I didn't end up playing for a Division I-A school. They couldn't grasp how I could be overlooked by 120 different programs.

Mike Gough, the head trainer at Athletic Edge, once told them, "It doesn't matter where you go to college, guys. If you're good enough, the NFL will find you."

It was the same exact message Michael Strahan had told me when he was buying jeans in the Garden State Plaza two years earlier.

Though I wasn't one of the 320 players invited to the NFL's annual Draft Scouting Combine in Indianapolis that February, Jack assured me that I'd still have a chance to work out for all thirty-two teams in the weeks prior to the NFL Draft in April. I acted as though not being invited to the Combine didn't affect me, but I was insulted. I looked at the list of the forty-four wide receivers who *were* invited to Indianapolis that week and learned all of their names. I wanted to know all of the guys who were considered better NFL prospects than me. I'd use those forty-four names as motivation to work even harder.

In March, I was invited to Boston College's NFL Pro Day. Scouts from fourteen NFL teams would be descending upon BC's Chestnut Hill campus to watch me and thirty other NFL Draft–eligible players from the area work out.

Because of a blizzard, we were all sent to Harvard's indoor facilities in Cambridge. Instead of running on a wet field, we ran on something called FieldTurf, a well-manicured synthetic grass. It was the same type of turf they had in Bradenton.

With thirty scouts watching, I ran the all-important forty-yard dash in 4.42 seconds. It was the fastest I'd ever run the forty. I then hit the bench press and did sixteen reps of 225 pounds.

I had an incredible workout. Jack said I was suddenly an NFL Draft "sleeper," a little-known prospect who had all the NFL scouts and media "draftniks" buzzing.

Two weeks after the Boston College Pro Day, representatives from all thirty-two NFL teams came to watch Vlad work out in Amherst. As always, Vlad brought the scouts' eyes up to western Massachusetts, and I tried leaving them with another guy to think about come NFL Draft day. I ran my routes to perfection and weighed in at 205 pounds, a good size for a speed receiver in the NFL.

The New York Giants hosted a local Pro Day in early April at the Timex Center in East Rutherford. The workout session consisted of all the guys who attended college in the New Jersey and New York area and some players from Philadelphia and Connecticut. Since I was living at home in Paterson, Jack suggested I attend. I came and performed well in front of the Giants scouts.

After that session, I went home and put my football cleats away in my bedroom closet. The auditions were all done. Now I just had to sit and wait. Those few weeks were grueling.

The NFL Draft was at the end of the month, but I wanted feedback and updates. I'd read things called Mock Drafts online and never see my name listed anywhere. I'd type the words "Victor Cruz" and "NFL Draft" into Google and get no results.

According to Jack, the Carolina Panthers were interested in me.

"They could take you in the sixth or seventh round, but you'll most likely have to try out for their team as an undrafted rookie free agent," he told me during one of our several pre-Draft phone calls.

Jack would be encouraged by news like that, but I'd be confused. I couldn't understand why teams weren't sold on me. Sure, I didn't put up huge statistics at UMass, and no, I wasn't built like Calvin Johnson. But I wanted it so badly. I knew I'd make it if I were just given an opportunity. Somebody just had to take a chance on me.

It was like the college recruiting process all over again.

A few days before the 2010 NFL Draft, Jack called and told me that a new team had inquired about me earlier that afternoon.

"The New York Giants have a scout, a guy named Chris Pettit, who really likes what you bring to the table," he said.

The Giants, huh?

I'd grown up fifteen miles from Giants Stadium but had never once stepped foot in the building. Though all my friends were Giants and Jets fans growing up, I was always a fervent Dallas Cowboys supporter. Rivals in the NFC East, I viewed the Giants as the enemies. When they beat the Cowboys in the NFC Divisional Round of the 2007 playoffs, I threw the TV remote control across our living room on East Eighteenth Street.

I hated the Giants.

But if they had even the slightest bit of interest in drafting me, I had no problem cleaning out my closet full of Deion Sanders and Michael Irvin Cowboys jerseys and replacing them with Phil Simms and Lawrence Taylor memorabilia.

I started to daydream about what it would be like playing for one of the two local NFL teams. Would my mother and Elaina get to attend all of my home games? Would the sports bars in Clifton put my jersey, with the word "Cruz" on the back, up on their walls? Would I be considered a "Hometown Hero" and loved by the fans? I'd been a Cowboys guy my entire life, but the thought of joining the New York Giants was suddenly incredibly appealing.

On the Tuesday morning before the 2010 NFL Draft, I sat at the computer in my bedroom and typed in the Web site URL www.NFL.com. I had to see what I was up against.

I clicked on the New York Giants logo, scrolled down to the "Roster" tab, and looked at all the wide receivers on the team.

The Giants were loaded at the position.

One by one, I saw first-round picks and guys I'd grown up watching on TV.

Steve Smith was a star at USC and a Giants hero from the team's historic Super Bowl win over the Patriots in 2008.

Mario Manningham was an up-and-coming talent out of Michigan who'd shown flashes of greatness in his first two years in the league.

Hakeem Nicks was a former first-round pick with some of the best—and biggest—hands in all of football.

Sinorice Moss doubled as a wide receiver and a kick return specialist.

Ramses Barden was a six-foot-six physical freak of nature.

In total, there were eight different wide receivers on the New York Giants roster. It appeared as though I'd gotten excited over nothing. With all of those veteran players under contract, there was no need for the Giants to add *another* wide receiver to the mix.

Out of curiosity, I decided to check out the Web site of the other team that had expressed interest in me—the Carolina Panthers. I printed out their roster, took out a yellow highlighter pen, and checked off all of their wide receivers whom I thought I could compete with for a spot on the active roster.

Then, because the computer was already on and I had nowhere else to be, I decided to do the same thing with the Dallas

Cowboys. And then I did the Jets. And then the Colts. Brandon Marshall had just been traded from the Broncos to the Dolphins. Maybe Denver needed a new receiver? I printed out their roster and marked it up with the highlighter.

Six hours later, the desk in my bedroom looked like it belonged in a mad scientist's laboratory. I had all thirty-two NFL teams' rosters printed out, marked up with a yellow highlighter pen, and spread out everywhere. The more I researched, the more I learned about each team. By dinnertime, I had Post-it notes all over my wall, too.

Before I went to sleep, I clicked on a popular NFL Draft-specific Web site called NFLDraftScout.com. I surfed around and discovered that I was ranked as the seventy-third-best wide receiver prospect in the 2010 NFL Draft.

Seventy-third.

I opened a Microsoft Word document and typed out the names, schools, heights, weights, and forty-yard-dash times of all seventy-two receivers who were ranked above me on the Web site.

Dez Bryant, a six-foot-two, 224-pound college superstar out of Oklahoma State, was ranked first. Preston Parker, a guy who transferred from Florida State to North Alabama, was ranked seventy-second. I looked at those two names and every single name in between them.

Then I stared at mine.

Seventy-third.

I started to get fired up. I did a set of push-ups on the floor next to my bed. I followed that with a set of five hundred sit-ups. I looked at the list of those seventy-two names over and over again and just nodded.

My mother walked into my bedroom around midnight and was alarmed by all the scattered paperwork and the enraged look in my eyes. "If only you had worked this hard during your freshman year of college," she laughed.

Even I had to smile at that one.

The NFL Draft was a painstakingly long, three-day experience. On the morning of the Draft's first day, I didn't wear an Armani suit or have a limousine drive me to Radio City Music Hall. There wasn't an ESPN camera crew set up in my living room.

I ordered a pizza and sat on my couch in my oversized Tim Thomas Playaz basketball shorts, alone, for the entire first round. My mother was a nervous wreck and was stressing me out. I told her to get out of the house. Elaina called a few times to check in on me, but I let her calls go to voice mail.

I watched every pick that first night with the understanding that my name probably wouldn't be called. Still, I thought there was a chance.

There wasn't.

The second day consisted of rounds two and three. Jack told me it'd be a "pleasant surprise" if a team selected me in either round on Day Two, but I kept my hopes up.

Two hours into the evening, the New York Jets were on the clock with the sixty-first pick. I was fixing something in the kitchen when I heard a familiar name announced on the TV.

"With the sixty-first pick in the 2010 NFL Draft, the New York Jets have selected Vladimir Ducasse, an offensive guard out of the University of Massachusetts Amherst," ESPN's Chris Berman said in his booming voice.

I was thrilled for Vlad. He'd been a great teammate and all of his hard work had paid off. I sent him a text message saying "Congratulations," and he wrote back, almost immediately, "Thanks, Vic. You're up next!"

The rest of the night went by, though, and my name wasn't called. The phone didn't ring once and Jack didn't have any updates for me afterward. "It's out of our hands, Vic," he told me. "Now try to get some sleep."

But I didn't sleep that night. I just stared at the ceiling in my bedroom and thought about my life. I thought about those days in The Sir's dojo. I thought about doing pull-ups with my father in Montgomery Park. I thought about the summer mornings spent running routes with Liam up in Amherst. I'd worked for this my entire life. I just needed a team to take a shot on me. I just needed an opportunity.

I'D WORKED FOR THIS MY ENTIRE LIFE. I JUST NEEDED A TEAM TO TAKE A SHOT ON ME.

The third day of the Draft covered rounds four through seven. After I'd stared five hours at the TV and seen receiver after receiver get selected, the seventh and final round of the 2010 NFL Draft began. Jack told me he'd call if he had any news.

I didn't hear from him all afternoon.

The Giants, the team I had daydreamed about playing for, had just one pick in the seventh round—the 225th overall selection. When they were on the clock, I stared at my phone and tried willing it to ring. I remember thinking, C'mon, Giants. Pick me. Pick me. Pick me!

They took a punter, instead.

The Carolina Panthers, the other team that had apparently expressed interest in me, had two seventh-round selections. They passed on me with both of them.

The Detroit Lions had the 255th and final selection in the 2010 NFL Draft. I looked at their roster, printed out and marked up with yellow highlighter pen in front of me, and thought there was a chance they'd draft a wide receiver.

They did.

But his name wasn't Victor Cruz. His name was Tim Toone and he was a five-foot-ten guy who went to a school called Weber State.

Tim Toone was the twenty-seventh receiver and the final player taken in the 2010 NFL Draft.

Seconds after he was selected and the ESPN NFL Draft crew bid their viewers farewell, my phone lit up with Jack's number flashing on the screen. "Victor, I've got some good news," he said with a cheerful tone.

I was all ears.

"Three teams want you to come in and try out for them. The Carolina Panthers, the Denver Broncos, and the Washington Redskins are all interested in bringing you in as an undrafted rookie free agent. You're going to have to pick one of those three teams tonight."

My head was spinning. Jack explained that for undrafted guys like me, the three hours after the NFL Draft were the most important three hours of the entire process. Teams called up all the agents of the players they still wanted and offered them the opportunity to come in for tryouts. If you impressed the team in the tryout, Jack explained, you'd be given an invitation to training camp. If you then impressed the team during training camp, you could make the regular season roster. It sounded like a million steps away from actually suiting up in an NFL game, but I was ready.

I'd already walked a million steps to get where I was. What was a million more?

"I need an answer, Vic," Jack said. "Do you have any preference between those three teams?"

I looked at my printed-out rosters and started weighing the pros and cons of living in North Carolina, Denver, and Washington, D.C. I called Elaina up and asked her what she thought.

Just as I was ready to give Jack an answer, he called again with the news that'd change my life forever.

"Vic, forget Carolina, Denver, and Washington," he shouted into the phone. "The New York Giants just offered you a contract, kiddo! You don't have to try out, either. They're skipping all that. You got an invite to training camp!"

It sounded too good to be true.

I asked Jack to explain what had happened and he said that the scout who liked me, Chris Pettit, went to bat for me in the New York Giants Draft "war room." He assured the rest of the scouts, the coaching staff, and the Giants front office that I'd make it worth their investment.

I'd only met Chris Pettit once in my life. He'd introduced himself at the UMass Pro Day. We exchanged brief hellos and didn't even have a real conversation. If I were asked to do so, I wouldn't have been able to pick him out of a lineup. He was a complete stranger.

But at that moment, I was ready to walk to Chris Pettit's house, wherever he lived, and give him a giant hug.

The New York Giants offered me a three-year contract, contingent on me making the team in August. It wouldn't be easy, but I had my opportunity.

That's all I ever needed.

CHAPTER 8

WILLIAM HAUSER © 2012

GOING IN

THE FIRST DAY of Giants rookie minicamp felt like my first day of school at Paterson Catholic. I'd been dreaming of stepping into an NFL locker room for such a long time that when it finally happened, nothing in the world could possibly wipe the little kid smile off my face.

Well, one guy could.

"I'm Coach Tom Coughlin" were the first words I heard the longtime head coach of the New York Giants say. "And I don't care if you were a first-round pick, a second-round pick, a high school superstar, or the greatest thing to ever step foot on your college campus. You're a rookie on the New York Giants now. You're at the very bottom of the barrel. I hope you're ready to work."

I didn't say a word to Coach Coughlin during that rookie minicamp. Part of that was because I decided I'd just let my actions speak for themselves. The other part was because I was simply too terrified of the man to even introduce myself.

He wasn't the most physically imposing person, but Coach Coughlin carried himself like a true leader of men. His staff respected him, his players never spoke ill of him, and he lived and breathed Giants football. When he walked into a room, everyone stopped talking. When he gave a command, everyone responded. He didn't waste his words and he never gave one player special treatment over another.

I couldn't wait to show Coach Coughlin everything I had. I couldn't wait to *give* him everything I had to give. I was ready to do whatever it took to be a part of his football team.

There were some real characters in the Giants 2010 rookie class. Jason Pierre-Paul was the team's first-round pick in April.

I'd never heard of him during the college season, but when I typed his name into YouTube before the Draft, a video of him doing seventeen consecutive backflips was the first thing that came up. I had no idea what kind of football player "JPP" was, but I was certain he was one hell of an athlete.

I COULDN'T WAIT TO SHOW COACH COUGHLIN EVERYTHING I HAD.

Mitch Petrus was a big offensive guard out of a tiny town in Arkansas. He listened to heavy metal music and wore leather cowboy boots. They didn't have many guys like Mitch Petrus on the streets of Paterson, New Jersey.

One familiar face at rookie minicamp was a guy named Tim Brown. We'd only met once before, but I'd known Tim's name since my senior year of high school. He was one of the three recruits that the Rutgers coach, Greg Schiano, was waiting to hear from before he could offer me a scholarship. Small world.

Nate Collins was a big defensive tackle out of the University of Virginia. The first time I met Nate, he was wearing an old-school 1980s Nike Windbreaker, listening to Jay-Z's *The Black Album,* and talking about White Castle cheeseburgers. I knew Nate and I would get along right away.

I roomed with another undrafted rookie wide receiver, a kid with a thick Southern accent from Memphis named Duke Calhoun. Duke had done some special things in college, but he, like me, wasn't one of the twenty-seven receivers drafted by an NFL team in April.

He was a bit embarrassed when he told me he'd never heard of me. I said it wasn't a problem, then promptly listed off his height, weight, and forty-yard-dash time. I also told him that NFLDraftScout.com ranked him as the thirty-fourth-best wide receiver in the 2010 NFL Draft. Duke shook his head and asked me if I was crazy.

I told him I was.

On August 1, all the veterans and free agent camp invitees reported to the University of Albany for training camp. The first time I walked into our locker room, I saw a blue jersey hanging on a locker with the number 3 and the last name "Cruz" on the back.

I took a moment before putting that jersey on.

It was a sight I'd always dreamed of seeing. At Passaic County Technical Institute, Paterson Catholic, Bridgton Academy, and UMass, the team's jerseys didn't have players' last names written on the back of them.

This was the first time I'd ever seen the name Cruz on the back of a jersey.

I savored the image.

More than just being my first NFL jersey, it was a symbol of my roots. The name Cruz didn't just travel back to the town of Paterson, but it traveled back to Puerto Rico.

The name on the back of that jersey didn't just identify Victor Cruz, the undrafted rookie wide receiver on the Giants. That jersey identified my *abuela*, my mother, and their incredible journeys to America. I'd wear that jersey with more pride than anything I'd ever worn before.

As I was taking it all in, Steve Smith, a veteran wide receiver on the team, stopped at my locker and put his arm around my shoulder.

"Cruz, huh?"

I nodded.

"Well, that's a last name you don't see very often in the NFL."

"No." I smiled. "It certainly isn't."

TRAINING CAMP WAS hard work, but I enjoyed the competition. Every day, we'd go out on the field and work our tails off. In addition to all the rookies and free agent invitees, the veterans on the team were all trying to make the squad, too.

Though Eli Manning was the Giants starting quarterback, I rarely got the opportunity to practice with him at training camp. The two quarterbacks I gelled the most with were Jim Sorgi and Rhett Bomar. Jim had served as Peyton Manning's backup quarterback for six years in Indianapolis. He had a Super Bowl ring but had never started an NFL game. Rhett, meanwhile, was once the most hotly recruited high school quarterback in the entire country. When I was in high school, Bomar was ranked as the number one overall player in the nation by the top recruiting Web site, Rivals.com. Rhett went to Oklahoma, where he was named the starting quarterback in just the second game of his sophomore year.

But Rhett's path to the NFL had some major bumps and detours along the way. The summer after his sophomore year, he was hired to work at a car dealership owned by a major University of Oklahoma donor. There were allegations that Rhett was being paid by the donor despite not actually showing up to the job. The NCAA investigated the claims and Rhett was promptly dismissed from the Sooners football team.

He transferred to Sam Houston State, a Division I-AA school like UMass, and had a nice, albeit far less publicized, college football career. He was a "small school" guy trying out for the Giants that summer, just like me.

Speaking with Jim and Rhett about their respective journeys to the Giants once again made me realize that everyone's NFL story is unique.

The Giants had a lot of talented wide receivers in camp that summer, but I was playing very well. Each day, I wanted to make one play—whether it was a catch, a block, or a special teams tackle—that made me stand out from the pack. For the most part, I did just that.

Every night after practice, I'd go back to the dorm room that Tim Brown and I shared up in Albany and I'd call Elaina. I'd brag about a one-handed grab or tell her something positive that a coach said to me, and she'd do her best to keep me grounded.

"Stay humble, Vic," she'd tell me. "You haven't made the team yet."

A week into training camp, though, I was turning heads and making plays. At the same time, some of the other receivers on the team were nursing injuries. Steve Smith, Mario Manningham, and Hakeem Nicks—the top three receivers on the Giants—all missed significant time during training camp, giving guys like Tim, Duke, and me the opportunity to make names for ourselves.

On one particular early August afternoon practice session, I made a move at the line of scrimmage and ran right past starting cornerback Terrell Thomas for a deep pass completion. It was the type of route I'd run a thousand times before, but this one was against one of the NFL's most talented cornerbacks.

The Giants fans in attendance that day, many of who saw me have a big game against Albany during my senior season at UMass, responded with a loud chant of "Cruuuuuuuz."

It was the first time I'd ever heard my name chanted.

It sounded incredible.

Though I still hadn't said a word to Coach Coughlin, he came up to me after the practice and patted me on the rear end. "Nice job today, son," he said.

Later that evening, I was watching the local news with Tim in our dorm room when the sports update came on. The anchor said something about a young receiver "creating buzz at Giants camp" and threw it to a video of Coach Coughlin standing at a podium.

"Victor Cruz! What do we need anybody

IT WAS THE FIRST TIME I'D EVER HEARD MY NAME CHANTED. IT SOUNDED INCREDIBLE.

for? We've got Victor Cruz," Coach Coughlin said. "How about the plays he made this morning, huh? I'm serious—he's made some outstanding plays. He's been going by people out here. Hey, it would be a great thing to just keep adding to the group."

Tim got up out off his bed and started jumping up and down. He crouched in front of my face and yelled, "Cruuuuuuuz!"

I couldn't believe it. I had no idea Coach Coughlin even knew my name, and here he was giving me praise during his post-practice press conference. It was tough staying *completely* humble after seeing that and even Elaina had to admit it was "kinda cool" when we spoke later that evening.

Our first preseason game was against the Jets at the brand-new MetLife Stadium in East Rutherford. During pregame warm-ups, I looked around the stadium and tried soaking it all in. Elaina and my mother were both in the building, Coach Wimberly and Jim Salmon each told me earlier in the week that they'd be coming together, and the game was going to be on in every bar and restaurant in Paterson. Perhaps the coolest part of all was the fact that it was a *Monday Night Football* game, meaning the entire country would be tuning in to Giants-Jets on ESPN. That morning, I received text messages from Liam, Pelli, and Courtney Greene. They all said the same thing: "Make me proud."

Kevin Gilbride, the Giants offensive coordinator, let me know in the locker room before the game that I probably wouldn't see much action in the first half.

"Just be ready to come in during the third or fourth quarter," he said. "We're going to try to get all of you guys in the game tonight."

Our teams went back and forth throughout the first half, and at halftime the Jets had a 13-10 lead.

"Cruz, you're going to get in during the second half," the wide receivers coach, Sean Ryan, told me in the locker room. "Make some plays."

I was ready. I just needed an opportunity.

With three minutes left in the third quarter, Coach Gilbride signaled me over to him on the sideline. "Cruz, you're going in."

The first time I ever touched the ball in a football game, I ran it sixty-four yards for a touchdown. It was for the PAL North Firefighters and I was twelve years old.

The first time I ever touched the ball in an NFL game, I did the exact same thing.

Jim Sorgi was in at quarterback and the play called in from the sideline had me running a straight Go route. Dwight Lowery, a five-foot-eleven cornerback, was lined up against me in man-to-man coverage. Jim took three steps back, looked in my direction, and lofted a pass toward me on the left side of the field. My right arm got tied up with Lowery's left, leaving me with just one arm to make a play. As the ball began its descent from the sky, I had only one option—I'd have to grab it with one hand.

It was a catch I'd made in countless practices in high school and college, but one I'd never actually attempted in a game. I stretched my left arm out, kept my eyes open, and hoped for the best. When I felt the ball land perfectly in my left palm, I cradled it like a baby, tucked it against my hip, and refused to let go. I heard the roar of the crowd and saw Dwight Lowery on the ground beneath me. I skipped out of his grasping arms and caught a glimpse of what was ahead of me—nothing but an open field.

I remember thinking, Don't fall, Vic. Don't fall.

I got my balance and ran my fastest toward the end zone. As I crossed the ten yard line, I realized I was going to score a touchdown on my first NFL reception. I glided past the goal line, placed the ball on top of the Jets logo, and turned around to see the rest of my teammates jumping up and down, celebrating the play.

As I saw the looks on their faces, I considered what my father's reaction would have been had he been in the building. He would have been going wild, shouting to everyone within fifty feet of him, "That's my son! That's my son!"

When I got back to the sideline, Coach Gilbride patted me on the behind and asked, "Got another one in you, Cruz?"

"Absolutely, Coach," I replied.

On our next offensive drive, Jim Sorgi drove us down the field with a few short completions to our running backs. On second and seven from our own thirty-nine yard line, Jim took another three-step drop and whizzed a pass my way. Lowery was draped all over me this time, but when I saw Jim's toss was going to come up short of both of us, I fought off Lowery and came back to the ball to make the grab. As I caught the pass, I danced past him, pushed myself off another Jets player, and picked up seven more yards. First down.

My adrenaline was running high. The crowd was going bonkers and I wanted more.

Two plays later, the Jets replaced Lowery with a longtime NFL starting cornerback named Drew Coleman. As we squared off at the line of scrimmage, Coleman said, "Sorry, man. You're not catching any more balls tonight."

Before I could even think about responding, Jim threw a perfectly lobbed ball aimed in my direction along the sideline. I fought past Coleman, made a strong cut toward the outside, and stretched out my arms.

The ball landed perfectly in my hands and I jogged into the end zone.

Another touchdown.

This time, instead of just placing the ball down, I took two steps and waved into one of the ESPN cameras.

"What was that?" my training camp roommate, Tim Brown, asked me when I got back to the bench.

"That was my 'Hi, Mom,'" I told him. "I've always wanted to do a 'Hi, Mom.'"

On our next possession, Rhett was in at quarterback. We'd bonded over the past few weeks, working long hours together after practice and eating lunch together every day. Rhett, like me, was doing everything he could to make the team. On his first pass of the game, Rhett threw me a five-yard slant that I caught for a short gain. A few plays later, he hit me on a sixteen-yard crossing route. After a couple more first downs, it was first and goal from the five yard line. I already had two touchdowns, but I wanted a third.

I never scored three touchdowns in a game at UMass.

Rhett looked at me in the huddle and said, "Vic, we've been practicing this play together all summer. Back shoulder fade. Let's go."

He took the snap, backpedaled a few steps, and threw a perfect pass over my right shoulder. I reached up, hauled the ball in, and landed in the end zone. Touchdown.

As I jogged back to the sideline, the reality of the situation started to dawn on me. In my first game in an NFL uniform, I'd just caught six passes for 148 yards and scored three touchdowns. More importantly, when I entered the game, we were losing 16-10. When the final whistle blew, we'd won 31-16.

A few of the Giants veterans came by my locker after the game to slap me five. As I started changing out of my pads, I reached into my jeans pocket to grab my cell phone. When I turned the phone on, I read the following words on the screen: "110 Text Messages; 40 Missed Calls; 20 Voice Mails."

That couldn't have been right, could it? As I started to scroll through some of the messages, I had to laugh.

For three straight days in April, I had stared at my phone, just begging for it to ring.

It never did.

Now it couldn't *stop* ringing. All I needed was an opportunity. I made the most out of the one given to me that night.

■ ■ ■

I MET ELAINA, my little sister, and my mother in the parking lot after the game and we drove home to Paterson in my mother's Ford Explorer. We were all smiling but were just too shell-shocked by what had occurred to really discuss the game yet.

Then, as we got on Route 3 and headed into Paterson in my mother's car, Elaina spoke up. "Vic, have you checked your Twitter?"

I'd signed up for Twitter back in 2009 but rarely used the social media service. I followed my favorite rappers, sneaker brands, and athletes. I'd tweet here and there about a new pair of Jordans that I liked, but I wasn't as active with it as some of the other guys on the team.

"Nah, are there people talking about the game?" I asked, assuming there might have been some chatter because of the game being on ESPN.

"Victor, LeBron James was tweeting about you tonight," she answered.

Excuse me? LeBron James?

Apparently, after my second touchdown grab, Miami Heat forward LeBron James—arguably the world's most recognized athlete—sent out a tweet to his four *million* Twitter followers that read "Victor Cruz going nuts on the Jets tonight on #MNF. Undrafted rookie from UMass. He's gonna have a job this year for sure."

I smiled and said, "I hope he's right. Do you think the Giants front-office guys follow LeBron on Twitter?"

I was only half kidding.

The next morning, I was ready to get back to the practice field and prove myself again. Though it obviously felt great to score three touchdowns on national television, the truth of the matter was that it was still just a preseason game. And despite my performance on Monday night, I was still likely the seventh or eighth receiver on the depth chart the next day. The Giants never kept more than seven receivers on their active roster. I'd need to do far more than make a few touchdown grabs in the fourth quarter of an early August preseason game if I wanted to make the squad.

When I got to my locker after that Wednesday's practice, a mob of reporters was waiting there to speak with me. I'd done a few interviews at UMass with the student-run school newspaper, but I'd never really dealt with "the media." The New York press was something entirely new to me.

"Victor," one of the local beat reporters began, "during Monday night's ESPN broadcast, Jon Gruden said that you were an *American Idol* story. He said that you had come 'out of nowhere.' Any thoughts?"

Cameras were flashing and recorders were being shoved in my face. I answered the only way I really knew how—honestly.

"I'm flattered by all that and I respect Coach Gruden's opinion, but I really haven't come from 'out of nowhere,'" I said. "I'm from Paterson, New Jersey—just a few miles away."

Pat Hanlon, the Giants longtime public relations director, swooped by my locker and leaned in toward my ear. "Hell of an answer, kid," he whispered. "I couldn't have written it better myself." He then patted me on the back and went on his way.

The New York media was enjoying their "Victor Cruz: From Rags to Riches" story line, but Jack and Elaina kept me grounded. That one game wasn't enough. I had to keep it going if I wanted to be anything more than just another "one-hit wonder."

We played the Steelers the following week and I had just two catches for thirty yards. "Sorry, LeBron didn't tweet about you tonight," Elaina said in the car ride home after the game. "But I still love you." She smiled.

I loved her, too, but I was disappointed with my effort. Two catches for thirty yards wasn't going to get me onto the Giants.

Our next preseason game was on the road against the Baltimore Ravens. My entire childhood, I'd watched Ray Lewis emerge from the Ravens' tunnel with Phil Collins's "In the Air Tonight" blasting on the stadium's loudspeakers during pregame introductions. Lewis had a signature dance and when he came bursting out on to the field, the home crowd in Baltimore exploded. I used to mimic Lewis's dance in my basement on East Eighteenth Street all the time, imagining I was coming out of a tunnel and onto the field on an NFL Sunday.

The New York Giant in me wanted to ignore what was going on in the Ravens' tunnel and just focus on the next sixty minutes of football that was ahead. The lifelong NFL fan in me wanted to see that dance up close and in person.

The fan won.

I snuck over to the Ravens' side of the field, crouched below a group of players, and watched Lewis energize the M&T Bank Stadium crowd. I got goose bumps.

Once I strapped on my helmet, though, I stopped being an NFL fan and became a football player desperately trying to make an NFL team. I was ready to do anything and everything I possibly could to help our squad.

But for the third straight week, I wasn't inserted into the game until late in the third quarter. "Don't be too concerned about *when* you're put in," Coach Ryan, our receivers coach, told me at halftime. "Just be ready to be special when your number *is* called."

With a little under seven minutes remaining in the third quarter, Coach Gilbride waved me over. "Hey, Cruz," he screamed, "go make something happen for us."

On third and two from our own twenty-one-yard line, Rhett threw me a twenty-yard pass toward the Ravens sideline that initially seemed out of my reach. I lunged forward, stretched my arms out as far as I could, and grabbed the ball with my fingertips. Thirty-five yards. First down. It was our biggest pass play

My *abuela* (grandmother), who taught me the salsa dance and so much more, always kept me smiling.

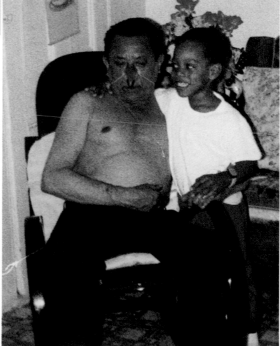

Papí, her husband, was my first best friend, and he gave me a love of music, wrestling, and adventure.

Above: My father, Mike Walker, with his two sons, my brother, Malik, and me.

Above: Dad was always proud of my tae kwon do championships. How about those glasses?!

The first football team I played for was the PAL North Firefighters. I didn't play receiver. I played center.

My dad was sometimes my coach but always my biggest fan.

Tae kwon do was my first passion. Long before I was hauling in touchdowns, I was mastering the flying roundhouse kick.

First-place finishes always felt great.

Malik and I were competitors on the basketball court. One of the craziest days was when we went up against each other in high school. Dad didn't pick sides.

My dad and me after we won the state title my senior year of high school. He never missed a game.

Coach Wimberly, a Paterson legend, who was not just my first coach but one of my first real mentors.

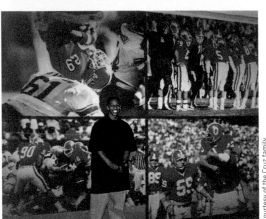

On my recruiting trip to Rutgers, the school I always wanted to play for.

With mom and dad signing my letter of intent to attend the University of Massachusetts–Amherst.

Before I even touched the football field at Paterson Catholic, I was the point guard on the hoops team. My chief responsibility? Getting my teammates the ball.

I met Elaina one month before I left for prep school; she's been by my side ever since.

I was always proud to wear my UMass jacket. Here I am during those years with my little sister Andrea.

My mother is the strongest woman I know. She's been with me through all the ups and downs, and I wouldn't be where I am today without her.

Top left: Keep your eye on the ball because you never know where it's going to land.

Top right: Eli Manning, not only a good quarterback but one of the elite pass throwers in the game.

Right: My big breakout game, a three-touchdown performance against the Jets on *Monday Night Football*.

Below: Doing the salsa dance after my first NFL touchdown was great, but beating the Dream Team Eagles in Philadelphia was what mattered most.

Saying a prayer before the Patriots game. *Papí* and my dad are with me on every play.

Our Christmas Eve game against the Jets was make or break for the season. If we had lost, our chances at the playoffs would have been slim to none.

My ninety-nine-yard touchdown reception against the Jets saved our season and cemented my place in the Giants' record books. It made for an incredible Christmas weekend.

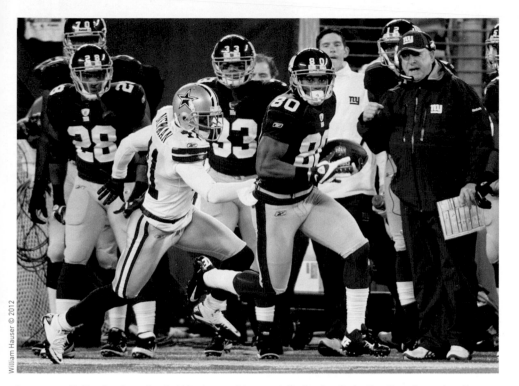

William Hauser © 2012

I grew up a Dallas Cowboys fan, but I had no problem contributing to eliminating them from playoff contention.

William Hauser © 2012

Our 31-14 win over the Cowboys clinched the NFC East. In front of our home crowd, nothing felt sweeter.

Right: James Ihedigbo took me around on my campus tour when I visited UMass as a high school senior. Eight years later, two undrafted "small school" guys went at it on the biggest of stages in the Super Bowl.

Below: Giants fans are incredible. They were out in full force in Green Bay.

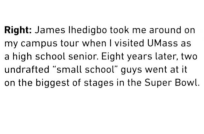

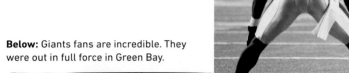

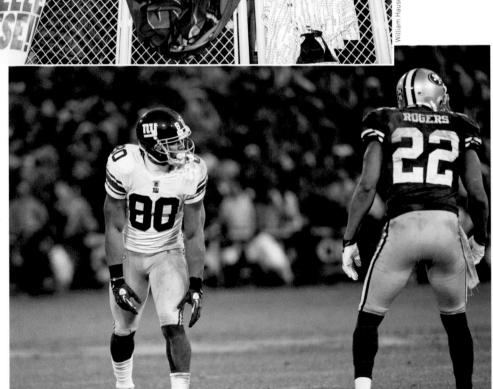

William Hauser © 2012

Top: Doing my best Michael Irvin impression, signaling for a first down against the Patriots in Super Bowl XLVI.

Left: Getting another shot against Carlos Rogers, the guy who outplayed me in week ten in the NFC championship game.

Touchdown!

Hoisting the Lombardi Trophy with my teammate, friend, and fellow receiver Hakeem Nicks.

Celebrating the big win with my brother, Malik, and my sister Ebony.

Marching down the Canyon of Heroes with my Giants teammates. Twelve months earlier I wasn't even sure I'd make the team.

Back in Paterson getting a hero's welcome with friends and family.

Move the chains! My story's still being written. It's first and ten with the rest of my life
ahead of me.

of the night. I had my first reception and now I was hungry for more.

For the casual NFL fan, the fourth quarter of a preseason game might not seem very interesting. All of the guys you'd ever draft in a fantasy football league are taken out at some point in the third quarter, very few of the players on the field are household names, and the football can be a bit sloppy at times.

But for an undrafted rookie fighting to make the team, the fourth quarter of a preseason game feels like the Super Bowl. Every single play from scrimmage is an opportunity to prove to the coaches that you're not only good enough to play in the NFL, but you're an indispensable part of the team.

With three minutes left in the game, I had just that one catch for thirty-five yards. It wouldn't be enough. I needed to do *more.*

I've never been a receiver to demand the football, but I was too hungry to just sit and let the clock—and perhaps my NFL career—bleed without doing something about it. I pulled Rhett aside before we jogged onto the field for our final drive and looked at him straight in the eye. "Rhett, we've worked all summer to make this team," I said. "Now let's *make this team.*"

The scoreboard read 24-3 and the stadium had long emptied out, but for Rhett Bomar and me, that final drive meant everything in the world. On first and ten, he hit me on a short pass to the right. I made a move on the cornerback and darted twenty-four yards for a big gain. On the next play, Rhett looked for me again but threw an incomplete pass.

After a handoff to one of our running backs, I ran to the line of scrimmage and linked eyes with Rhett one more time. "Again," I said sternly. "Again, Rhett!"

Rhett didn't smile or object; he just nodded.

He went back three steps and tossed me a dart right in my numbers. I hauled the pass in, made the man covering me miss, and bolted a few more yards for the first down.

On the next play, he connected with my rookie minicamp roommate, Duke Calhoun, for a twenty-yard pass completion.

It was now first and goal from the one yard line, and I wanted the ball.

Rhett set up in a shotgun formation, took the snap, and threw a high, floating fade pass toward the back of the end zone. So many things were going through my mind as that ball wobbled in the air. I thought about not knowing what a fade route was during my first week of practice at Paterson Catholic. I thought about my second year at UMass when I just wasn't good enough to get on the field. I then thought about making the New York Giants' fifty-three-man roster.

I had to make this catch. There were no alternatives.

I snuck behind the Ravens cornerback, a guy named Prince Miller, did my best to keep my feet inbounds, and extended my arms high into the sky. When my fingertips felt the football, I secured it with all of my might. My feet were in, I'd caught the ball, and it was a touchdown.

Tim Brown, the other wideout who was in the game at the time, came running over to chest-bump me. I looked at Rhett and he was flat on his back, having been hit hard on the play. He was lying on the ground, but he was pumping his fist in triumph.

I HAD TO MAKE THIS CATCH. THERE WERE NO ALTERNATIVES.

I may not be in charge of the Pro Football Hall of Fame, but I'm fairly certain that score was the most meaningful meaningless touchdown in NFL history. Or at least that's how I'll always view it.

We lost 24-10 that night, but I'd made an impact. I led the team in receptions, receiving yards, and scored our only touchdown of the evening. Coach Coughlin was in no mood to hand out praise after the loss, but he came up to me in the locker room and patted me on the rear. "Fine work out there, son," he said. "Way to come to play."

Our fourth and final preseason game was against the New England Patriots at MetLife Stadium. The tension in the locker room before the game was high as many of us knew there was a chance it'd be our last time putting on a New York Giants uniform.

I caught three passes, including a twenty-four-yard pass from Rhett in the second quarter, and felt good about my final audition for the squad. Deon Grant, an eleven-year NFL veteran who was acquired by the Giants in the off-season, came by my locker after the game.

"Cruz, I've been through ten different NFL training camps and preseasons," he said as he watched me pack up my belongings. "Sometimes these things work out. Other times they don't. You did all you possibly could, man. Just know that if you *don't* make this team, it's not because you didn't give it your best effort."

I'd watched the way Deon handled himself throughout training camp. He was a true professional and the perfect example of a respected team leader. Though he wasn't necessarily the biggest star in the league, everyone knew and admired Deon Grant. For him to go out of his way to speak to me after our final preseason game meant a lot.

I left MetLife Stadium that night with my future uncertain. I didn't know if I'd done enough to catch the eye of our general manager, Jerry Reese, or if I was viewed as an indispensable player by the coaching staff. I *did* know, however, that I had given the New York Giants my absolute everything that summer.

Of the seventy-five players who had arrived at training camp in Albany on August 1, only fifty-three of us would make the final roster.

Over the course of the next several days, the Giants' front office would be making decisions that'd alter many of our lives. Earlier in the summer, D. J. Ware, a running back who'd bounced from team to team over his first three years in the league, explained the process to me.

"You sit and you wait," he said. "Remember NFL Draft day? It's like that all over again, but it's the exact opposite. You don't want that phone ringing. If you get a phone call, it means they're calling you to come in to turn in your playbook."

D.J. was in a situation similar to mine. He'd played very well in our preseason games, but there were other guys—players who were actually drafted by the Giants—vying for the backup running back spots on the roster.

"You just don't want that phone ringing, Vic," he reiterated. "If it does, be ready to pack your bags and move the family to another NFL city."

The Sunday after the Patriots game was "Cut Day." I had a long talk with Elaina that morning. She was the love of my life and my biggest fan. She was also the one person who always kept me grounded. We looked at the different wide receivers on the roster and discussed my chances of making the team.

Smith, Nicks, and Manningham were locks. Sinorice Moss was on the injured reserve list, but he'd likely make the team, too. Ramses Barden was a Giants third-round pick back in 2009, and though he hadn't done much in his rookie year, he was all but assured a spot on the team in 2010. The Giants kept six receivers on their active roster in 2009, meaning there was more than likely just one spot left to fill for the 2010 squad.

It'd be between me, Duke, Tim, and a veteran wide receiver named Derek Hagan. We'd all played well that summer and offered different skill sets to the team.

"You did all you could," Elaina told me. "You've already made everybody so proud."

At around eleven a.m., my phone rang. When I looked at the number, though, it wasn't one of the Giants' coaches. It was my agent, Jack.

"Hey, I wouldn't read too much into this," he began, "but I just wanted to let you know that the Giants traded for a backup quarterback and a wide receiver this morning."

I felt a pit in my stomach.

I'd thought that among Tim, Duke, Derek, and me, the Giants had a hard enough decision to make about their sixth wideout spot. If they were trading for a veteran wide receiver, though, I assumed that the four of us just hadn't done quite enough.

Heartbroken, I looked up Darius Reynaud, the player they'd just traded for, on Google. While researching, I learned that Reynaud actually wasn't a true wide receiver with the Vikings in 2009. He was a utility type of guy—playing wide receiver in some formations but also getting work at running back and return man. Maybe, I thought, they'd still roll the dice on one of us.

"They could just want him for special teams," Jack added. "You never really know."

The hours went by and I heard nothing.

"No news is good news," Elaina would tell me every ten or fifteen minutes.

I then got a text message from Rhett Bomar: "Hey, buddy, it was an honor playing with you this summer. They just cut me. Hoping to get a contract somewhere else."

Rhett had had a hell of a preseason, but when the Giants acquired another quarterback, Sage Rosenfels, in the Vikings trade, Rhett was made expendable.

A few minutes later, I got a text from my training camp roommate, Tim Brown: "Just got the call. Headed in there now."

Soon after that, I found out that the Giants had also cut Derek Hagan.

It was a strange feeling. These were guys I'd come to know and love over the past several weeks. But with each one of their releases from the team, my chances of making the squad improved. I felt terrible, but optimistic about my own future.

"It's a business, Vic," Elaina said. "You can't feel guilty if you make it over them."

The next few hours came and went and I heard nothing from anyone. It was the Sunday before Labor Day and the rest of the world was enjoying a gorgeous summer afternoon. I was cooped up in my house, on the couch, unable to eat a thing.

At around seven p.m., the phone finally rang. It was Sean Ryan, our receivers coach.

"Whatever he says, just know that I love you, your mother loves you, Malik loves you, and your sisters love you," Elaina said as I took the phone into the other room.

"What's up, Coach?" I asked, knowing my future as a New York Giant had already been determined. I held my breath and waited for his response.

"Congratulations, Victor," he said. "You've made the fifty-three-man roster. Come down to the facilities tomorrow and we'll get you situated. Our first game is in a week versus the Carolina Panthers. No time to celebrate. Be ready to hit the ground running."

I dropped the phone and ran into the other room to find Elaina.

"I made it!"

She hugged me and screamed so loud that I'm still shocked the neighbors didn't call the police. She immediately called my mother on her phone, shouting "Oh my God! Oh my God!"

As Elaina spread the news to just about everyone, I took a few steps outside the house and sat down in the setting sun. Having been glued to the couch for the past twelve hours, the fresh air felt good on my face.

I'd done it.

I knew it was just the very start of my NFL career, but it meant so much on so many levels to make the team. Beyond the football, it'd change things in my life forever. By making the squad, I got a three-year contract from the Giants that'd pay me enough money to move out of my mother's home and into a new apartment with Elaina. I could also help pay for my little sister's college tuition. And by playing for the Giants, and not one of the thirty other NFL teams not based in New Jersey, I got to pursue my life's dreams in front of all the people I grew up with. Coach Wimberly, Jim Salmon, the guys on East Twentieth Street—they'd all be a part of my NFL journey.

As I sat on the front stoop of my mother's house, I noticed a pack of kids playing touch football in the street. I saw the smiles on all of their faces as they pretended they were NFL superstars like Larry Fitzgerald, Philip Rivers, and Percy Harvin. I watched those boys play in the street for twenty minutes, each one of them trying his very hardest to make the other guys miss.

I'd be playing that sport for a living. I'd be getting paid to do what I truly loved.

I WAS THRILLED to hear that in addition to me, Duke Calhoun also made the team as a wide receiver. Duke and I had come a long way since we walked into rookie minicamp in April as two undrafted guys who none of the Giants veterans were familiar with.

D. J. Ware, the tough running back who'd bounced around the league from the Jets to the Titans to the Giants, made the team as well.

On top of the fifty-three players who make the active roster, the NFL also allows teams to carry eight players on their practice squads. I was upset when Rhett told me that he'd been cut, but the Giants added him to the practice squad the very next day. Nate Collins, the big defensive tackle whom I'd become close with during rookie minicamp, accepted a spot on the practice squad, too.

I got a call from Tim Brown a few days after he was released by the Giants. His NFL dreams didn't die when he was given his walking papers from New York. In fact, he signed a deal to join the Arizona Cardinals practice squad. It was probably a better situation for Tim, anyway, as his former college offensive coordinator at Rutgers was the new Cardinals quarterbacks coach.

Everyone's story is unique.

I ARRIVED AT practice the next day eager to start my NFL career. I had made the fifty-three-man roster, but nothing was guaranteed. I could be released at any point in the season if I wasn't playing well or if the front office guys felt they needed the roster space to make room for another player. "You're never safe in the NFL," Deon Grant told me after our first team meeting. "Never."

Though I'd played well throughout training camp and the preseason, I still hadn't worked much with Eli Manning, our starting quarterback. Because of my Dallas Cowboys allegiances growing up, I was never much of an Eli fan. Troy Aikman was my favorite quarterback as a kid, and when Tony Romo took over as the Cowboys starting quarterback in the middle of the 2006 season, I became a Romo guy.

I always assumed Eli Manning was a decent enough NFL player. After all, he was the first pick in the 2004 Draft and the MVP of Super Bowl XLII. But I had no idea just how good Eli Manning was until I got the opportunity to practice with him every day.

It seemed as though every single pass Eli threw was perfectly accurate. If you ran the right route, he'd hit you in the exact location where you needed the ball, threading the needle on just about every pass. He also was eternally calm. Nothing ever rattled the guy. Watching Eli play quarterback was a pleasure, but watching him handle the New York media was an even greater sight to behold. He had the whole thing perfected. No question the reporters ever asked him was too big; no cameras were ever too bright. Eli just went about his business, on the field and off, and demanded the same out of his teammates. He was the leader of our locker room and the face of our franchise. I was honored to work alongside him every day.

Before our first regular season game, Coach Coughlin let me know that I'd be listed as "inactive." I'd get to dress and run out on the field with the team, but I wouldn't be getting any playing time in the game. He made sure I knew that it wasn't a reflection of the way I'd been practicing or any sort of knock against me as a player. It was just a coaching decision. We won 31-18 and were off to a promising start to the season.

The next week, a Sunday night affair versus the Colts in Indianapolis, marked my first appearance in an NFL regular season game. I played on the special teams unit, chasing down punts and kickoffs, and blocking for our return man, Darius Reynaud. Special teams isn't the most glamorous part of the game, but it's one that any backup receiver or running back needs to master if he wants to stick around the league. I was willing to do whatever it took to stay on the active roster, and if that meant being a special teams guy, I'd make the very most of it.

Eli's older brother, Peyton, carved our defense up and we were blown out of the building in a 38-14 loss. The following week, the Tennessee Titans beat us 29-10 in MetLife Stadium.

We were 1-2 and the Giants fans weren't happy. All week, I heard callers complaining about our effort on the sports radio shows and saw the talking heads on ESPN criticizing Coach Coughlin. I came to practice that Tuesday and asked the veteran guys if they had heard what Skip Bayless said on TV or what Mike Francesca ranted about on the radio.

"You can't listen to that stuff," Deon Grant told me. "If you are getting caught up with what guys are saying in a recording studio somewhere, you're not focusing on what really matters."

He was right.

I had a job to do, and on that Monday night we'd be playing in a pivotal game against the 3-0 Chicago Bears. I still hadn't taken one offensive snap but was starting to make a difference on special teams. Our biggest challenge of the season would come against Chicago's All-Pro punt return specialist, Devin Hester.

All week, we prepared for Hester. Our special teams coach, Tom Quinn, instructed us to keep him contained, pushing him to the outside any time he touched the football. Our punt coverage unit silenced Hester, and after our defense sacked Chicago's quarterbacks ten times, we had our second victory of the season wrapped up.

We were 2-2 and I was starting to get more comfortable with Coach Gilbride's offense, actually working with the starting unit quite a bit in practice. The following week, we beat the Houston Texans, improving our season record to 3-2. I still hadn't recorded a reception or touched the ball, but I was feeling good about my work on special teams and the squad's recent string of victories.

My entire life, it seemed as though I had to wait a little bit longer than most to get an opportunity. But once that opportunity presented itself, I usually delivered. I was confident that my chance would come in 2010. I'd just have to be patient.

It never did.

The Monday after the Houston game, I was running wind sprints before practice when I felt a sharp pain shooting down my right hamstring. It was as if I'd been stung by a million bees at once.

"You okay, Cruz?" my teammate Hakeem Nicks asked as I fell to the ground.

I thought I was fine, and nodded. When the training staff noticed me limping around, they urged me to get off the field.

In all my years playing competitive sports, whether it was tae kwon do or AAU basketball, I'd never once gotten hurt. I couldn't imagine I really did anything too serious from just running some sprints. But as I tried walking, I realized the pain wasn't going away. I was injured.

The doctors' initial prognosis was that I had strained my hamstring and I was told that I'd be back at full speed by the end of the week. When Friday came, though, I was still in a tremendous amount of pain. I couldn't walk.

I was listed as "inactive" for our next game, a matchup against the Lions, but focused on getting healthy for the week seven battle against the Cowboys. I'd had that one circled on the calendar since I got to rookie minicamp in April.

Unfortunately, the pain in my hamstring wasn't going away. When the doctors looked at it a second time the next week, my greatest fear was confirmed—I didn't just strain my hamstring; I tore it.

"So, how long will I be out, Doc? Another two weeks? A month?" I asked Dr. Russell Warren, the Giants' lead physician.

He shook his head and broke the news I didn't want to hear. "It means you're likely done for the year, Victor. I'm sorry."

And just like that, my 2010 season was over.

I'd made the team, but in five weeks with the Giants, I had zero catches, had zero yards, and scored zero touchdowns. Worst of all, I didn't particularly make much of an impression on the coaches. I was given a golden opportunity to step up and shine, but I'd done nothing to separate myself from the rest of the wide receivers looking for jobs in the NFL.

I'd have to wait until next season.

Of course, there almost was no next season.

RISING TO THE OCCASION

I SPENT THE REMAINDER of the 2010 NFL season rehabilitating my hamstring and watching the Giants compete from afar. I was still considered part of the team, but because I was placed on the injured reserve list, I couldn't play as active a role as I would have hoped. I got to attend home games, but I didn't travel to opposing stadiums.

"Out of sight, out of mind" is a phrase that's motivated me my entire life. During the two spring semesters I spent in Paterson after getting kicked out of UMass, I'd obsess over what was going on up in Amherst without me. I'd want to know about every practice session and hear which receivers were making plays and catching the coaches' eyes. I'd call Liam and ask for detailed reports each week, pressing him to give me every last morsel of information. There was a constant fear that I'd be forgotten, that my presence on the team could be replaced.

After my being put on the shelf at the start of week six, the paranoia of being "Out of sight, out of mind" drove me wild for the next three months. I'd see the other Giants receivers making spectacular catches or important plays on special teams and it'd burn me up inside. Of course, I was happy to see my teammates excelling. But the lingering thought of "That could have been me" would fester in my mind.

We had a 9-4 record heading into a week fifteen matchup with the Philadelphia Eagles. With a win, we'd be in a very strong position to make the NFC Playoffs and perhaps a Super Bowl run. I watched the game from our sideline, dressed in street clothes, making sure to stay out of everyone's way. With the score tied at 31 and just fourteen seconds remaining in the fourth quarter,

Coach Coughlin sent our punter, Matt Dodge, onto the field with the instructions to punt the ball out of bounds.

Matt took the snap and instead of kicking it toward the sideline, he booted the ball up the middle to DeSean Jackson, the Eagles' dangerous punt return specialist. Jackson initially bobbled the ball, only to find his balance and evade three Giants defenders behind the fifty yard line. He made a move at midfield and had an opening. Jackson ran past Dodge, made his way toward our sideline, and began to position himself for a dead sprint toward the end zone.

As he glided by us, I felt the urge to run out onto the field and make a game-saving tackle.

But I was in jeans and a winter coat.

Jackson ran the punt back sixty-five yards for a score and we lost the game 38-31.

The following week, the team traveled to Lambeau Field for a "must win" game against the Green Bay Packers. I watched that one from my apartment, alone on the couch, eating a bowl of cereal in my pajamas. We lost 45-17.

Not being able to do anything to help the team in either of those losses made for some long, sleepless nights.

We finished the season with a win in Washington, but our 10-6 record left us one victory shy of the playoffs. We had a final team meeting the next day and said good-bye for the winter. "We'll get back at it in April," Eli assured the team as we packed up our bags and lockers one last time.

But we didn't get back at it in April. In fact, we came very close to not getting back at it at all.

THROUGHOUT THE 2010 regular season, there were whispers in our locker room about a potential NFL lockout that would postpone or, worse, cancel the upcoming 2011 season. Shaun

O'Hara, one of our team's National Football League Players Association representatives, let all of us know that the NFLPA was going to do all it could to prevent a work stoppage, but that it was a distinct possibility.

I wasn't sure what all that would mean at the time, but when the NFL lockout was announced in late March, the significance of the situation became strikingly clear.

In addition to not being able to communicate with any of the Giants coaches, team management, or office staff, I wouldn't be getting paid a dime until the lockout was lifted.

And that was a problem.

Unlike most other working Americans, NFL players' yearly salaries are not spread out over the course of a fifty-two-week calendar. Instead, players get paid per game during the NFL season, with the occasional roster bonus in April and training camp payments in July. I received my last check from the Giants two weeks after the regular season ended in January.

By the middle of March, funds were starting to run a little low.

People assume that just because you wear an NFL uniform on Sundays, you're a multimillionaire, capable of buying fancy cars and summer homes on the beach. But my rookie contract wasn't for millions, and with the costs I'd incurred moving into a new apartment with Elaina over the previous summer, things were getting tighter and tighter as the winter turned to spring.

With no paychecks coming in, I had to make some lifestyle changes. Elaina and I stopped going out to $100 dinners and treating our friends to big nights in New York City. We cooked five nights a week, and when we did order in on the weekends, it was usually a few pies and breadsticks from Pizza Hut.

I considered taking a second job, perhaps working as a trainer at a nearby gym or going back to the Garden State Plaza for a gig at a clothing store. Elaina was having a lot of success with her brand management company, but I didn't want to rely on her for emotional *and* financial support. I was growing restless, and without checks coming in, I needed something to keep me occupied.

So I focused on rehabilitating my hamstring. If there was one positive to the time away from the Giants, it was that it gave me the opportunity to get healthy without missing any significant team-sponsored events.

I linked up with a new physical trainer, a guy named Sean Donellan, and hit the gym hard. Sean had worked with Packers running back Ryan Grant and my Giants teammate Justin Tuck in the past, and I was ready to commit to whatever workout plan he had in mind for me. Every day, I arrived early and stayed late. I thought about making the Giants during every exercise, stretch, and sprint. The dream of making the NFL motivated me in 2010. The desire to hold on to my roster spot did even more in 2011.

The NFL Draft was on April 30. As much as I wanted to deny it, I knew that I hadn't done anything to separate myself from the other Giants receivers in 2010. I had a few good preseason games, but I was a nonfactor once the regular season began. I desperately feared the possibility of the Giants drafting a receiver with one of their early-round picks.

Steve Smith, one of our starting receivers in 2009 and 2010, was coming off a season-ending injury and would be a free agent when the lockout ended. Hakeem, Mario, and Ramses were all under contract for at least another year and weren't getting cut. My situation, however, wasn't as stable.

Twelve months earlier, I'd watched the first three rounds of the NFL Draft with interest in all thirty-two teams. In 2011, I watched it with my eye on just one—my own.

In the first round, the Giants took a cornerback out of Nebraska named Prince Amukamara. In the second, they selected Marvin Austin, a big defensive tackle. With the eighty-third pick in the 2011 NFL Draft, they drafted someone named Jerrel Jernigan.

"Jernigan's a five-ten, 190-pound speed demon who can really help out on special teams," one of the ESPN announcers on TV explained. "Beyond Nicks and Manningham, the Giants don't have much depth at wide receiver. Jernigan will make for a great third wideout."

It was the wake-up call I'd needed.

The next morning, I headed to the gym and elevated my off-season training to another gear. My hamstring still wasn't 100 percent, but I pushed myself harder than ever before. If the Giants were drafting Jerrel Jernigan—a receiver with a physical build and forty-yard-dash time nearly identical to mine—I couldn't just kick back and watch it all happen. I had to respond. I became an animal in the gym, lifting weights and watching my diet as if I were training for a prizefight.

As the lockout extended into the summer months, I'd check my phone for updates from our NFLPA team representatives. Seldom did those e-mails reveal good news.

But I was ready to play football again. I was salivating at the thought of getting the chance to prove myself on the field. I was finally healthy, I was hungry, and I hadn't touched a football since October 10. Hell, I hadn't caught a pass since our final preseason game against the Patriots in September. Every new day of the lockout meant another day I wasn't playing football. It was burning me up inside.

Then, one day in May, I got an e-mail from Eli Manning. It was addressed to the entire team and suggested we meet him at Hoboken High School for some informal workouts.

It was the e-mail I so desperately needed. I didn't care when, where, with whom, or what the workouts even entailed—if it meant getting back on the field and playing football, I'd be there with bells on.

I got to Hoboken High School at seven o'clock that first Wednesday morning and was pleased to see that I wasn't alone. Eli,

Hakeem, Ramses, Duke, D. J. Ware, Kevin Boss, Sage Rosenfels, and veteran receivers Sam Giguere and Michael Clayton were all dressed and ready to go.

"If you go too long without playing football, you start to forget things," Eli told us as we stretched before taking the field. "Let's go through all the terminology, all of the routes, and be the most prepared offense in the league when the season starts in September."

"And, guys, I'm not thinking about the lockout right now," he said. "I'm confident that'll all work itself out."

Eli then paused for a moment and looked at each one of us. "I'm thinking about the Super Bowl."

We looked at each other and nodded. Though opening day was scheduled for the second Sunday in September, the 2011 New York Giants season started that morning in Hoboken.

We began going through all of our drills and went at it hard. One by one, kids would walk by the field, stop, and spend the rest of the day cheering us on. I made one particularly nice catch on a Curl route and heard a chant of "Cruuuuuuuz."

It'd been a while since I'd heard it, and I'd be lying if I didn't say that it sounded awfully good.

When the crowds of fans became too large and the media contingent too invasive, Eli moved our workout sessions to Bergen Catholic High School. We practiced even harder there. The temperature was topping 100 degrees every day, but I couldn't tell. I just cherished being outdoors, in the sun, playing the sport I loved.

After one of our workouts at Bergen Catholic, Eli pulled me aside in the parking lot. "Hey, we're expecting big things out of you this year," he said as we strolled toward our cars. "I love the way you've come ready to work each morning. Keep it up during training camp."

I couldn't resist opening up to him. I told Eli how much it

killed me to not be able to help the team in 2010; how I watched the Eagles' and Packers' losses from afar, feeling like I'd let the rest of the squad down. I described how I felt when Jernigan was selected with the Giants' third-round pick. I told him I'd learn the offense and be ready to step up when my number was called.

"Hey, just use all that as fuel for your fire, man." He nodded. "Stay motivated. Stay hungry. You're playing well. Keep it up. Master the offense and make a difference this year."

Eli wasn't really quite the nurturing type of quarterback that Liam was, but they had a few traits in common. Neither Eli nor Liam just spoke for the sake of hearing his own voice. They weren't the guys who screamed in the huddle or spiked the football after big scores. They led by example and wisely chose their moments to be vocal.

That weekday morning parking lot chat was one of the first times Eli and I really connected on a one-on-one level.

We'd connect many more times—both on the field and off—in the months to come.

ON JUNE 6, I started my day like I had started any other morning that summer. I made myself a bowl of cereal, went to the gym, and came home to my apartment at eleven a.m. When I got back to our place, though, Elaina was sitting on the couch with a concerned look on her face.

"What's up, babe? Everything okay?" I asked, knowing something was obviously up.

"Vic, I've been feeling really weird lately," she said with a look of apprehension.

Was she breaking up with me? Had I done something wrong? Was she worried that I was still out of work? All sorts of ominous questions were racing through my mind.

"Vic," she said, and smiled, "I'm pregnant."

They were the most beautiful words I could ever have imagined hearing her say. I ran to the couch and gave her a hug and a giant kiss. It was amazing news. I loved Elaina. She was the only girl I'd ever loved and I wanted to spend the rest of my days on Earth with her. Learning that we'd be spending those days with a beautiful baby was one of the greatest moments of my life.

"VIC," SHE SAID, AND SMILED, "I'M PREGNANT."

"When are you due?" I asked, unable to do all of the necessary math in my head.

"Well, I'm at twelve weeks now. So I guess I'll be giving birth sometime in January," she answered.

"Perfect. Our baby will be able to watch Daddy in the Super Bowl!" I shouted sarcastically.

She punched me in the arm and we both had a laugh. I then looked at her in the eye and told her I loved her.

"I love you, too," she replied.

I'd never been happier.

THE OWNERS AND the NFL Players Association did figure out the labor situation, and the lockout ended on July 24. Two days later, the NFL's free agency period opened with a flurry. Minute after minute, teams were signing free agents to big contracts with the added pressure that training camps were opening across the league in less than a week. Teams completely retooled their rosters, and the look and feel of several NFL franchises changed in a matter of days.

The squad that made the most headlines was the Philadelphia Eagles. By signing Nnamdi Asomugha, a player widely considered to be one of the best cornerbacks in all of football, and stars Cullen Jenkins, Jason Babin, and Ronnie Brown, the Eagles made a bold statement to the rest of the league: they were committed to winning Super Bowl XLVI.

When Vince Young, a former Pro Bowl player who the Eagles signed as their *backup* quarterback in July, referred to Philadelphia as the "Dream Team," the veteran guys in our locker room took notice.

"The Dream Team? The *Dream Team?*" Brandon Jacobs, our boisterous running back, bellowed during stretches before our first practice at training camp. As other teams continued to load up on new players and bask in the media spotlight, our team remained quiet throughout the final week of July. Everywhere you looked online or on TV, the Giants were being labeled as the 2011 off-season's "biggest losers" for not signing any prominent free agents.

One move the Giants *didn't* make ended up greatly impacting my chances of making the team. Steve Smith was one of the team's top receivers for many seasons, but after he suffered a season-ending injury at the end of 2010, the Giants opted not to re-sign him in 2011. He signed with the "Dream Team" Eagles, instead.

Steve was a good friend and one of the veteran guys on the squad who had looked out for me when I was a clueless rookie in 2010. But his departure created an opportunity for me to step up and grab one of the top three receiver spots.

I was concerned when the Giants drafted Jerrell Jernigan in the third round of April's draft and spent the bulk of the summer doing the numbers game in my head, trying to figure out how many receivers I'd be competing with in camp. With Steve out of the picture, I had no more excuses, no more numbers to compute. A spot on the 2011 Giants roster was mine for the taking.

I just had to grab it.

Training camp in 2011 was much shorter than training camp in other years because of the lockout. With less opportunity to turn heads, I had to make an impact immediately.

I did just that.

My hamstring was back at full strength and I was in the best shape of my life. I was making hard cuts and displaying the same type of confidence in my routes that I had during my final two years at UMass. Working with Eli all those mornings in May made for a smooth transition into training camp in August. We were on the same page on nearly every pass he threw me, and the rest of the team began to acknowledge our newfound chemistry.

A SPOT ON THE GIANTS 2011 ROSTER WAS MINE FOR THE TAKING. I JUST HAD TO GRAB IT.

"Hey, Cruz, did you and Eli have sleepovers during the lockout or something?" Brandon Jacobs joked after we connected on a back shoulder fade.

We were gelling, but it wasn't just Eli and me who were already in midseason form. Hakeem, Mario, Ramses, and Domenik Hixon, a veteran returning from a season missed because of a torn ACL, were all playing very well right from the start. Jernigan was taking a while to get acclimated to the NFL, but it looked like he had a bright future ahead of him. All six of us appeared to be in good shape to make the final fifty-three-man roster. Devin Thomas, a former second-round pick of the Redskins, had a tremendous camp with us as well.

When "Cut Day" rolled around forty-eight hours after our final preseason game against the Patriots, I didn't sit on the couch biting my nails like I had done twelve months earlier. I was confident that all the hard work I'd put into the off-season had paid off and that the coaches would recognize the improvements in my overall game. I was more familiar with Coach Gilbride's offense, I had proven myself on special teams, and Eli and I had found an obvious rhythm. I knew that I had given it my best effort. It was out of my hands at that point.

Coach Ryan called me at seven p.m. and I asked him the same thing I had a year ago: "What's up, Coach?"

He let me know that I'd made the squad and told me to be ready at the facilities the next morning. Before hanging up the phone, I told him that I was ready to do whatever was necessary to make the 2011 Giants a better football team.

I put the phone down, shared the good news with Elaina, and kissed her belly. I wasn't playing for just the two of us anymore. There was a new member of our team on the way.

NONE OF THE "experts" on TV picked us to be much of a factor in the NFC East prior to the season. The Eagles were supposed to finish in first place in the standings, and the Cowboys were penciled in as the division's second-best team. The Giants and Redskins were predicted, by just about everyone, to finish in the NFC East's bottom half.

Our first game of the 2011 regular season was at Washington on the tenth anniversary of September 11. I'd been thinking a lot about my father of late. When Elaina told me she was pregnant, I couldn't help imagining the joyous reaction he would have had when he heard the news. When I made the Giants roster for the second straight year, I felt the urge to call him and let him know. My dad never got the chance to see me play a down of college football, and here I was, standing at midfield, in uniform, on NFL opening weekend. It was surreal.

Only a few of the guys on the team knew my father was a firefighter, and I'm not sure any of them were aware that he had volunteered his services in Lower Manhattan in the days following 9/11. When we rose for the National Anthem that afternoon, I looked around the stadium and savored the moment.

There were close to a hundred thousand people in the building, but for those two minutes and twenty seconds, it was just

Mike Walker and his son Victor—the NFL football player—taking it in.

ON OUR VERY first drive of the game, Coach Gilbride signaled for me on the sideline. "It's third and eight, Cruz," he shouted as I hustled toward him. "Go in there and get us the first down." This was it. I was finally going in at receiver and being given the chance to show what I could do in a regular season game.

I ran my route and Eli threw me a perfect pass. I planted my feet, extended my hands, and dropped what should have been an easy first down.

It was a terrible error and a momentum killer. I got to the sideline and Coach Gilbride was shaking his head. "Can't be dropping the easy ones, Cruz," he said. "I can't put you in the game if you can't catch them when they matter."

We lost the game 28-14 and Eli only threw one more pass in my direction the rest of the afternoon. I tried shaking the first quarter drop-off, but I'd have to wait another week for redemption.

Hakeem was nursing a bruised knee throughout the following week in practice, and I'd been making plays in his absence. But on September 15, just four days before our week two game against the Rams, the Giants signed a free-agent deal with thirteen-year league veteran Brandon Stokley.

I'd grown up watching Stokley play slot receiver for the Colts, and I tried not taking the news too personally. If anything, I told myself, I'd use the opportunity to play alongside Stokley to better myself.

"You could do a lot worse than watching a guy who's made 330 career receptions every day in practice," Coach Ryan told me after one of our weight room sessions that week. He was right. Brandon Stokley was my competition, but he came in and immediately showed me some of the tricks of the trade that he'd picked up over the course of his thirteen-year NFL career. He was an invaluable resource.

Hakeem, Stokley, and I all dressed for our week two meeting with the Rams, and in the third quarter I was inserted into the game in another big third-down situation. "Make a play! No drops this time," Coach Gilbride screamed to me as I jogged on the field.

As Eli was calling out orders at the line of scrimmage, I noticed that two Rams defenders were on my side of the ball, set to blitz him from his blind side. Though the play originally called for one pattern, I had to adjust to what I was seeing on the field and run what's known as a "hot route." Essentially, instead of going deep down the field, I'd have to make a play at the line of scrimmage. Eli would see that I'd made a blitz read, he'd get the ball out of his hands faster than usual, and I'd have to gain the necessary yards after the catch for a first down.

He took the snap, both blitzers flew in as I suspected they would, and Eli threw me a short pass at the line. I caught the ball, made my move, and lunged for extra yardage.

First down!

I was so excited with my first NFL reception that I got up and did an exaggerated first-down signal with the ball, pointing it toward the Rams' end zone. It was a move I'd grown up watching Michael Irvin do after first downs my entire life. It probably wasn't the time or the place to be celebrating, but I was so thrilled with my first catch that my emotions took over.

When I got to the sideline, the coaches were all thrilled with the play. It was one thing to run a nice route and make a catch. It's an entirely other thing to perfect a blitz read at the line of scrimmage. To the casual fan, that play might not have looked like much. But in the film room later that week, I got a lot of praise for using my head and being quick on my toes.

The truth was that I never would have been able to make that play had I not spent all those summer mornings practicing it with Eli. We went through that very situation on countless simmering-hot days. He'd explain, "Vic, if two guys come from this side in this protection, you have a hot route. If I call out 'Ricky, Ricky,' you don't have the hot route."

I made a lot of big catches in 2011, but that blitz read in the third quarter against the Rams might have been the one I needed the most. We won the game 28-16 and I'd played a notable, albeit small, role.

After the game, Dan DePalma, one of the rookie wide receivers on our practice squad, walked up to my locker with a curious look on his face.

"Hey, Vic," he began. "I've got to ask you—was that first-down celebration a shout-out to Michael Irvin?"

I smiled and explained, "I hadn't made a catch in a football game since November of 2009. I had to do *something.*"

Week three was a game many of us circled on our calendars when the schedules came out in April. Even before they signed half a dozen big stars in the off-season, we had a score to settle with the Philadelphia Eagles for the way they ruined our 2010 campaign.

Prior to the game, Coach Gilbride sat me down and told me that I'd be starting at wide receiver. Domenik Hixon tore his ACL for the second straight year in the game against the Rams, and Mario was still feeling the effects of a concussion. Though Stokley would get some action, he still wasn't as familiar with Coach Gilbride's offense as I was.

As I tried keeping my emotions in check and somehow focusing on the task ahead, Coach Sullivan, our quarterbacks coach, casually strolled over and stood above me at my locker. Kickoff was less than three hours away, but he had something else he wanted to discuss to with me.

"You know, Victor, this month is Hispanic Heritage Month," he said, fully aware that Hispanic Heritage Month was the last thing on my mind a few hours before my first NFL start. "If you score a touchdown, you should do something to celebrate the month in the end zone."

Was he kidding? I was so nervous I couldn't think straight and Coach Sullivan was talking about doing an end zone celebration after a touchdown? I was just hoping to put my pants on the right way.

"Okay, Coach, I'll try," I said, deflecting the conversation and quickly returning to my playbook.

It was an absurd thing to even consider on game day. But it *did* give me something to think about other than the fact that I'd be starting. At the very least, it was a distraction from all the stress and anxiety I had boiling inside me.

How would one even show Hispanic heritage in an end zone celebration? I asked myself, trying to think through all the various possibilities. I loved my grandmother's cooking, but I wasn't going to pretend I was serving rice and beans after a touchdown. That wouldn't have made much sense. I remembered the roosters and their cock-a-doodle-doos down in Puerto Rico, but how would I even attempt to symbolize that in an end zone celebration?

Then it hit me.

I'd dance.

My *abuela* taught me the salsa at a very young age. I was a rambunctious little kid, always running around and causing trouble in our apartment on East Twentieth. One day, when I was about five years old, she sat me down and told me she was going to focus my energy into something fun. We did it all—the merengue, the bachata, and the samba. My favorite dance of all, though, was the salsa. She'd put her favorite Tito Puente vinyl record on the record player, and we'd dance for hours in the kitchen. *Papí* would smile and laugh, sipping on his black coffee in his rocking chair.

I'd seen Terrell Owens shake pom-poms, Joe Horn break out a cell phone, and Clinton Portis do a cartwheel, but no one had ever done the salsa in the end zone. It'd be a tribute to my grandmother and my Puerto Rican roots. It'd also be pretty fun.

I just needed to score a touchdown.

AFTER TAKING AN early 7-0 lead, we got the ball back, deep in our own territory late in the first quarter. It was third and two, and Coach Gilbride gave me the same look he'd given me the week before against the Rams. It was time for me to make a play.

I jogged out onto the field and saw the man lined up across from me inching his way toward the line of scrimmage, getting in position to attack Eli with a blitz. I ran five yards to the left, caught Eli's bullet pass, and shook off a tackle from Kurt Coleman, the Eagles' safety. I had the first down, but I wasn't done. After a few steps, I saw Nnamdi Asomugha—the Eagles' newly acquired All-Pro cornerback—coming my way.

I'd never played against Asomugha, but I'd heard and read all about him over the summer. Widely viewed as the best free agent signing of the off-season, he rarely missed a tackle or ever made a mistake. As he approached me with his arms out and his shoulders square, I knew I needed to do something special to evade his tackle.

I planted my left leg hard in front of me, shifted my hips to the right, and turned my entire body around. Asomugha lunged at me, but I slid out of his grasp. I took a hop step forward, realized I was past him, and saw nothing but the open field up ahead. I raced down the sidelines, focusing on turning a fifteen-yard third-down reception into the first touchdown of my NFL career.

There was only one Eagles defender who had a chance to bring me down, and when Hakeem threw a block on him at the ten yard line, I knew I was in for the score. I crossed the goal line and immediately thought of Coach Sullivan.

Should I really do this? I asked myself, weighing out the pros and cons of doing the salsa in front of arguably the most hostile road crowd in the entire NFL.

I then looked at the mass of Eagles fans, standing together, above the end zone. They were booing me, swearing at me, and clad in all shades of green.

I figured, Ah, why not?

And without much second thought, I broke out the very same salsa dance my grandmother had taught me on East Twentieth Street twenty years before.

Step, step, step. Move your arms. Shake your hips.

The salsa!

I jogged to the sideline and the entire team was waiting for me, most of them in shock. First, they congratulated me on the play. It was huge. Then they wanted to discuss the celebration.

"What in the *hell* was that dance?" Michael Boley, our starting linebacker, asked me, in between laughs.

Even Brandon Stokley, a thirteen-year veteran who never once did a touchdown celebration over the course of his career, had a smile on his face. "That was pretty good," he said as he slapped me on the back of the helmet.

I saw Coach Sullivan and he was shaking his head with a smile from ear to ear. "I've seen a lot of crazy stuff over the years, Cruz," he laughed. "But that right there might take the cake."

The salsa end zone celebration was officially born.

But my afternoon wasn't done.

We were trailing 16-14 in the fourth quarter when Eli threw me a high, floating pass at the Eagles' goal line. As I positioned myself for a

THE SALSA END ZONE CELEBRATION WAS OFFICIALLY BORN.

leap into the air, I noticed that not only was Nnamdi Asomugha grabbing me, but his teammate Jarrad Page was in the area, too. It was two-on-one, and I was the odd man out.

I jumped up in the air when the ball hit its apex, and grabbed it from the sky. As I was coming down, I remember thinking, Don't drop it. Don't drop it.

I didn't. I landed on my feet, stretched the ball over the goal line, and looked for the official's ruling. When he swung his arms upright, giving the sign for touchdown, I jumped and pumped my fist. I didn't do the salsa, but I gave my teammate Henry Hynoski a powerful chest bump in the middle of the end zone. We'd just taken a late fourth quarter lead on the "Dream Team" in *their* home building.

We scored one more time and left Philadelphia that afternoon as victors. We were 2-1, tied for first place in the NFC East, and I'd played a major role in the victory. After the game, Eli came to my locker and smirked. "I probably shouldn't have thrown that last one," he said, acknowledging the fact that he'd tossed the ball into double coverage. "Way to make a play."

I got a call from my mother that evening and she was excited to share some news. "Your *abuela* heard about your salsa dance from all of her friends. She loves it. She wants you to do it every single time!"

Coach Sullivan got a kick out of that one. "See," he laughed, "I told you!"

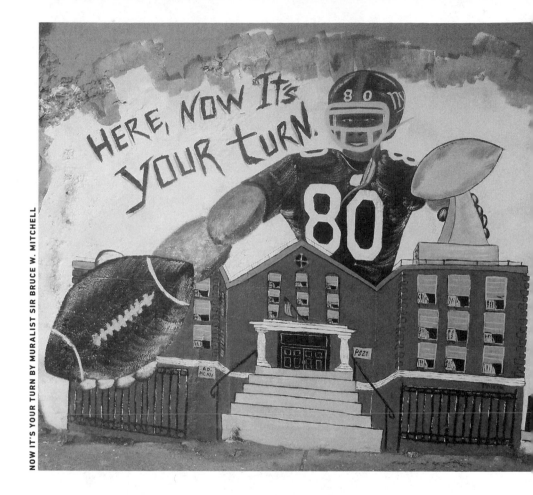

CHAPTER 10

NOW IT'S YOUR TURN BY MURALIST SIR BRUCE W. MITCHELL

HOMETOWN HERO

THE FOLLOWING SUNDAY, we traveled to the desert to play the Cardinals in Glendale, Arizona. Before the game, I was stretching at midfield when I saw a player with a familiar face stroll past me.

I racked my brain, trying to figure out how I knew the guy and when our paths had crossed. Did we compete in college? Was he one of the players I'd gone against at Bridgton Academy?

Then, as he turned his back, I saw his last name—Doucet.

Early Doucet was the physical freak of nature who had dominated the University of Virginia seven-on-seven football camp I attended after my junior year of high school. I remember being a seventeen-year-old kid, watching Early do things I'd never seen done on a football field before, and assuming he'd someday make it to the NFL.

Well, he did.

But so did I.

As I headed back to the locker room for Coach Coughlin's pre-game speech that afternoon, I couldn't help taking some pride in knowing that I'd be suiting up against Early Doucet in an NFL game.

Sure, Larry Fitzgerald—Early's teammate on the Cardinals—was considered the best wide receiver in all of football. But for me, playing against Early Doucet meant that we'd both reached the sport's pinnacle. We were two boys from completely different worlds dropped off at a random football camp in the middle of Virginia back in 2003. Eight years later, we were both on the football field together, once again. Our paths were different and mine wasn't quite as direct as his, but he and I both made it to the NFL. It seemed nearly impossible in that University of Virginia dorm room, but I'd somehow caught up to Early Doucet.

We got off to a sluggish start and were trailing 27-17 late in the fourth quarter. Fitzgerald was catching everything thrown remotely near him, and the Cardinals' running back, a guy named Chris "Beanie" Wells, scored three touchdowns. As our offense took the field with less than five minutes remaining, Eli urged us to fight for every yard possible and to hold on to the ball.

"We can't afford a turnover here," he explained. "A turnover means the game is over and we lose."

On second and ten, Eli dropped back for a pass and threw a laser to Hakeem along the sideline for twenty-six yards. On the next play, he found our tight end, Jake Ballard, in the back of the end zone for a score.

We'd cut the lead to 27-24 and needed a defensive stop. Our D responded by stuffing the Cardinals on three straight plays, forcing Arizona to punt us back the ball on fourth down. We'd have one last opportunity to either tie or take the lead.

Four years earlier, the Giants had beat the Patriots in Super Bowl XLII on the very same field. In the fourth quarter of that game, Eli made a miraculous play where he evaded three defenders behind the line of scrimmage, wiggled out of what appeared to be a surefire sack, and connected with David Tyree for a game-saving first down.

As we stood in the huddle, down three points with less than four minutes remaining in the fourth quarter, Eli reiterated what he'd told us prior to the previous drive, "No turnovers. Hold on to the ball tightly. If we turn it over, we lose."

On first and ten, he took the snap out of the shotgun and rolled to his left. A defender came sprinting toward him, but Eli—like he'd done four years earlier in nearly the same exact spot on the field—ducked and evaded the sack. Free for an instant, he threw me a perfect pass twelve yards down the middle. I caught the ball, broke a tackle, and fell to the ground before an oncoming defender could hit me.

After I went down, I let go of the ball and started to think about the next play. Yet, as I began to get up on my feet, I saw a Cardinals player scoop up the football and run with it the other way.

In college, once you go down, the play is ruled dead. In the pros, however, it's usually a live ball until a defender touches you.

My initial reaction was one of horror. We'd fought so hard to get back into the game, and I'd just carelessly fumbled everything away.

Before the Cardinals defender could take the ball into the end zone, though, I heard a series of whistles blowing in the air.

It turned out that Jerome Boger, the game's lead official, had called the play dead immediately after I'd fallen to the ground. Ken Whisenhunt, the Cardinals' longtime head coach, threw a red challenge flag out on the field, requesting that the ruling on the field be reviewed.

As the officiating crew huddled together to discuss the play, I stared at the ground, simultaneously hoping for the best and fearing the worst.

The game went to a commercial break, meaning we'd have to wait even longer for the officials' decision. During those three, long minutes, I was too scared of Coach Coughlin and Coach Gilbride to even consider heading to the sideline. I'd made a tremendous error, recklessly dropping the football before being touched by an opponent, and I knew it. If the call was put up for review, the ruling would most likely be overturned and we'd lose the game.

I'd be wholly responsible.

As Boger emerged from the officials' huddle, I closed my eyes and held my breath.

"The ruling on the previous play was that the receiver gave himself up by going to the ground," he said into his microphone.

"That cannot be challenged. So there is no challenge allowed by Arizona. It is first down, New York."

It wasn't a fumble. It was a first down and we were still alive!

On the very next play from scrimmage, Eli threw a beautiful twenty-nine-yard touchdown pass to Hakeem. Our defense stopped the Cardinals on their final drive and we survived our trip to the Arizona desert with a come-from-behind 31-27 win.

I very easily could have been the biggest goat in all of New York City that week, but I wasn't. Just as we'd escaped Arizona with a victory, I'd escaped the wrath of the New York media and one of the sport's most passionate fan bases.

My teammates, of course, weren't letting me get away with my careless play scot-free. Michael Boley, one of my closest friends on the team, teased me all week in practice. "Hold on to the ball, Cruz," he shouted from across the field. "Please!"

We'd won three straight games and I'd made some crucial plays—*mostly* good ones—in the second half of all three victories.

A quarter of the regular season was officially in the books.

But we were just getting started.

THE NFL CAN be hard to figure out sometimes.

You can beat the "Dream Team" Eagles in their building one week, then find a way lose to the 1-3 Seahawks, playing without their starting quarterback, at home just two weeks later.

That's exactly what happened to us in week five.

We were riding high after our big win in Arizona and got caught sleeping by Pete Carroll's team. I had several highs and two terrible lows in the game, continuing the roller-coaster ride that was my 2011 season.

We were trailing 19-14 at the start of the fourth quarter, and we needed a spark to get us going. On third and thirteen, Eli gave me a look in the huddle and I knew I was getting the ball.

He took the snap, backpedaled a few steps, and heaved one thirty yards in the air in my direction. When I spun around, I realized the ball was thrown a few yards short and made a quick adjustment to compete with Kam Chancellor, the Seahawks' Pro Bowl safety, for the grab. It was a classic game of "jump ball," and though I made a strong effort of cutting my pattern short and making a go at it, it looked like Chancellor had the edge on me with this one. As we both went up for the grab, our hands hit the ball at the same time, springing it upward in the air.

> I WAS ON TOP OF THE WORLD. LESS THAN THREE MINUTES LATER, I WAS AT THE BOTTOM.

Chancellor's teammate, a cornerback named Richard Sherman, had come over to help on the play, but seemed to lose sight of the ball when it was deflected. I got my balance, looked up, and saw an opportunity to make a play. With the ball floating in the air, I reached out my right hand, tipped it one more time, and hauled it in. Chancellor was behind me, Sherman had his back turned, and I had a clear path to the end zone. I secured the ball with both hands and sprinted twenty yards. Touchdown.

It was my first ever score in front of the Giants' home crowd, and they responded with a resounding chant of "Cruuuuuuuz." In return, I broke into my salsa dance celebration. Ahmad Bradshaw converted the ensuing two-point conversion and we took a 22-19 lead. I was on top of the world.

Less than three minutes later, I was at the bottom.

On the following drive, we were faced with a third and seven on our own twenty yard line. Eli fired me a pass and I caught it in stride, but after I'd made a move toward the middle of the field, a Seahawks defender poked the ball out of my hands. Fumble. I coughed it up in our own territory, a Seattle defender recovered, and they tied the game on a field goal shortly thereafter.

I'd get an opportunity to redeem myself in the game's final minutes. Trailing by four with less than three minutes on the clock, Eli led us on what had all the makings of another thrilling game-winning drive. On second and ten, he rolled to his right and floated me a perfect pass. I had a step on my man, grabbed the ball, and shuffled out of bounds after a forty-one-yard gain. We were in striking distance and I knew he was coming back to me on the very next play.

Eli took the snap out of the shotgun and hit me for a nineteen-yard gain. It was now first and goal from the ten yard line, and Coach Gilbride's play called for me to run an eight-yard slant pattern toward the end zone. I fought my man off at the line of scrimmage, saw Eli winding up to throw me the ball, and felt my feet give out beneath me.

I slipped.

Eli tossed the ball where I should have been and I managed to get a hand on it, but it was too late. Brandon Browner, the Seahawks cornerback, intercepted the ball and proceeded to run it back ninety yards for a touchdown.

We lost 36-25 and I couldn't help blaming myself for the defeat. My fourth quarter fumble and Eli's intercepted pass directly led to eleven points—the exact margin of the Seahawks' victory.

"That's football," Deon Grant told me after the game as I sat with my head buried in a towel in front of my locker. "One minute, you're running in a touchdown and the crowd's chanting your name. The next, you're sitting with your head in a towel at your locker. If you beat yourself up too much, you won't be able to rebound the following week. Shake it off, Vic."

He was right. I'd have to forget my errors from week six if I was going to do the team any good in weeks seven, eight, nine, and so on.

The Buffalo Bills were the toast of the league in October, jumping out to a surprising 4-1 start with big wins over the Patriots and Eagles already under their belts. You couldn't turn on the television and not hear about Ryan Fitzpatrick, their Harvard-educated quarterback, or their opportunistic defense that recorded an interception in each of the team's first five games. Our meeting with Buffalo was CBS's number one game of the day, which meant that most of the country was getting our game in their living rooms.

We were tied at 24 and the Bills were driving the ball late in the fourth quarter when Corey Webster, one of our starting cornerbacks, intercepted a Fitzpatrick pass deep in our own territory. With less than four minutes left in the game, Eli took the ball at our own nineteen yard line and did what he always does when we need him most—he led us down the field. A few Ahmad Bradshaw runs, a pair of pass interference penalties, and a Bear Pascoe reception got us within field goal range.

Lawrence Tynes, our kicker, booted one through the uprights to give us the three-point lead, and we turned to our defense to seal up the win.

Fitzpatrick had 1:32 on the clock and a few time-outs at his disposal. Yet, as they'd end up doing all season long, our defense rose to the challenge. They stuffed the Bills on two straight plays, and on fourth and five, Jason Pierre-Paul batted down a Fitzpatrick pass at the line of scrimmage.

I knew "JPP" was a very special athlete the first day I'd met him at rookie minicamp in April of 2010. In just his second year in the league, though, he was exceeding everyone's wildest expectations. JPP was quickly proving himself to be one of the best defensive players in the NFL. That play wouldn't be the last time he'd save a game by batting the ball down at the line.

The win over the Bills improved our record to 4-2 and we had our bye the following week.

With thirteen days before our next game, I finally had some time to relax and go back to visit my mother and little sister in

Paterson. I'd had an idea that everybody was cheering me on at home, but I didn't realize just how proud everyone was of my success until our bye week. Everywhere I went in town, people on the street were slapping me five and showing me love.

I took my mother to breakfast at the same IHOP restaurant that we'd gone to a thousand times before, and we had kids coming up to me, asking to pose for photographs that they'd post on Facebook. Grown men and women, people twice my age, were telling me how much joy I was giving them on Sundays.

GROWN MEN AND WOMEN, PEOPLE TWICE MY AGE, WERE TELLING ME HOW MUCH JOY I WAS GIVING THEM ON SUNDAYS.

I was flattered and a bit overwhelmed by the outpouring of support I was receiving. I had lunch with Jim Salmon one afternoon and he helped put the situation in perspective for me. "Remember when you were thirteen years old and you worshipped the ground Tim Thomas walked on?"

Of course I did. I wore my shorts like Tim Thomas, took jump shots like Tim Thomas, and even walked like Tim Thomas.

"You're the town's new Tim Thomas, Vic," he said with a grin.

I shrugged the comment off and tried changing subjects. Tim Thomas was a Paterson icon; I was just catching some footballs for the hometown team.

"These kids see where you're from and what you've overcome to get where you are today. They see all that and believe they have a chance to do the same," he continued. "You may not realize it, but just by suiting up on Sundays and having fun, you're giving all of these kids hope."

It was a lot to take in, but Jim was speaking the truth. I knew full well that if there were a New York Giants player from Paterson when I was growing up, I'd look to him as an inspiration, too.

Seeing what my success was doing for the town only made me want to work harder. I wasn't just playing for myself, Elaina, and the bulge in Elaina's belly anymore.

I was playing for the thirteen-year-old kid at School 21 who thinks there's no other option than the streets. I was playing for the boy at the park who has to decide between a game of pickup hoops and an aluminum can of beer. I was playing for all my old classmates who were just never given the chance.

I was playing for Paterson.

LIVING THE DREAM

AFTER OUR WEEKEND off, we came out of the gates looking rusty in our week eight matchup with the Dolphins. Winless coming into the game, Miami jumped out to a 14-3 lead, meaning we'd have to play from behind yet again. Eli hit Mario for a touchdown late in the second quarter and we trailed 14-10 at the half.

The Dolphins added a field goal in the third quarter, leaving us with a 17-10 deficit as we headed into the fourth. I'd had a few catches earlier in the game but hadn't done anything to fire up our team. As we jogged onto the field to start the fourth, Eli looked at me and nodded.

He didn't have to say a thing.

On third and nine from our own twenty-seven yard line, Eli threw a deep pass to me over the middle of the field. With a catch, I could keep the drive alive. A drop would mean we were punting. I went up for the ball and grabbed it. First down. A few plays later, I made a seven-yard reception that put the ball in field goal range. After a Lawrence Tynes field goal, the Dolphins' lead was cut to four.

Our defense came up huge, stopping the Dolphins on their next drive, and we got the ball back with a little over eight minutes remaining in the game.

"Someone make a play for us," Coach Coughlin pleaded as we took the field. Ahmad Bradshaw answered, scampering for a first down on second and eight. Eli then connected with Hakeem for a seventeen-yard completion. Two plays later, it was third and twelve from the Dolphins' twenty-five yard line. Third downs were my time to shine and I knew I had to step up.

ELI SET UP IN THE SHOTGUN AND GAVE ME THE LOOK. IT WAS COMING TO ME.

Eli set up in the shotgun and gave me the look. It was coming to me.

He took the snap, I made a cut toward the middle, and he threw a bullet pass right in my numbers. As I caught the ball, I felt a Dolphins defender grab me with both arms from behind. I decided to spin, hoping to jar myself loose from the tackle. As I swung my body around in a 180-degree motion, I felt the defender let go of my jersey. There was now just one man to beat and I sidestepped him with a shimmy move. I saw the blue paint of the end zone and ran the ball in for a score. Touchdown.

I did the salsa dance and the crowd erupted with a "Cru-uuuuuz" chant.

When I got to the sideline, Michael Boley was the first teammate to greet me. "You're the number one salsa dancer in the entire NFL," he said.

Who was I to argue?

Our defense came up huge on the Dolphins' final two drives, sacking Matt Moore, Miami's quarterback, four times and intercepting his final pass of the game. It wasn't easy—it never was—but we had the W.

We were 5-2 with a trip to New England up ahead.

THE PATRIOTS CAME into our week nine matchup having won their twenty previous regular-season home games. The streak dated back more than two complete NFL seasons, and Tom Brady had thrown a touchdown pass in each of his last twenty-four games played in Gillette Stadium.

None of that seemed to matter to the leaders in our locker room.

Eli, Brandon Jacobs, David Diehl, Justin Tuck, and Corey Webster were just some of the guys who'd played large roles in the 2007 team's upset win over the Patriots in Super Bowl XLII. All week during practice, the message from the veterans was the same: "Who cares about their streak? We've got their number. They're scared of *us*." It'd been more than three years since that game, but our team leaders carried it with them into this one. Their confidence was contagious.

Both offenses failed to get much going in the first half, and when we walked into the locker room after the second quarter, the score was tied at 0. Our defensive game plan was working perfectly, as Tom Brady, the Patriots quarterback, appeared frustrated throughout the first half. After getting sacked by JPP late in the second quarter, he threw his hands up in disgust.

But we were having our troubles, too. There were drops, penalties, and mental errors in both the first and second quarters.

"Be patient," Coach Coughlin told us in the locker room. "Make the plays when they're there in the second half."

Though we scored the first ten points of the game, the Patriots fought back and took a 20-17 lead with less than two minutes remaining in the fourth quarter. Eli had already led us on fourth quarter comebacks in four of our five wins in 2011. In Super Bowl XLII, he took the Giants the length of the field in the final minutes against the Patriots and threw a game-winning touchdown pass to Plaxico Burress. I looked at him before we took the field for our final march of the game, and it might as well have been the middle of May.

Nothing ever seemed to faze Eli Manning.

"You ready?" he asked me in the same tone he would have asked me any other random question at any other random time.

I strapped on my helmet and rubbed my hands together. "Yeah, I'm ready."

And then Eli went to work.

On first and ten, he hit me on a nineteen-yard pass play over the middle. First down. After two more throws in my direction, he connected with Jake Ballard for a clutch twenty-eight-yard gain on third down. We rushed to the line in the no huddle and Eli quickly took the snap. I wasn't open and Mario was completely covered, so Eli cradled the ball under his arm and took off. We *never* saw Eli run. But there he was, with less than a minute to go in Foxborough, ripping off a twelve-yard gain for a first down.

Coach Coughlin called time-out and the offense gathered on the sidelines in a small huddle. "Victor, I'm looking for you in the end zone," Eli told me. "Get to the goal line and let's win this game."

As we lined up, I tried reading the defensive end. I knew that if I could make a move at the line of scrimmage and break free in the play's first few seconds, I had a path to the goal line. Eli snapped the ball and I maneuvered my way out of the defender's grasp and headed for the end zone. I looked up at around the five yard line and saw Eli winding up for a pass. As it came down from the air in my direction, I felt a Patriots player hit me from behind. The ball dropped to the ground, but there was a yellow flag on the play.

Pass interference. We'd get the ball on the one yard line with thirty seconds on the clock.

Eli threw an errant pass to Ballard, and Brandon was stuffed at the line on second down. It was now third and one and we had no time-outs remaining. An incomplete pass would send the field goal unit onto the field to likely force the game into overtime. A touchdown would end things right then and there.

Eli wasn't throwing an incomplete pass.

He took the snap, faked a handoff to Brandon, and threw a dart off his back foot toward Ballard in the corner of the end zone. Jake stretched out his arms, caught the ball with both hands, and pulled it in for the score. Touchdown. Eli had done it yet again.

Our defense stuffed Brady in the game's final drive and we all ran off the field, jumping up and down.

Even Coach Coughlin was smiling after the victory, shaking all of our hands as we entered the locker room. Then, in a moment I'll never forget, we got in a circle and started jumping around him like we were in a mosh pit. Michael Boley started chanting, "See you Wednesday! See you Wednesday!" and we all chimed in.

We usually came to the facilities to watch tape and get light workouts in on Mondays. Tuesdays were our off-days. But after rare wins or particularly tough road trips, Coach Coughlin would give us both days off and we'd be able to rest our bodies until Wednesday. After the win over the Patriots, all any of us wanted to hear was Coach Coughlin say, "See you Wednesday!"

We were jumping around him like little kids and he was laughing hysterically. Brandon lifted Coach Coughlin up off the floor and started bouncing him up and down. The emotions of the week and the joy of victory were just pouring out of each of us.

"Now, listen," Coach Coughlin said as we all quieted down to let him address the team. "You are nine-point underdogs and there's *no way* you can win," he shouted, repeating what all of the talking heads were saying on TV during the week leading up to the game.

We all cheered.

"We've got a *good* football team," he continued. "And when we play together like that and when we have a physical nature to the game, and we believe in ourselves that we're never out of it . . . well, that's a hell of a win."

We cheered again.

"You've got to come in and lift tomorrow, but I'll see you on Wednesday."

The locker room erupted.

"One thing right now, though," he said, interrupting the celebration. "That team next week, we're not going on a six-hour trip to lose that game."

The San Francisco 49ers were 7-1 and the hottest team in all of football. They played physical defense and ran the ball hard up the middle behind a punishing offensive line.

We knew we were in store for a battle, but we were ready.

THE 49ERS DEFENSE was unlike any unit we'd seen before. Justin Smith, their All-Pro defensive end, was nearly impossible to stop with just one offensive lineman, and Coach Gilbride built our entire offensive game plan around his presence. Their linebackers—Patrick Willis, NaVorro Bowman, and Ahmad Brooks— were among the league's best, and their defensive backfield was filled with incredibly talented players at all four spots.

The 49ers play in a rustic, beat-up stadium called Candlestick Park. The place is filled with history and just smells of tradition. The locker rooms are anything but luxurious, and the field's conditions are among the worst in the league. In one of the end zones, the sun shines in your eyes, making it incredibly difficult to see the ball. Jim Harbaugh's 49ers played football just like their stadium— they were old school. They roughed you up on defense and they shoved it down your throat with their running game.

Both offenses struggled in the first half, as we exchanged field goals throughout the first and second quarters. Less than a minute before halftime, Eli threw me a pass toward the middle of the field. I broke to my right, but the ball was out of reach.

Carlos Rogers, San Francisco's top cornerback, got a good step on the play and intercepted the pass. I grabbed him from behind and made the tackle, but the 49ers were now in good position to put some additional points on the board before the end of the half. As I was on the ground, I looked above me and saw a circle of 49ers players surrounding Rogers.

Then with his teammates cheering him on, he did a sarcastic salsa dance over me.

The Candlestick Park crowd went ballistic, but I wasn't laughing. It was a sign of disrespect. Instead of getting up and retaliating, though, I sat and watched Rogers finish his cheap Victor Cruz imitation. I promised to never forget it. I wasn't sure when the opportunity would present itself, but I was confident I'd get payback for that dance.

The 49ers beat us 27-20.

We all sat at our lockers in disbelief after the game. We'd been red hot the past few weeks, but we came up short in our toughest battle to date. Whereas the veterans were lifting a jovial Coach Coughlin off his feet seven days earlier, they weren't saying a word after this one. We were physically outplayed and Eli—for what felt like the first time all season—was unable to pull a rabbit out of his hat in the final seconds.

"Philly's next," Deon Grant said as we headed to the buses. "We'll see these guys again. Don't worry."

As he usually was, Deon was right.

AFTER A LONG flight home, a few of my friends suggested we go out and celebrate my twenty-fifth birthday. I was so focused on the 49ers game the previous week that I almost forgot the occasion on November 11. After some back-and-forth, a bunch of us headed into Manhattan for a Tuesday night out on the town. When we got to the spot, a place called Juliet Supper Club on West Twenty-first Street, there were a few tables in the corner set aside for our crew.

Elaina didn't make the trip in, so I spent the bulk of the night just hanging out and catching up with my boys. At around midnight, a bunch of the guys on the team said good-bye and headed out of the club to go home.

I should have left with them.

Instead, I stayed a little longer, enjoying a rare night out in

Manhattan. My *abuela* always told me that nothing good ever happened after five p.m. Around the league, there was a saying that nothing good ever happened after midnight. We were off on Tuesdays, though, and with no curfew—I thought I had earned a night off to celebrate.

There were bottles, celebrities, and a DJ playing a great set. Every half hour, I checked my phone. Elaina was long asleep and had stopped texting me around eleven. The way I saw it, walking through the door at one in the morning or walking through the door at three in the morning really made no difference at that point. The party was still going strong and I was having a blast.

Then, at two thirty a.m., I heard gunshots. Unfortunately, it was a sound I knew all too well.

"Get down!" I shouted. In an instant, everyone in my party ducked for cover, holding on to each other under our table.

Wap-wap-wap!

There was a second round of shots fired.

As women were screaming and men were pushing to get out the front door, I sat under a table, frozen.

Everything was going so right in my life. I'd made it to the NFL, Elaina was seven months pregnant with our first child, and I was representing my family and my town better than I could ever have imagined.

And yet, despite all that, there I was—sitting under a table during a nightclub shoot-out.

With absolute mayhem surrounding me, I just sat there crouched like a baseball catcher, asking myself, Why?

Why was I in a Manhattan nightclub at two thirty in the morning?

I simply had too much at stake to be putting myself in dangerous situations anymore. And though I was with a good crew of trusted friends and teammates, I didn't need to be partying after midnight on Tuesday evenings. I'd worked too hard to have some freak accident throw a wrench in my dreams.

I sat under that table, waiting for the chaos to finish.

When it did, I left the Juliet Supper Club with a new outlook on the way I'd approach things off the field. My life—and all the new responsibilities that came with it—was simply too valuable to be putting it at risk. And though I'd done nothing wrong or illegal, I decided there'd be no more nights out in New York—or anywhere, really—until two thirty in the morning.

THE NEXT DAY, I LEARNED THAT A MAN HAD BEEN SHOT AND KILLED IN THE GUNFIGHT.

The next day, I learned that a man had been shot and killed in the gunfight. The news shook me to my core. It can happen just like that. Be in the wrong place at the wrong time and everything you've worked so hard to earn can be taken from you.

I showed up to practice knowing I'd have to explain myself to Coach Coughlin.

What I didn't expect was a mob of reporters waiting for me at my locker.

Three years earlier, in the winter of 2008, Giants receiver Plaxico Burress had brought an unlicensed gun into a New York City nightclub and accidentally shot himself in the leg. It was a national news story and a black eye for both Burress and the New York Giants franchise.

Clearly, my situation from the night before was far different than the one with Burress, but the fact that I was out so late during the middle of the season was sure to make headlines. I handled each reporter's question as well as I could and when they asked me if it was the first time I'd ever heard gunshots, I told them the truth. It wasn't.

"Just when you think you've strayed away from that lifestyle and you're one of the fortunate few to get away from that, it happens again," I explained. "I'm going to take it down for right now. I'm going to play it real easy. I have a baby on the way, so I can't be involved in that anymore."

Coach Coughlin didn't scream or yell when I met with him in his office. He didn't fine or suspend me, either. His first questions were about my family and my friends. He wanted to know if everyone was okay. He heard about the man killed in the shooting, and Coach Coughlin was most concerned about the safety of my loved ones.

"You're a grown man, Victor," he said after shutting the office door behind him. "I'm not going to tell you what you can or cannot do on your free time, but as someone who genuinely cares about you as a man, I can't understand why you'd be out at three in the morning. You've got too much ahead of you, son. Use this experience and move on."

We shook hands and I thanked him. I was scared of Coach Coughlin for a very long time. He can be tough and he gets on you for mental mistakes on the football field. But when it came to real life—the things that really mattered—there wasn't a more genuine and caring guy in the world. I'm sure he was disappointed with me that day, but he didn't lecture me or lose his voice.

He saw it in my eyes. He knew I'd already learned a valuable lesson.

OUR NEXT GAME was at home against the Eagles. After giving themselves their "Dream Team" label in August, Philadelphia started the season with losses in six of its first nine games, giving away many of those with late fourth quarter collapses. They were without their starting quarterback, Michael Vick, and their top receiver, Jeremy Maclin, for our Sunday night showdown.

For whatever reason, we couldn't get anything going on offense during the game's first three quarters. As we took to the field in the fourth, we trailed 10-3. It was familiar territory for us, as it seemed like we entered every fourth quarter trailing by a touchdown or two. On third and long from our own twenty-nine, Eli found Hakeem deep down the right sideline for a first down. Two plays later, Eli rolled left out of the pocket and looked for me going deep down the field. I had a step on Nnamdi Asomugha and thought if Eli could drop the ball right in my hands, we could tie the game.

The pass was perfect, I caught it, and I ran it in for a touchdown. I dropped the ball on the ground and did my salsa, pumping the crowd up in the process.

The Eagles answered with a touchdown score of their own, though, giving Philadelphia a 17-10 lead with less than three minutes on the clock.

"Do you guys have another one in you?" Coach Sullivan yelled to Hakeem, Mario, and me.

Then, on third and three, Eli called my number out of the shotgun and hit me on a quick slant pattern across the middle. I had the first down, but it wasn't enough—we needed more. I'd made a move on Asomugha in the open field the first time we played the Eagles, and I was ready to do the same, here. As he squared up to tackle me, I shifted my hips inside, then popped my body to the outside. I left him in the dust and ran thirty more yards to the sideline. We were in striking distance and it felt like we were going to pull off some more last-second magic.

But on the very next play, Eli scrambled to his right and got the ball poked out from behind. The Eagles recovered the fumble, converted a first down, and ran out the clock. Another game, another loss. And our schedule didn't get any easier. Over the course of the next three weeks, we'd be playing the red-hot New Orleans Saints, the defending Super Bowl champion Green Bay Packers, and the Cowboys in Dallas.

■ ■ ■

I'VE BEEN TO a lot of loud sporting venues—places like Cameron Indoor Stadium at Duke or the RAC at Rutgers—but I'd never been in a building as loud as the Superdome for our Monday night game versus the Saints.

Neither team scored in the game's first fifteen minutes, but their offense caught fire in the second. We were trailing by eighteen points at halftime, and things didn't get much better in the third quarter. After Drew Brees connected with Jimmy Graham for a touchdown, we found ourselves down 35-10 going into the fourth quarter.

Down more than three touchdowns, Eli faked a handoff to Brandon and looked deep down the field for me. Because he had bit hard on Eli's play fake, I had several steps on my defender. The ball was thrown perfectly. I made the catch and ran it to in for a seventy-two-yard touchdown. It felt great to get in the end zone, but we were still down three scores. There'd be no salsa this time.

A few drives later, I scored another touchdown, but it was too little too late. We'd lost again, our third straight defeat, and were suddenly 6-5 for the year with the undefeated defending Super Bowl champions up ahead.

I GREW UP wanting to be the next Charles Woodson. As a guy who played both cornerback and wide receiver in high school, I used to always point to Woodson's Heisman Trophy–winning season at Michigan as proof that I could play both positions at the collegiate level. Woodson eventually stuck with just cornerback and instantly became one of the NFL's best defensive players.

At thirty-four years old, he won the 2009 Defensive Player of the Year and his first Super Bowl ring. At thirty-five, he was lined up against *me* at the line of scrimmage.

I played well against Woodson, catching several passes and making some key blocks on him downfield. Our two teams exchanged touchdown scores over the course of three quarters, and with 3:29 left to go in the game, Eli led us on yet another fourth quarter scoring drive. We went seventy yards for the touchdown, and with the score 35-33, D. J. Ware converted a two-point conversion to tie the game at 35.

MetLife was the loudest it'd ever been and we all rallied for our defense to make a stop.

But Aaron Rodgers was just too good. The Super Bowl MVP from a year earlier took the Packers on a heartbreaking game-winning drive, hitting Greg Jennings for eighteen yards and setting up a Mason Crosby thirty-yard field goal for the win.

It was our fourth straight loss.

"We'll see them in the playoffs," one of the veterans said after the game.

At the rate we were going, there'd be no playoffs.

MY FIRST STEPS inside Cowboys Stadium in Dallas were memorable. Though I'd grown up watching the Michael Irvin, Emmitt Smith, and Deion Sanders teams play at Texas Stadium, the new building preserved the look and feel of Dallas Cowboys football. Eli and I walked onto the turf hours before the game and went through our routes, and I remember just being amazed by the size of the two scoreboards hanging above us. They must have been 160 feet long and eighty feet wide apiece, and the HD picture quality was perfect. Everything was just *big*. It felt like we were playing in a Six Flags amusement park. The only things missing were the roller coasters.

As Eli and I practiced all of our patterns, I considered what was at stake. A win, and we were still in the driver's seat of the NFC East. A loss, and our Super Bowl dreams would essentially be over.

I also thought about my father.

He had raised me a Cowboys fan, and when his firefighter buddies used to say, "Your son is going to make it to the pros someday, Mike," he'd always smile and ask them if they thought I'd be wearing the Dallas Cowboys star on my helmet. He would have enjoyed seeing me compete anywhere, but he would have absolutely *loved* watching me play in Dallas.

Early in the first quarter, JPP got behind the Cowboys' offensive line and sacked Tony Romo in the end zone. Safety. JPP was having an incredible season, and that play got us off to the start we needed. He'd make an even bigger play later on in the game.

We went back and forth with the Cowboys for much of the first three quarters, and though I had a couple of bad drops early on, I was confident if Eli gave me another shot to make a play, I'd respond.

Things didn't look good, though. With just over five minutes remaining in the fourth quarter, Tony Romo threw a fifty-yard touchdown pass to a wide-open Dez Bryant. Bryant, wearing the same number 88 Dallas Cowboys jersey that my childhood hero Michael Irvin made famous, celebrated the score with a salsa dance in the end zone. He was the first-ranked wide receiver on NFLDraftScout.com's 2010 Draft rankings. I was seventy-third. Now he was mimicking *my* touchdown celebration.

We're down 34-22. From an outsider's perspective, things looked bleak. We were down twelve on the road in a rowdy building, we hadn't won a game in over a month, and they'd answered every time we put points on the board. A loss would give us a 6-7 record for the season, putting us two games behind the Cowboys in the NFC East standings.

But I knew the types of guys we had on our team, and I knew that our quarterback wasn't going to let us down. Eli's last three fourth quarter comeback attempts had come up short. I just couldn't see it happening again. We'd fought too hard and played too well for our season to end in that giant Six Flags amusement park that night.

Eli led us down the field. He hit me for eleven yards and then again for eight more. Then, on a crucial third and one, I ran a deep square out, and Eli found me for a twenty-three-yard pickup. Two plays later, he connected with Hakeem for twenty-four yards. Then, on second and eight, the offensive line protected Eli well, giving him enough time in the pocket to rifle a pass into Jake Ballard. Jake, with a man hanging on his back, extended his arm over the goal line for a touchdown.

We'd cut the lead to five, but the Cowboys' controlled the ball and the clock. We needed either our defense to make a big play or a stroke of good luck. We got the latter.

On third and five, Miles Austin, the Cowboys' star receiver, broke free off the line of scrimmage and was wide open down the right side of the field. Romo immediately spotted him and lofted what looked like a perfectly thrown, surefire touchdown pass. A catch would have meant that the game—and ultimately, our season—was over.

But Romo's pass wasn't perfect. It was thrown a few too many yards in front of Austin. He didn't dive for the ball, it bounced off the ground incomplete, and we were, somehow, still alive.

Two minutes left, down five points, and a hostile opposing crowd calling you every name in the book—there's nothing better in the world.

Eli drove us right down the field again. He hit Ballard for twenty yards, me for eight, and then Ballard for another eighteen. On first and goal from the one, Brandon ran the ball up the gut of the Cowboys' defense for the go-ahead score. Touchdown. D. J. Ware converted the two-point conversion and we took a 37-34 lead with just 1:30 left on the clock.

The Cowboys marched down the field with a pair of pass completions and their rookie kicker, Dan Bailey, trotted onto the field for the game-winning field goal attempt. I could hardly watch.

The ball was snapped and Bailey booted the ball right through the uprights. Tie game. We were going to overtime.

Only, there were whistles being blown. Though I didn't see it, Coach Coughlin apparently signaled for a time-out seconds before the Cowboys snapped the ball on the kick.

There'd be a do-over.

Bailey trotted back out onto the field, and I crouched on the sideline, just thinking to myself, Man, somebody please block this kick. We practiced defending against field goals all season, and our special teams guys pride themselves on batting down kicks and blocking punts.

We needed one of them to break through and make a play.

JPP did just that, bursting through the line and getting his fingers on Bailey's kick. It fluttered in the air and hit the ground. Game over.

We went wild on the sideline, jumping all over each other and rushing onto the field to celebrate with JPP and the rest of the special teams guys.

The party carried over to the locker room, where we hugged and cheered.

Coach Gilbride, grinning from ear to ear, approached me at my locker. "Did you see what they were doing to you on those last few drives?" he asked.

I'd realized I was having trouble getting open but didn't know what the Cowboys were doing to keep me contained.

"They put a double vise on you, Victor," Coach Gilbride explained with his smile getting bigger. "That's the ultimate sign of respect for a wide receiver, son. The *ultimate*."

A "double vise" meant that Rob Ryan, the Cowboys' defensive coordinator, ordered two different players to cover just me.

He thought so highly of my skills that he risked leaving another player on my team completely open.

"Some of the very best receivers in the entire league don't see a double vise," Coach Gilbride said as he patted me on the head.

We all congregated in a huddle in the middle of the locker room and Coach Coughlin instructed us to take a knee.

"Way to reach down, deep inside, and come up with the final courage to pull this thing out," he said as we clasped hands. "What a hell of a fourth quarter and what a great win for our football team."

Coach Coughlin then raised his right hand, and said, "What a tremendous job *in the division*. You can now take the star down off the mountain and put the N-Y-G up top. Now, listen, you've got to keep it up there now!"

"Let's enjoy this now," he started, "and I will see you . . . Wednesday!"

We all screamed in delight with that one.

OF COURSE, WHEN we took to the field the following Sunday against the 4-9 Redskins, we came out completely flat. The whole day had an incredibly weird feel to it. Sometimes you can just sense it in the air. And as we continued to make errors, the home crowd started to grumble. We'd lost our last two home games, and after the big win in Dallas, the Giants faithful wanted to see us put together a similar type of effort.

But we just didn't have it.

The Redskins jumped out to an early 17-0 lead and we never came close to catching up. We lost 23-10 and were back where we'd been the previous week—in a must-win situation.

THE JETS WERE 8-6, we were 7-7, and our seasons were both on the line. Though our loss to the Redskins was bad, the Jets' week fifteen loss to the Eagles might have been even worse. There was a desperate feeling from both fan bases, and throughout the week it was the biggest news story in New York.

Prior to the game, I heard from what felt like every single person I knew. At least thirty-five different people told me that they'd be coming to the game.

If the area's crosstown rivals playing in a "do-or-die" game on Christmas Eve wasn't enough of a story line, the New York media helped create an additional one. After practice one afternoon, one of the local paper's Giants beat reporter, a woman who'd asked me a thousand questions over the course of the season, said, "Victor, it seems as though teams aren't scared to throw at Darrelle Revis anymore. They've been coming at him a little more this season. Would you agree?"

She was right.

I didn't have the opportunity to watch the Jets every Sunday, but from the game film we had watched earlier in the week, it did appear as though opposing quarterbacks were throwing to receivers covered by Revis more than they had in the past. Nobody doubts how good Darrelle Revis is. He's the top cornerback in the league and one of the best defensive backs to ever play the game. I thought it was an accurate observation, though.

"Teams aren't really scared of him anymore," I answered. "He's got to earn his money this year. Teams aren't really backing down. I feel like we're going to do the same thing. We're going to go all out. Until he physically stops us, we're going to throw the ball on him."

Maybe I shouldn't have said a thing. Maybe I should have known better. But I answered the question honestly, not intending to insult or disparage an opposing player.

Sure enough, the next day, all the newspapers ran with the same blurb—"Cruz Says Teams Aren't Scared of Revis Anymore."

Then it got out of control. Mario said something, Antonio

Cromartie answered back at Mario, and Revis got the last jab. On the Thursday before our Saturday game, one of the Jets' beat reporters asked Revis what he thought of me.

"I don't even know who this guy is," he said.

I'd heard a lot of trash talk throughout the year from opposing players on the field. They called me a "One Year Wonder," they made fun of my salsa dance, they called me "Mighty Mouse" for being less than six feet. None of that bothered me.

But Revis's and Cromartie's comments stuck with me in a different way than the other insults.

They brought me back to the Paterson Catholic locker room, where after every game I'd see college coaches huddle around Chenry Lewis and Kit Pommels and ignore my presence. They took me to Greg Schiano's office at Rutgers, where he told my mother and me that he had to wait and see if ten other players were going to accept or deny scholarship offers before he could consider giving me one. They took me to the NFL Draft training facilities in Florida, where Juice Williams and Trindon Holliday asked why they'd never seen or heard of me before.

I was one of the NFL's leaders in receiving yards, a local guy playing in the New York market, and making big fourth quarter plays every single week. And yet these guys—Revis and Cromartie—still didn't seem to think that I belonged. They still saw me as an outsider, or worse, someone whose name wasn't on their radars.

I'd have to make them remember me.

Our team was fired up, the Jets were fired up, and both of our fan bases were ready to explode in the hours leading up to the game. During player introductions, the Jets introduced their entire defense— and ex-Giants Super Bowl star Plaxico

THEY STILL SAW ME AS AN OUTSIDER, OR WORSE, SOMEONE WHOSE NAME WASN'T ON THEIR RADARS.

Burress. The Jets' home crowd, decked in green, went absolutely nuts.

Both teams looked sluggish at the start of the game. We had a horrible twelve-men-on-the-field penalty, the Jets had a bad missed field goal, and our teams went back and forth with punts throughout the first half. Our defense was keeping us in the game, though, and we were fortunate to be trailing by just four points late in the second quarter.

Third and ten.

Two minutes, twenty-seven seconds left in the first half.

The ball was on our own one yard line.

The play would change our season and my life forever.

So much was going through my mind before the snap. Elaina was in the stands, eight months pregnant and just about ready to burst. Cromartie had been running his mouth all game and nailed me with a big hit in the first quarter. Kyle Wilson, a name I remembered seeing on all of the recruiting Web sites when I was a "one star" recruit in high school, was giving me some room on the line. When I saw Wilson nervously backpedal two steps before David Baas, our center, snapped the ball to Eli, I knew there was some sort of miscommunication on their side of the ball.

I caught Eli's pass, broke free of Wilson and Cromartie, and ran my fastest down the sideline, surging past the Jets' safety, Eric Smith.

Eric Smith wasn't getting me.

No one was.

I raced past the goal line, threw the ball, and did the salsa in front of eighty thousand screaming fans just fifteen miles from the kitchen where I had learned to dance twenty years earlier.

Emotions were running high and as I ran to the sideline to celebrate the score with my teammates, I found myself repeating the same refrain, "They know my name now. They know my name now."

The play not only gave us the momentum in the game, but it flipped a switch on our season. Like we'd found ourselves all year long, we were backed into a corner and in dire need of a game-changing moment. The touchdown sucked the life out of the Jets' "home" crowd and gave our defense the breathing room it needed to stay aggressive.

We never looked back.

We beat the Jets 29-14, extending our season one more game and essentially ending theirs.

After the game, Peter John-Baptiste, one of the Giants' public relations guys, told me that there'd only been twelve niney-nine-yard touchdown receptions in NFL history prior to mine. None were by a New York Giant.

The play also meant that I was the new Giants' single-season record holder for receiving yards in a season, breaking Amani Toomer's long-standing record of 1,343 yards.

It was a childhood dream of mine to someday get a shot in the NFL. Now I was a record holder for one of the most storied franchises in the sport. The whole thing was surreal.

That night, I went out to dinner with some friends in Manhattan's Meatpacking District.

When we got to the restaurant, there was a line wrapped around the block.

It was cold and I had Elaina waiting up for me in our apartment. I wasn't standing in a line in freezing temperatures.

As I started to leave the restaurant, I looked at the front of the line and saw a familiar face.

"Is that *Revis*?" I asked my friend Josh, who poked his head out to see.

It was.

We didn't get the chance to speak after the game and I wanted to explain my comments from earlier in the week. The line was long, though, and he was already headed inside. It'd have to wait until the next time.

Just as it looked like he had disappeared into the mob of people inside the restaurant, he came back out, looking for one of his friends in line. We linked eyes and he broke out in a smile.

Revis waved me over to him and I pushed through the crowd to get to the restaurant's front entrance. When I got there, he embraced me with a hug. "Listen, man," I started, wanting to say my piece and tell him how my words got distorted and placed out of context.

But he cut me off before I could get any of it out.

"We know who you are, Cruz," he said as he leaned in toward me. "Good game today. You played well."

I was home by eleven, in bed on Christmas Eve with my pregnant girlfriend cuddled up next to me.

And Darrelle Revis knew who I was, after all.

Life was good.

WE PICKED UP right where we left off the following week. Our Sunday night week seventeen showdown with the Cowboys was hyped as "the Game of the Year" and the NFC East title hung in the balance, but we never had any doubts we'd beat Dallas in our building.

The crowd came ready to lift us and we responded with our best all-around effort of the regular season.

In the first quarter, with the score still tied at zero, Eli hit me on a timing pattern on the left side of the field. When I hauled the ball in, I realized I'd gotten past Terence Newman, the Cowboys' cornerback who'd been lining up against me all game. I looked ahead and saw green grass. I ran hard, knowing both Newman and his teammate Gerald Sensabaugh were a step or two behind me. Instead of losing a second by turning around, I looked up at the scoreboard to gauge how much space I had. Using the scoreboard's video screen as my rearview mirror, I was able to separate from both of them and took the ball seventy-four yards for another score, my ninth touchdown reception of the season.

I did the salsa in the rain and was greeted with hugs by everyone on the sideline. "Ladies and gentlemen, the number one salsa dancer in the league!" Michael Boley screamed, again, as he and Antrel Rolle swarmed me.

We were up 7-0 and we didn't look back.

The Cowboys had had their chance to win the division in week fourteen, but Tony Romo overthrew Miles Austin on third and five.

We were given an opportunity and we made the most of it. Three quarters away from the playoffs and the first Giants NFC East title since 2008, we weren't going to leave anything to chance. Eli led us on two more scoring drives before halftime and we led 21-0 at the end of the second quarter.

We won the game 31-14 and celebrated our division title in the locker room. We were playoff-bound and would be hosting the first-ever postseason game played at MetLife Stadium in exactly seven days.

My teammate Chris Canty, a former star on the Cowboys, approached me in the locker room after the win. "We're not division champions if you don't step up this season, Cruz," he said, patting me on the shoulder.

Winning the NFC East title was a great team accomplishment, but it wasn't the goal Eli had set for us back in May during those scorching-hot mornings at Hoboken High School.

Chris Canty had been in the league seven full seasons and hadn't played in a Super Bowl. I looked at him and thanked him for the complimentary words. I then assured him that we weren't finished yet.

NEW RESPONSIBILITIES

ON JANUARY 8, we hosted the Atlanta Falcons in the first post-season game ever played at MetLife Stadium. Elaina was in the stands, now nine months pregnant, with my mother seated next to her.

Twelve months earlier, I had been sprawled out on my living room couch in Paterson, watching the playoffs, uncertain about the NFL future of an injured rookie with zero career receptions.

On January 8, 2012, I was starting an NFL postseason game in front of the two women who'd been with me through it all.

Eli had never won a playoff game at home, and during the week leading up to our wild card matchup with Atlanta, many of the ex-players and analysts on TV picked us to lose.

That wasn't going to happen.

Our defense stopped the Falcons on two big fourth-and-one plays, our running game took charge, and we had a 17-2 lead heading into the fourth quarter.

I'd been having trouble getting open all game, and though Hakeem and Mario were more than picking up the slack, I was growing frustrated with my performance. I wanted to make a difference.

"You see what they're doing to you, right?" Coach Ryan asked me after an offensive series in the second half.

"They've got the double vice on you."

He was right. On nearly every play, I'd had either Dominique Franks or Chris Owens, two of the Falcons' cornerbacks, covering me one-on-one at the line of scrimmage. Then, the second I'd break into my route, Thomas DeCoud, the Falcons' safety, would shade over to give the cornerback help.

Hakeem caught six balls for 115 yards and scored two touchdowns. Mario had four receptions for sixty-eight yards and put the game away with a twenty-seven-yard touchdown reception in the fourth quarter. I caught just two balls for twenty-eight yards.

I couldn't have been happier.

We won 24-2 and Eli was finally able to celebrate a playoff victory in front of the home crowd.

After the game, I was in the tunnel waiting for the rest of my teammates when I spotted Justin Tuck, our team's defensive captain, coming my way.

"Cruuuuuuuz!" Tuck yelled from the field.

Then he broke into his own version of the salsa.

"How am I doing, Cruz? Can I salsa or what?" he asked me as reporters snapped photos of him dancing up a storm.

It wasn't pretty, but I gave him a "10" for the effort. "Looks good, dude," I laughed. "You're a natural."

ELAINA AND I got back to our apartment and I started to prepare us some dinner. The Broncos-Steelers AFC wild card game was on the television, and Elaina was in the bedroom getting changed into something more comfortable.

"Victor!" she screamed.

"What is it, babe?" I answered, running over to see if she was okay.

"I think my water just broke."

The next few hours are a complete blur. I don't remember much, but I do know that I packed clothes in a gym bag. Lots and lots of clothes. I packed three changes of clothes for Elaina, two changes of clothes for Elaina's mother, some shirts for Malik if he decided to stop by, and some clothes for my mom and Andrea, my little sister.

What I forgot to pack was a change of clothes for *me*. No underwear. No socks. No second T-shirt. Nothing. I'd wear the same shirt, jeans, and underwear for the next eighteen hours.

I placed Elaina in the backseat of the car and rushed to Hackensack Hospital. It felt like we were in a movie. She was screaming, "Hurry! Hurry!" in the back as I was trying my best to get her there as quickly as possible while still respecting New Jersey's traffic laws.

When we got to the hospital, the nurses took Elaina into a room and I immediately called my mother.

"What's up, Victor? Are you watching this game?"

I'd later learn that Tim Tebow, the quarterback of the Broncos, was leading his team to a victory over the defending AFC Champion Steelers. I couldn't possibly have cared less.

"No, no. Mom—Elaina's giving birth!"

"What? Now?" she asked.

"Well, soon. But yeah!"

Elaina's mother was there with me in the hospital, and as January 8 turned to January 9, we excitedly waited for our new addition to arrive.

At ten twenty-four a.m. on January 9, 2012, Kennedy Ryan Cruz entered the world. She weighed seven pounds, two ounces and had beautiful, piercing gray eyes that lit up the room.

"Vic, she has your eyes," Elaina said as she held our daughter in her arms.

She did, but she also had something else—my father's smile. Even in those first few hours after being born, I could see her giving little smirks. She knew she was the most beautiful girl in the world already.

I held Kennedy in my arms and for a moment tried processing all that was going on in my life. The past twelve months had been a complete whirlwind.

Then I stopped and just looked at her sparkling gray eyes. My baby girl. She put me at ease.

"You've got a beautiful mother, Kennedy. You know that?" I asked, rocking her in the hospital room while smiling at Elaina.

I was the father of a wonderful, healthy baby girl.

I was truly blessed.

IT WAS DIFFICULT to focus on football that week, but I tried my hardest. Every minute of every day, Elaina and Kennedy were on my mind. But when I got within the walls of our facilities, I shifted my attention to something else—the defending champion Green Bay Packers.

The Packers finished the regular season with a 15-1 record and went a perfect 8-0 at Lambeau Field. Aaron Rodgers, the quarterback who had torn our hearts out with a last-second scoring drive in our building back in December, had an all-time great NFL season. Rodgers would go on to win the league MVP award, and rightfully so. He threw forty-five touchdowns and six interceptions in just fifteen regular season starts.

But we believed there was a chance Rodgers could be rusty when he took the field against us that Sunday. Though he'd had an incredible season, he hadn't thrown a pass in a game in twenty-one days. He also hadn't been sacked in twenty-one days. Rodgers's coaches sat him in week seventeen against the Lions, and the Packers had a bye during the first week of the playoffs. If our pass rush could get to him early, maybe he'd be off his game. Even if he was a *little* rusty at the start, we could use that to our advantage.

The 2007 team had won an all-time classic NFC Championship Game at Lambeau Field during their Super Bowl run. The squad last year had lost that season-ending game in week sixteen. But I'd never been to Lambeau. It was a sight to behold.

Walking around the field before the game, I thought about all the NFL Films highlights I'd watched as a kid. Bart Starr, Vince

Lombardi, Brett Favre—they had all played in this very building. I was amazed to see that instead of the fancy luxury boxes you see in other NFL stadiums, Lambeau Field actually had old-school benches in the stands. Cold, hard benches—like the ones you'd find at a high school field in New Jersey. If we didn't have a football game to play, I could have walked around the stadium for hours. All of the NFL's legends had gone through Lambeau Field at some point in their careers. Now I was getting that opportunity.

During that entire week of practices, Hakeem told the other receivers that we were going sleeveless. He was insistent. I'd played football in the Northeast my entire life, so the cold weather really never bothered me. I'd gone sleeveless before and I'd go sleeveless again. I just loved that it was Hakeem—the guy who was born and raised in North Carolina—who was pushing the sleeveless thing so hard.

Fortunately, the sun was shining before kickoff and it wasn't as cold as we'd anticipated it to be. The Packers were nine-point favorites, but we'd won four straight games and felt very good about our chances.

As we hoped they would, our defensive line got to Rodgers early and often, pressuring him from all angles. He also wasn't getting much help from his teammates. We were up 3-0 in the first quarter when Rodgers had his Pro Bowl receiver, Greg Jennings, wide open toward the goal line. He threw the ball a bit too high and it bounced to the ground. Incomplete. It could easily have been seven points, but their timing was off on the play.

On third and eleven from deep in our own territory, the offensive line gave Eli enough time to operate and he threw a bullet pass to Hakeem across the middle. First down. On the very next play, Eli went back to Hakeem. This time, he not only caught the ball, but he bounced off a Packers defensive back and broke free in the open field. Sixty-eight yards later, he was beating his chest like a caveman in the end zone. Sleeveless. We were up 10-0 on the defending Super Bowl champion Packers in Lambeau Field.

Green Bay answered, though, and after leading his offense right down the field, Rodgers hit John Kuhn, his big fullback, for a touchdown pass that cut our lead to three. They blocked a field goal attempt on our next drive and had the ball again, looking to score once more.

The NFL's hard to figure out, though. Much in the same way that you can beat the Eagles in Philadelphia and lose to the Seahawks at home, sometimes players who never drop balls just drop balls.

Play after play, Rodgers was throwing perfectly thrown passes to his trusted receivers, and they were dropping them. In the first half alone, the Packers' running backs, receivers, and tight ends combined for four dropped passes.

"They're rusty," Justin Tuck shouted as our defense came off the field after James Starks, the Packers' running back, dropped an easy one in the flat. "They haven't played a big game in months."

Back and forth we went in the second quarter, and after Mathias Kiwanuka knocked the ball loose out of Kuhn's hands, we recovered the fumble in Packers territory with less than four minutes remaining in the half. Hakeem made a big catch along the sideline, but we couldn't punch the ball in for a touchdown. We settled for a field goal, giving us a 13-10 lead late in the second quarter.

Rodgers had a third and five and was moving his team down the field, but Michael Boley—a guy who'd been coming up huge for us all season—sacked him to end the drive. We got the ball back but had the entire length of the field to go and just forty seconds on the clock.

I expected Coach Gilbride to instruct Eli to kneel the ball a few times and preserve the three-point halftime lead. He had just the opposite in mind. "Let's go score some points," Coach Gilbride blared as our offense jogged back onto the field.

Eli hit Bradshaw for a few yards, then threw an incomplete to Jake Ballard. The Packers, now seeing an opportunity to get the ball back one more time before the end of the half, called time-out.

It was third and one and you could feel the momentum of the game swinging back and forth on every play.

During the time-out, Coach Gilbride drew up a running play for Ahmad and urged him to get out of bounds after converting the first down.

"If you pop it to the outside, be sure to get out of bounds," he shouted continuously. We had no time-outs left and though everyone *wanted* Ahmad to pick up a big gain, getting out of bounds and stopping the clock would give us two plays to set up for a field goal attempt before the end of the half.

Eli pitched it to Ahmad and he picked up the first down running behind David Diehl on the left side of our offensive line.

"Get out of bounds! Get out of bounds!" I shouted.

But Ahmad wasn't ready to just do that. Instead, he cut back and ran across the entire length of the field, picking up fifteen more yards, and somehow getting out of bounds on the *right* sideline.

It was a risky, but downright incredible, play. The clock stopped and we were now at the Packers' thirty-seven yard line with just eight seconds left in the half. The ball was out of Lawrence Tynes's field goal range, meaning Eli would have to give heaving a prayer toward the end zone a shot.

I'd never seen a team complete a Hail Mary pass in person. Not in high school, not in college, and certainly not in the pros. You see them from time to time on the highlights on *SportsCenter*, but they're extremely rare.

But extremely rare things seemed to be happening for us.

The play is literally called "Trips, Hail Mary." It's in Coach Gilbride's playbook and the instructions are as follows: "Run to the goalposts as fast as you can and try to catch the ball when it's thrown."

I remember running down the field alongside Hakeem and Devin Thomas and looking around, thinking, There's nobody wearing green in this end zone. Usually on a Hail Mary pass, there are eight or nine defenders, but for whatever reason, we actually outnumbered them. When Eli threw his pass high into the sky, Hakeem boxed his defender out like a basketball player positioning for a rebound and jumped as high as he could. The ball came down and landed perfectly in his hands.

He caught it.

A Hail Mary!

I couldn't believe it. Not knowing what to do, I just started slapping Hakeem on the helmet over and over again. He'd just caught a Hail Mary pass in the playoffs—at Lambeau Field!

The play sucked the life out of the entire stadium. Lambeau was so loud during pregame warm-ups that it was shaking. After the Hail Mary touchdown, it was completely silent. You could have heard a pin drop. We had a ten-point lead going into half-time, and our offense hadn't even played particularly well.

A HAIL MARY! I COULDN'T BELIEVE IT.

The defense carried us in the third quarter, sacking Rodgers play after play and keeping their high-scoring aerial game under wraps. Osi Umenyiora, JPP, Canty, and Tuck seemed to be in Rodgers's face every time he dropped back for a pass. Boley and Kiwanuka were getting good hits on him, too. The entire unit was fearless.

Lawrence Tynes hit a field goal to make it 23-13 at the start of the fourth quarter, and we pleaded with our defense to stop the Packers one more time.

Rodgers tossed a screen pass to his running back, Ryan Grant, and Grant made a few nifty moves to pick up some extra yards. As he fought for a few more, Kenny Phillips, our strong safety, knocked the ball loose. Chase Blackburn scooped the ball up off the ground and ran with it forty yards the other way. He was brought down at the five yard line, and we were in great scoring position.

"Put 'em away!" Justin Tuck screamed as our offense took the field.

On the very next play, Eli faked a handoff to Ahmad, waited for each one of us to break out of our routes, and threw a perfect pass to a streaking Mario in the back of the end zone. Touchdown.

Everyone talks about my salsa celebration, but Mario has a pretty great touchdown dance of his own. When he scores, he blows on an imaginary pair of dice and rolls them in the end zone. It was amazing to see him do his whole routine—dice blowing, dancing, and all—in front of seventy-three thousand stunned Packers fans in Lambeau.

But the Packers wouldn't go away. They answered again with another touchdown, making the score 30-20.

"Hands team, get in there," shouted Coach Quinn. Green Bay was lining up for an onside kick, meaning I'd be entering the game on special teams. As one of the guys on "the hands team," I had to line up at the very front of our kickoff return formation and recover the onside attempt. There's nothing glamorous about being on the hands team, but if you get your mitts on the ball, you need to do everything—and anything—you possibly can to ensure that you do not let it go. The number of receptions, touchdowns, and salsa celebrations I'd had over the course of the season didn't matter anymore. They were all meaningless now. On the hands team, all that matters is your toughness. You're asked to do one thing—grab the ball and never let it go.

Mason Crosby, the Packers' kicker, faked going to his right and booted the ball to the left in my direction. As it bounced off the ground, I kept my eyes on its laces, knowing it could take a funky twist or turn once it ricocheted off the Lambeau Field grass. The ball took a hop, I got both of my hands on it, and I fell to the ground, gripping it tightly to my chest.

The bottom of a pile-on is never fun, and in that particular one, there were guys clutching my face mask, pulling my jersey, and grabbing my crotch.

It's all in the name of the game and you can't take it personally. I just closed my eyes and held on to the ball as tightly as I could. I didn't care if there were a million Packers grabbing for that ball—no one was taking it from me.

The official signaled that we'd recovered the kick and the pile of players was slowly ripped off me one by one. When I got back to the sideline, there was a mob of Giants teammates and coaches waiting to greet me. I'd caught five passes that night—four of which went for first downs—but recovering the onside kick was my biggest play of the evening.

I'd had a few terrible drops at the start of the season. I woke up in the middle of the night once with a nightmare about the one on our very first drive of the year against the Redskins.

To now have *my* hands be the ones that secured the victory was incredible.

The defense came up big on our next few drives, and after Brandon Jacobs scored a touchdown late in the fourth quarter, it became real—we were knocking the defending champs out of the playoffs and advancing to the NFC Championship Game.

Next stop: a rematch in San Francisco.

CARLOS ROGERS.

It was the only name I heard about in the six days leading up to our NFC Championship Game against the 49ers.

Carlos Rogers.

All week, the beat reporters asked me if I'd be looking for revenge after he mimicked my salsa dance in front of our sideline in week ten. I played it cool, telling the media that I thought it was a "sign of disrespect" but didn't really let it bother me.

The truth was that I'd been hoping to get another shot at him since the second we boarded the plane back to New York that Sunday night.

I'd had a few catches when we played the 49ers the first time around, but we lost the game. And Rogers didn't just have that one interception; he had another one, too. I'd had big days against some of the top cornerbacks in the league—Nnamdi Asomugha, Charles Woodson, and Terence Newman to name a few—but Rogers got the better of me in our regular season matchup.

Salsa dance stuff aside, I didn't like that he'd outplayed me. I didn't like it when *any* cornerback outplayed me, and he'd done it in front of millions of people on a nationally televised stage. I had a score to settle with Carlos Rogers and was being given an opportunity to get the last word.

We watched tape of our week ten loss in San Francisco and picked some things up in our film study sessions. We saw that their safeties—Whitner and Goldson—tried to get in and make a hit on every running play. They don't just want to be in on the play as support; they want to make contact on the backs *every single time.*

Seeing this on tape, our crew of receivers knew that we'd have to do more than just catch balls in our rematch with the 49ers. We'd have to really lend a hand in the blocking game, too. Our effort in protecting Eli and our running backs would end up being as important as our duties as pass catchers.

I never was too interested in the blocking aspect of the game in high school and didn't truly grasp it in college. But in 2011—

watching guys like Hakeem, Mario, and Stokley do it so effec-tively—I started to realize just how important it was for a receiver to be a sound blocker, too.

It was all a cycle. If I blocked well for our running backs, they'd have a better chance at success. If they were having success, it'd force defenses to respect our ground game. If defenses were concerned with our ground game, it meant more opportunities for me through the air.

WE WEREN'T WALKING INTO THIS BATTLE ALONE; WE HAD ALL OF GIANTS NATION IN OUR CORNER.

We all knew that this was going to be the most physical game of the year, and we were ready. We arrived in San Francisco craving the contact, wanting the pain. It was raining and it was dark the day of the NFC Championship Game, but we saw a sprinkling of blue in the stands.

Giants fans are incredible. Here we were, twenty-five hundred miles from home, and there were Big Blue supporters in all parts of the crowd. Hearing the "Cruuuuuuz" chant in MetLife was one thing, but hearing it screamed over a mass of rowdy 49ers fans was something else. We weren't walking into this battle alone; we had all of Giants Nation in our corner.

Before every game, Hakeem gathers the receivers in a small circle in the locker room for a prayer. He wishes us good safety and good fortune on the football field. Before the NFC Championship Game, though, he pointed Mario out specifically. Hakeem put his hand on Mario's shoulder and said, "God, grant Mario the hands to catch the game-winning touchdown that takes us to the Super Bowl."

Mario looked at Hakeem and nodded.

We finished our prayer and took to the field. We were ready.

■ ■ ■

RIGHT FROM THE start, we tried establishing the run and I threw my body hard into Whitner and Goldson. I held my ground and did my best to help Ahmad and Brandon get some room on the edge. It felt good getting a few solid hits on those guys. And as strange as it sounds, it also felt pretty good getting hit *by* them. The rain was coming down hard, my jersey was covered in mud, and we were playing tough NFC-style football. Giants-49ers. It just felt right.

As our running game got going, I found myself isolated one-on-one with Carlos Rogers. He wasn't talking trash, but he was grabbing me at the line. Eli spread the ball out over the first few drives, hitting Hakeem, Mario, and me early in the first quarter. But after the 49ers scored on a long pass play to make it 7-0, Eli told me he'd be coming to me more in the second quarter.

I'm not sure if he'd seen something in our film study sessions during the week, at the line of scrimmage during the game, or if he just felt comfortable playing catch with me on a rainy day— but in that second quarter, I became his first, second, and third target.

On a big third and six, he hit me for a thirty-six-yard completion. I grabbed the ball right over Rogers. On the following third and four, we connected for six yards. First down. Four plays later, Eli tossed a beautiful pass to Bear Pascoe, our backup tight end, for a touchdown.

Over on our sideline, Eli pulled Hakeem, Mario, and me close to him. "You guys are open. They're blitzing me from all over and they're honoring the run. You're all one-on-one with these corners. I'll find you."

He hit me for fifteen yards on our next drive, but we didn't put up any points. After both teams exchanged some punts, our offense took the field with less than two minutes remaining in the first half.

On second and ten, Eli found me for fifteen yards. I caught the ball, fought Rogers off, and picked up an additional four. Two plays later, he hit me for eleven more. Again, it was on Rogers. On the very next play, Eli threw one deep to me. I had a step on Rogers, but the ball fell to the ground, just out of my grasp.

We got back to the huddle and I told him, "It's there."

The very next play, out of the shotgun, Eli threw me a seventeen-yard pass and I hauled it in to my body. Rogers, still covering me with no additional help, brought me to the ground.

We hurried to the line and Eli spiked the ball, stopping the clock.

In the huddle, he looked at me again. I knew he was coming right back to me.

Rogers was gasping for air and so was I. We'd been going at it all afternoon, but the past few plays were essentially an Eli Manning and Victor Cruz versus Carlos Rogers bullying session. It was like we were picking on the guy.

It's what I wanted. It's what I'd been pining for since he outplayed me on November 13.

On the next play, Eli took the snap and I made a hard cut over the middle. I had a step on Rogers and was thrown a laser. I caught it with both hands and went down to the ground at the 49ers' twenty-one yard line. First down.

I couldn't breathe. I was exhausted.

We hustled to the line and Eli stopped the clock with a spike.

Lawrence Tynes then ran onto the field and booted one right through the uprights for three points.

We had a 10-7 lead going into halftime.

The drive was classic Eli Manning. He had to lead us seventy yards in 1:34, and he did exactly that with poise and efficiency. Nothing ever rattled the guy; he just got it done. Always.

I was thoroughly drained after the offensive series. On that scoring drive alone, I caught four balls for fifty-six yards and was tossed another one deep down the middle of the field. In total, I had eight catches for 125 yards in the first half. Carlos Rogers was covering me on just about every single one of those plays. I knew that, and so did he.

Neither of us said a word to each other. Neither of us was doing the salsa. We were just going at it, two competitors, leaving everything we had on the football field.

The 49ers scored on a Vernon Davis touchdown midway through the third quarter and we found ourselves trailing 14-10. Our offense stalled on our next few drives, and Eli took a beating behind the line of scrimmage. Even when he wasn't getting sacked, he was taking good licks from the San Francisco defensive attack. Aldon Smith, Patrick Willis, and Justin Smith were making their presences felt just about every time Eli went back to pass.

But he got up whenever he was knocked down. The guy never seemed to flinch.

At the start of the fourth quarter, we trailed 14-10 and knew that our season could be finished within the hour if our offense didn't get something going. We had the ball on our own twenty yard line with a little over eleven minutes remaining, and the Candlestick crowd was as loud as it'd been all game. Eli had that look in his eyes and I thought we were about to begin one of those legendary Eli Manning fourth quarter drives.

But after three failed plays, it was fourth and fifteen and our punt team was shuffling onto the field.

I stood with Hakeem and Mario on the sideline, the three of us just hoping for a big play.

Steve Weatherford, our punter, booted one down the field and Kyle Williams, the 49ers' punt return man, watched as it bounced off the ground and rolled past him. As the ball dribbled by Williams, Devin Thomas, our special teams "gunner," sprinted toward it and picked it up.

It didn't appear as though the ball had touched Williams at all, but Devin was acting as if it had.

The officials ruled that the ball hadn't made contact with Williams and it was the 49ers' football.

But Devin insisted. From the field, he urged the coaches to toss a red flag, challenging the ruling on the play. Coach Coughlin went for it, and the play was reviewed.

It turns out that Devin was right. The ball *had* hit Williams. On the replay, you could see the ball just slightly nick his knee. How Devin noticed that, I'll never know. But it was the game-changing play that we so desperately needed. Ed Hochuli, the official, came back on the field and awarded us the ball.

Then, on third and fifteen, from the 49ers' seventeen yard line, Eli took the snap out of the shotgun and waited for us to break out of our routes. I was open six yards over the middle, but he was going for it all.

He wound up and threw a perfect pass in the middle of the end zone, where Mario was crossing at the exact moment the ball arrived. He jumped, and seconds before one of San Francisco's safeties could lay him out, he hauled it in for a touchdown.

Hakeem, D. J. Ware, Jake Ballard, and I all raced over to Mario in the corner of the end zone and celebrated the score.

We were all jumping on him, and I couldn't stop screaming at Hakeem, "You called it! You called it!" He had prayed for that very play to happen just a few hours earlier.

We hadn't won the game yet, though. And on the 49ers' next possession, they tied it up at 17 with a field goal.

Over the course of the next few drives, I was dinged pretty hard by Patrick Willis, clocked by Donte Whitner, and brought down by Carlos Rogers. Though I'd had my way with Rogers in the first half, the 49ers' coaching staff started to shade Whitner over toward me throughout the third and fourth quarters. I was doing everything I could to get open, but I was taking a beating. On one play, I slipped on a route and my left foot came right out of its shoe. I walked back to the huddle with a soaking-wet foot, my jersey covered in grass stains, and my voice nearly gone from all the screaming.

It was the toughest, most physical game I'd ever been a part of, and after eight more minutes of our two teams exchanging punts—it was headed to overtime.

We won the coin toss and got the ball first, but were stopped on our first drive. Then our defense came out and forced the 49ers to punt after three plays. It'd gone this way the entire game.

When we started our next drive at our own thirty-five yard line, it appeared as though Eli was getting into a good flow. He hit my roommate, Travis Beckum, for five yards and then our fullback, Henry Hynoski, for three more. But just as we were moving the ball, Justin Smith got behind the line of scrimmage and sacked Eli for a ten-yard loss.

Our punt team hustled back onto the field.

Devin Thomas had already made one game-changing play in the fourth quarter. We needed another one from our special teams in overtime.

Weatherford's punt was a rocket in the air, and Kyle Williams caught it cleanly.

Jacquian Williams was a sixth-round pick in the 2011 NFL Draft. Like I had a year earlier, he'd shown up to Giants training camp in August with a goal to make the team. A linebacker and teammate of JPP's in college at South Florida, he earned his roster spot through hard work and dedication on special teams. Nobody owned a Jacquian Williams jersey or bought his football card on eBay. But it was Jacquian Williams who came up with the biggest play of the game.

As Kyle Williams took a few strides with the ball, Jacquian

sprinted forty yards with a full head of steam. He let up for just a second, stretched his right arm out, and knocked the ball loose out of Williams's hands.

"Fumble!" I screamed, watching from the sidelines with Mario.

Devin Thomas, the guy who'd been our best special teams player all season long, jumped on the ball.

Four plays later, Lawrence Tynes kicked a thirty-one-yard field goal right through the uprights, sending us to the Super Bowl.

As the ball sailed through, I ran onto the field with my helmet in my hand, just screaming, "We're going to the Super Bowl! We're going to the Super Bowl!"

It was amazing.

I sat down on the wet grass at midfield, and just took it all in. My white jersey was now completely green and brown. My body was sore all over. I had no voice left.

But I was going to the Super Bowl.

I SPENT THE next three days on the couch next to Elaina, just savoring some quality time with her and Kennedy. Our daughter was so tiny that she fit in the palm of my hand. I was still getting used to holding her, but I was starting to get the knack of some of my other fatherly duties. I was learning how to warm her bottle, burp her, and even change her diapers.

My body was a mess after the San Francisco game, and I enjoyed having an entire week off with my baby girl before we headed to Indianapolis. Sometimes when I was holding her, she'd stretch her arms out, making it look like she was giving the touchdown signal. "Touchdown!" I'd say. Kennedy would smile back at me.

She was a natural.

Kennedy was my good luck charm. Since she'd entered the world, we'd won both of our playoff games and I was happier than ever. Now we were headed to the Super Bowl. I always liked when we had a few days off between games, but being able to spend an entire week with my newborn baby daughter was truly a gift. I'd be going to Indianapolis with a clear head and a fulfilled heart.

On the Saturday before we left for the Super Bowl, the town of Paterson threw me an old-fashioned pep rally. I'd gotten word of it earlier in the week and thought it would consist of a few of my friends and family members wishing me well with a party.

When I got to School 21, the site where the rally was being held, I was greeted by the warmth and love of *thousands* of Paterson residents.

I couldn't believe my eyes.

The word VICTOR-Y was spelled out in the windows of the school, and there were handmade signs that read CRUZ CONTROL. Congressman Bill Pascrell, the congressional representative from our district, was dressed in a blue Victor Cruz Giants jersey. The Eastside High School marching band was there in full force, playing the drums. The school's cheerleaders were dressed in their uniforms, doing Victor Cruz cheers. All of my old teachers, coaches, and friends from childhood flooded the streets, just going wild. I saw several of my father's old firefighter buddies in the crowd, smiling proudly back at me. Even Sister Gloria, my old principal from Paterson Catholic, made it to the rally.

I was introduced over a loudspeaker, and the entire crowd erupted with cheers.

I tend to have an answer for everything. I'm usually fairly quick on my toes when it comes to words.

But when I grabbed that microphone, I was speechless. I was overcome with raw emotion, just bowled over by the outpouring of support. When I finally got myself together, I thanked Coach Wimberly, Jim Salmon, and all the positive role models who helped make me the player—and more importantly, the man—that I had become. I thanked the teachers who helped me along the way, too.

I also thanked Paterson.

This was my homecoming party, something I'd never dreamed of seeing as a kid. I wanted to soak it all in.

WHEN I GRABBED THAT MICROPHONE, I WAS SPEECHLESS.

The crowd chanted my name and after being nudged by a few of the city officials, I even led a "Cruuuuuuuz" cheer and did the salsa.

As I walked through the mob of kids, parents, and old familiar faces from the neighborhood, I linked eyes with an older woman off in the distance, a few hundred feet away. I recognized her immediately and felt my chest tighten when I saw tears flowing from her eyes.

I pushed through the jubilant crowd and wrapped my arms around her. I hugged the woman, bringing her close to me, and I started to cry on her shoulder.

"This is for him," I wept. "I'm living out his dreams. I'm living out *our* dreams."

The woman was Jordan Cleaves's mother. Hours before Jordan passed away in the fatal car accident back in 2004, he and I had spoken about our futures while strolling around the fair. We spoke about someday winning Super Bowls and buying mansions for our hardworking moms. We talked about being "small school" guys who'd make it to the NFL. We talked about making all the folks in Paterson proud to call us their own.

Jordan was my big brother on the football field and one of my best friends off it. He saw things in me that very few others had. When he died, I lost one of my most trusted friends.

I held Ms. Cleaves-Thompson in my arms, assuring her that I wasn't achieving my goals and chasing my dreams alone. Jordan was with me on the journey, and this outpouring of love and support wasn't just for me.

It was for both of us.

"He would have been so happy for you, Victor," she said as we dried our tears and smiled. "He would have been so proud."

Two days later, as we boarded the plane for Indianapolis, Deon Grant came and sat alongside me. In my life with the Giants, Deon played a role similar to Jordan's at Paterson Catholic. Any question, any advice, any wisdom I ever needed—I went to Deon for guidance.

"Hey, Cruz," Deon said. "You good, man?"

I looked out the window of the plane. It was all happening so fast. Super Bowl–bound, I gave him a giant smile and a shake of the head.

"Yeah, man. I'm good."

CHAPTER 13

WILLIAM HAUSR © 2012

FINISHING
THE JOB

T**HE TUESDAY MORNING** before Super Bowl Sunday is known as "Media Day." I'd heard all about it from my teammates who'd been through one before, but I still wasn't prepared for the sheer number of people that were on hand to ask us questions.

Some of those questions were about football.

Some.

The rest? Not so much. There were guys dressed as superheroes from Nickelodeon, supermodels asking questions about Tom Brady's UGG shoes and Wes Welker's eyes, and comedians doing bits.

I got a kick out of getting the opportunity to answer some questions in Spanish. ESPN Deportes, Univision, and Telemundo all had camera crews in attendance, and Ciara was there, wearing a Victor Cruz jersey. At one point, one of the stations took out a boom box and a disco ball and asked me to do the salsa. I, obviously, obliged.

I was even asked to don a sombrero, which I think is more of a Mexican thing than a Puerto Rican tradition. But I didn't push back or ask any questions. I tossed it on and posed for photos. It was all in good fun.

I loved connecting with the Spanish-speaking reporters because it was something I rarely get the chance to do during the season. I take such pride in seeing the name Cruz on the back of my jersey every day when I get to the locker room and love what it represents. Though there have been others before me, I didn't really have a Hispanic football or basketball player to look up to as a kid. If I could be that guy for a young boy or girl, it's a tremendous honor.

As I was getting peppered with questions from all types of reporters, I heard a familiar voice ask a question from the crowd beneath me.

"You're an undrafted free agent. What's it mean to you to be seated at that podium today?"

It was Deion Sanders, one of the Dallas Cowboys players I'd idolized as a kid.

I stammered through an answer, just shocked that *Primetime* was asking *me* a question.

Super Bowl week, as a whole, made for a series of surreal moments. On Monday night, a few of us went to dinner at a restaurant called St. Elmo's and there were hundreds of fans lined up outside, just wanting to get a glimpse of us. I'd gone out to dinner with Elaina in New York City several times throughout the season and nobody ever noticed us. That night in Indianapolis, though, it was as if we were rock stars. Everywhere we went in town, there were Giants jerseys, lining the streets. A lot of them were my number 80. Seeing the Giants' fans, out in full force, meant a lot.

On Thursday, I was walking back to the hotel after practice when Antrel Rolle, our starting safety, asked me, "You know about the Madonna stuff today, right?"

I had no idea what he was talking about. I knew Madonna was performing during the Super Bowl halftime show on Sunday, but I hadn't heard any major news about her.

"She did the salsa at her press conference today. Actually, she did *your* salsa dance at her press conference today. YouTube it," Antrel said.

When I got into my hotel room, I immediately took out my computer and typed the words "Madonna" and "Salsa" into a

> I TAKE SUCH PRIDE IN SEEING THE NAME CRUZ ON THE BACK OF MY JERSEY AND LOVE WHAT IT REPRESENTS.

Google search. The first result that came up was a video of Madonna doing the salsa.

Madonna.

As crazy as things were during Super Bowl week, I was happy to have both Elaina and Kennedy in town with me the entire time. There was no way I could have spent an entire week away from them.

In addition to Elaina and Kennedy, I secured Super Bowl tickets for Coach Wimberly, Jim Salmon, my brother, Malik, and my sisters, Andrea and Ebony. My *abuela* called me on the Friday before the game to tell me she'd be watching at home.

"And if you score," she said in Spanish, "don't forget to do your dance."

I told her for the millionth time that I'd be doing the salsa every time I scored for the rest of my career. It was my tribute to her.

The coaching staff had two weeks to review the Patriots' game tapes from the season and came to Indianapolis prepared with a game plan that we worked on at practice throughout the week. During walk-throughs, we were focused and energized. There were no distractions, no major hiccups, and nothing standing in our way.

We'd beaten the Patriots earlier in the season and we knew that we had what it took to beat them again. If we stuck to our game plan, played confidently, and didn't make mental errors—we'd be Super Bowl champions.

We just had to go out there and play New York Giants football.

I'VE ALWAYS TALKED to myself before games. I did it in high school, I did it at UMass, and I do it every week in the NFL.

Sometimes I psych myself up. I'll recite lyrics to a song that gets me going. Jay-Z and Kanye's "Who Gon Stop Me" usually works. Drake's and Wale's stuff tends to do the job, too.

Other times, though, I just say what's on my mind.

In the hours leading up to kickoff on Super Bowl Sunday, I couldn't stop talking.

I was saying all the names of the Super Bowl greats I'd watched with my father as a kid—legends like Steve Young, Joe Montana, and Troy Aikman. I was telling myself that we'd come too far not to come home as champions. I reminded myself that no one remembers the team that *loses* in the Super Bowl, just the teams that hoist the Lombardi Trophy.

At one point, as I was stretching, I repeated the same refrain over and over again: "It's about this team, man. It's about this team, man. It's about this team, man."

As a high school player, I'd sit and I'd stir when I saw the college coaches talk to Chenry and Kit, jealous and confused as to why they weren't interested in me. In college, I'd call Liam from Paterson and ask him how all the other receivers were performing but never think to ask about how the team looked as a whole. Even in my rookie year, I sat and pitied myself because of my injury but didn't feel the same kind of pain when the rest of the guys lost up in Green Bay.

Now, though, the *only* thing that mattered on the football field was whether we won or lost. I looked around and saw guys I loved and respected. I wanted to play my hardest and be spectacular so *they* could be winners. Guys like Deon Grant, Michael Boley, and Chris Canty—veterans who'd played football their entire lives and still hadn't gotten a Super Bowl ring.

It wasn't even about me anymore. It wasn't about Victor Cruz—the overlooked, undersized kid with the Hispanic last name—proving his doubters wrong.

It was about the team.

It was about the New York Giants.

■ ■ ■

WE GOT THE ball first and the moment I stepped onto the field, all the nervous energy, anxiety, and impatience of Super Bowl week disappeared. We were just playing football, like the kids on the street in front of my mother's house on East Eighteenth.

On the third play of the game, we were faced with a third and six from our own twenty-seven yard line. I'd been Eli's third-down go-to guy all season, and the Super Bowl would be no different. I made a move on my man and got open. Eli hit me with a pass, I picked up an extra yard, and we were on the move. First down.

I heard a recognizable roar in the crowd. "Cruuuuuuuz!"

Eli took us a bit farther down the field, but on third and thirteen, he was sacked for a loss. We punted the ball away and shifted our attention to the defense.

All week Justin Tuck and Osi Umenyiora, two of the guys who'd starred in the team's Super Bowl XLII victory over the Patriots, stressed being ready for the "moment."

Tom Brady was going to come out firing, Aaron Hernandez and Wes Welker were going to get their catches, and Bill Belichick was going to have a few things up his sleeve. We knew that going into the game. But if our defense stayed true to its game plan and didn't allow the moment to become too large, we knew that we'd be in the game until the very end.

The defensive unit—from the most seasoned veterans like Deon to the young guys like JPP—came ready for the moment on February 5.

On the Patriots' very first offensive play, Tom Brady faked a handoff and looked deep for an open receiver. Our linebackers and defensive backs had each one of their wideouts and tight ends covered. As Brady continued to search for an open man, Justin broke through the offensive line and dove at his legs. Brady, under pressure in his end zone, heaved the ball as far as he could to nobody in particular.

Flag on the play. Intentional grounding.

Safety.

We needed our D to come up with a stop, and they did that and much more, getting us our first points of the game.

It was early, but with a 2-0 lead, we had the momentum.

Our offense took the field and Eli led us on another long drive.

He hit Henry Hynoski for thirteen yards. D. J. Ware popped open for eight more. Ahmad tore off a twenty-four-yard run. Eli then connected with Bear Pascoe and Hakeem for consecutive completions. We were moving the ball and he couldn't miss. Everything Eli threw was perfectly on target.

On third and three, Eli gave me the look. I knew the ball was coming my way. He hurried to the line and threw a short pass over the middle. I caught it with two hands and tried fighting for some more yards. As I pushed forward, though, Patrick Chung, a safety on the Patriots, took his hand and jarred the ball loose.

Fumble.

The Patriots recovered.

I thought I might have been down before the ball got ripped from me, but I wasn't. I glanced at the guys on our offensive line, veterans like Chris Snee and David Diehl, and felt my heart sink. They'd been working so hard to give Eli the time he needed to complete his passes, and I'd just let every one of them down. Coach Gilbride, Coach Ryan, and Coach Sullivan preached "protecting the ball" all season long, and in the biggest game of all— I'd done just the opposite.

I had started to walk toward the sideline when I saw a yellow flag thrown in front of me.

It was a penalty against the Patriots. It turned out that New England had twelve men on the field during the play, one more than they were allowed to have. The penalty not only meant that we'd be getting the ball back but that we'd get a first down, too.

I'd been given a second chance.

Two plays later, I got to the line of scrimmage and looked at the man standing five feet in front of me in a blue Patriots jersey.

It was James Ihedigbo.

Back in the fall of 2003, I fell in love with UMass because of the two guys who took me around on my campus tour. They were older players whom I immediately connected with. Shannon James was one of those two guys. The other was James Ihedigbo.

Now here James and I were, going up against each other in front of 111 million viewers in the biggest game of our lives.

Staring at James, I thought of what Michael Strahan had told me that day in the mall. "The NFL will find you if you're good enough."

The NFL found both James and me. Neither of us was drafted. But we were given opportunities and we'd made the very most of them.

Now we were lined up, face-to-face, in the Super Bowl.

Eli took the snap and I ran directly at James. When he lunged to make contact with me, I made a quick slant to the inside and lifted my head. As I got a step on him, I saw the ball coming at me with one eye and a Patriots linebacker flying toward me with the other. Eli slipped the pass in between both James and the linebacker and I felt the ball hit my chest. I bobbled it slightly and then clutched it with both hands. I wasn't dropping this one.

I got my feet planted, bounced off Hakeem, and heard the roar of the thousands of Giants fans in the stadium.

Touchdown.

I BOBBLED IT SLIGHTLY AND THEN CLUTCHED IT WITH BOTH HANDS. I WASN'T DROPPING THIS ONE.

I knew Coach Wimberly and Jim Salmon were seated above the end zone and I briefly looked up into the stands, trying to spot them. When I couldn't locate them right away, I just did what I always did when I scored. My tribute to my *abuela*.

I danced the salsa.

Hakeem and Jake Ballard celebrated the touchdown with me in the end zone and I remember screaming, "Let's go! Let's go!"

We were up 9-0 on the Patriots and they'd run just one offensive play the entire game.

I'd scored a touchdown in the Super Bowl, but what it meant for me personally didn't really register at the time.

We were up 9-0.

That's all that mattered.

THE PATRIOTS ANSWERED. We knew they would.

Brady took New England the length of the field. But on third down, JPP batted a pass down, forcing the Patriots to settle for a field goal.

With a little over four minutes remaining in the second quarter, Brady got the ball back on New England's one yard line. He got hot. Pass after pass, Brady moved the Patriots down the field. When it was all said and done, he'd led the Patriots on a fourteen-play, ninety-nine-yard scoring drive. With just eight seconds on the clock, he hit Danny Woodhead for a four-yard touchdown pass, giving the Patriots a 10-9 lead as we headed into the locker room for halftime.

Halftime seemed to last forever. Usually, it's a quick fifteen-minute break, and then we head back onto the field for the third quarter. But because of Madonna's halftime show, we were in the locker room for close to thirty-five minutes.

Justin, Osi, and Deon addressed the defense, and Eli said a few words to the offense. Both Hakeem and I were seeing double coverage all night, meaning that Mario, Bear, Jake, and the running backs were the ones the Patriots were leaving open. Mario had been making clutch plays for us all season. If he was going to be the guy who'd have to make the big catch down the stretch, I had no doubt he'd find a way to make it happen.

He'd get that opportunity in the fourth quarter.

When we finally got back onto the field, the Patriots received the kick and Brady went back to work. He led New England eighty yards, mostly out of the no huddle, and extended their lead with a touchdown pass to Aaron Hernandez. Though we'd started the game by taking an early lead and owning all of the momentum, we were now trailing 17-9 early in the third quarter.

On our next offensive drive, it became clear—Hakeem and I weren't going to be the ones to beat the Patriots. It'd have to be the other guys. Every time we lined up for a passing play, there were two men grabbing and clutching us. A cornerback would man up against us at the line, and then a safety would shade over after we broke into our routes.

Eli identified and adjusted to the double coverage and threw a series of passes to Jake, Bear, and Mario. Though we didn't score a touchdown on that drive, we picked up three points and cut the Patriots' lead to five.

Our defense needed to somehow stop Brady. On New England's last two drives, he'd moved the Patriots efficiently down the entire length of the field and they scored both times.

On third and eight, Brady went back to pass and looked for an open receiver. One second. Two seconds. Three seconds. After four seconds in the pocket, he took a step forward. Dave Tollefson, one of our defensive ends, hit Brady at the line and Justin gobbled him up and tossed him to the ground. Quarterback sack. It was a huge play. Brady had been on fire the last few drives, and our defense had finally cooled him down.

"That's what we needed!" I shouted to Mario and D. J. Ware, standing next to me on the sideline. "Let's go!"

On the ensuing drive, Eli faked a handoff and threw a perfect pass to Hakeem. He took one step with the ball and had it stripped out of his hands.

Fumble.

Henry Hynoski had been running hard on the play and jumped on the ball when it bounced off the ground.

What if Henry wasn't there? What if he'd run the wrong route? What if the Patriots took the fumble back for a touchdown? Every play, every route, every step matters in an NFL football game. Henry was in the right position to make a play and he made one. Twenty years from now, no one will say, "Hey, remember when Henry Hynoski recovered that fumble in the Super Bowl?"

But twenty years from now, Hakeem, Henry, and the rest of us will all remember it vividly. It would never be a "Top Ten" play on *SportsCenter*, but that fumble recovery was huge. It kept us alive.

On third and eight, Eli looked for me, but I wasn't open. He was sacked and we were forced to settle for another field goal. It was 17-15 Patriots.

"We need another stop, D!" I pleaded from the sideline.

New England had put up huge offensive numbers all season long and hadn't lost a game since we beat them in their building on November 6. I knew if our defense could just stop Brady and the Patriots' offense one more time, we'd be able to find the end zone and win this game. We just needed the D to come up with a stop. Someone had to step up and change the game.

Chase Blackburn was the Giants' leading special teams tackler for six seasons. When I was trying out for the squad in 2010, it was Chase who had served as our special teams unit's captain. He was hardworking and respected by every player and coach in the locker room.

After the Giants opted not to re-sign him over the summer, Chase waited for a shot with another team. For whatever reason, that shot never came. He waited and waited, and as the 2011 NFL season got under way, he was an NFL football player without an NFL team.

He'd made some money with the Giants, but not enough to stop working. So he looked at other career options and decided to become a substitute teacher at a middle school up in Ohio.

Chase was an undrafted guy like me. He'd been given a shot in the league and made the most of it. But after six seasons, it looked like his NFL playing days were over. He kept a packed suitcase in his bedroom with jeans, underwear, a few T-shirts, and a suit—just in case a team called and he was needed to be somewhere in a moment's notice.

After a string of injuries decimated our linebacker corps in December, Chase's phone rang. The Giants needed him to be in New Jersey the very next day.

He was ready.

Two months later, Chase Blackburn was our starting middle linebacker in the Super Bowl.

On the second play of the fourth quarter, Brady took a snap out of the shotgun, avoided a sack, and rolled to his right. As he evaded the pressure of our surging defensive line, he looked deep for his six-foot-seven tight end, Rob Gronkowski. Brady wound up and heaved a beautifully thrown ball deep down the field.

We all held our breaths on the sideline.

Chase isn't the fastest guy in the world, but he kept up with Gronkowski, running with him stride for stride on the play. When the ball came down from the sky at around the five yard line, Chase jumped in front of Gronkowski and snatched it out of the air.

Interception.

"There we go, Chase!" I screamed, running onto the field with my helmet.

We were back in business.

Chase Blackburn, the middle school teacher with the packed

suitcase by his bed, had just made one of the biggest plays of Super Bowl XLVI.

Everyone's story was unique.

DOWN 17-15 WITH fourteen minutes remaining, Eli took us on what we had hoped would be another one of his classic fourth quarter drives. But we couldn't score any points. After a few completed passes—including an eight-yarder over the middle to me—we were stopped on third down and forced to punt the ball back to New England.

The Patriots' next drive felt like it lasted even longer than half-time.

Brady was milking the clock on every play, and anytime it was third down, he'd make a play to move the chains and make it first and ten.

As minute after minute ticked off the clock, I began to wonder if our offense would even get back onto the field. On second and eleven, Brady threw a deep pass to his top receiver, Wes Welker. There was a mix-up in our defense's pass coverage and Welker stood alone, wide open, at the twenty yard line. A touchdown would put the game—and ultimately, the season—away.

Brady and Welker had connected on 122 passes during the 2011 regular season. They'd connected on 331 passes over the course of the previous three seasons, making them the most productive quarterback/receiver duo in the entire league over that span. They'd likely practiced this very same route over ten thousand times in their lives.

But when the pass left Brady's right hand and came spiraling toward Welker, their timing was one second off. Welker jumped in the air, stretched both arms out, and went for the grab.

The ball flicked off his fingers and fell to the ground.

Incomplete.

I looked at Mario in shock. Had that really just happened? He shook his head in disbelief.

We shouldn't have been surprised. Those kinds of plays had been happening throughout our Super Bowl run.

Had Tony Romo hit Miles Austin on third and five in week fourteen, our season would have been over before Christmas.

Had Aaron Rodgers hit a wide-open Greg Jennings in the first quarter of our Divisional Round game versus the Packers, the rest of that afternoon could have gone a completely different way.

Had Brady hit Welker on a play they probably could nail ninety-nine out of one hundred times in their sleep, our year likely would have ended with 4:11 left to go in Indianapolis.

But Romo didn't hit Austin, Rodgers didn't hit Jennings, and Brady didn't hit Welker.

Coach Wimberly once said, "Strange things can happen over the course of a football game. You're better off not thinking too hard about the last play."

In our case, strange things were happening every week. Strange, wonderful things. Brady's and Welker's misfortune was our gain. After another incomplete pass on third down, we were punted the ball back with 3:46 left on the clock.

We'd get one last shot.

Coach Gilbride called in "Otter W Go" from the sideline. The play is designed for the two receivers lined up to the right of the line—Hakeem and me, in this case—to be the primary and secondary targets. Hakeem's supposed to go seven yards and cut inside, and I'm supposed to do a double move and go deep.

The third option on the play, one that's really not expected to be used, is the receiver lined up to the left of the offensive line. That receiver, which in this case was Mario, is supposed to run a straight Go route down the sideline.

All game, Patrick Chung, the Patriots' safety, had been cheat- ing off our other receivers to provide double coverage on Hakeem and me. Eli must have had a hunch that he'd be doing it again on "Otter W Go."

When he took the snap from the shotgun at our own seven yard line, Hakeem and I both ran our routes hard, fighting to get open. Eli looked at Hakeem, he looked at me, and then he shifted his hips to the left.

Without even taking a second to see what was downfield on the far sideline, he tossed a high, spiraling pass into the air.

Essentially, it was a no-look pass.

It was an incredibly risky decision, a gamble in every sense of the word.

But Mario's end zone celebration all season long had been the craps player blowing the dice at the casino.

If ever there was a receiver worth rolling the dice on, it was Mario Manningham.

The pass went thirty yards in the sky and started to descend along the Patriots' sideline. Eli guessed right on Chung, as the safety was a tenth of a second late getting to the landing spot of the pass. Sterling Moore, the cornerback covering Mario, trailed him by a step.

As the ball came down, Mario stretched his arms out as far as he could, simultaneously trying to keep both of his feet inbounds and avoid any contact from the two Patriots' defenders.

He caught the football, dragged his feet, and got pushed out of bounds by Chung. Mario went tumbling into a sea of Patriots players and coaches on their sideline. I looked over from my spot on the middle of the field to see if he'd caught it.

He held on!

But did he have possession of the ball? Did he keep both feet inbounds before getting hit?

The ruling on the field was a catch, but Bill Belichick didn't buy it. He immediately threw the red challenge flag.

Mario and I gathered together at midfield and watched the replay in slow motion on the stadium's video scoreboard above us.

"Look," I said to him. "Catch. Right. Left!" He had control inbounds. It was a catch! It was as clear as day.

John Parry, the official, returned to the field and ruled it a reception. Thirty-eight yards. First down. Mario gave a big Michael Irvin first-down signal of his own and we slapped each other five. It was the play we'd been looking for the entire second half.

Only, Eli and Mario weren't done.

Two plays later, they connected for sixteen yards. The play after that, they linked up for another two. Then Eli found Hakeem open along the sideline for fourteen. We were moving.

After another completion to Hakeem, we were well within Tynes's field goal range. There was a minute left to go and we trailed by two points. A field goal would be enough to win the game.

On second and six from the Patriots' six yard line, Eli handed the ball off to Ahmad, and the Patriots gave him a free path to the end zone. I'd never seen anything like it. The entire defense just let him run the ball up the middle with absolutely no resistance. They *let him* run the ball in.

It was a smart decision. If the Patriots let Ahmad score a touchdown, Tom Brady and the New England offense would get the ball back, down four points with about a minute left in the game. If their defense had tackled Ahmad, Eli could have taken a few knees, killed the clock, and Lawrence Tynes would have kicked a game-winning field goal with no time left for a Patriots response.

Ahmad got to the goal line, saw what was going on, and sort of awkwardly fell backward into the end zone for the touchdown.

It was the most anticlimactic last-minute touchdown score in Super Bowl history. None of us really cheered or congratulated him. We were too damn scared of Tom Brady.

It was 21-17, there was less than a minute left, and our season would come down to one final defensive stand.

"We've done it all year, boys," I shouted to the D as they took the field.

Brady strolled out there like it was no big deal. Just another Sunday. All the great quarterbacks act that way in high-pressure situations. Eli does the same thing.

They're different guys, though, Eli and Brady.

Brady gets fired up. He plays with a lot of emotion and wills his team with his charisma and energy. It's not uncommon to see him scream at a receiver, yell at a coach, or pump his fist after a big play.

Eli doesn't really do any of that. He's even-keeled. His body language isn't much different after a twenty-yard completion than it is after an interception.

Brady's Brady and Eli's Eli. They're both elite quarterbacks. They just carry themselves differently.

Brady broke from the huddle and I couldn't stomach watching from our bench. Standing there with Ramses, D. J. Ware, Mario, and Hakeem, I just paced back and forth along the sideline, hoping for our defense to stand its ground.

After two incomplete passes, Brady went back and looked deep for an open receiver on third down. Osi was pressuring him off the left edge and forced him to shift to his right. Just as Brady took that step, Justin came surging up the middle and wrapped him up for the sack.

It was fourth and sixteen and the Lombardi Trophy was just one defensive stop away.

Unfortunately, it wouldn't be that easy.

Brady hit his receiver, Deion Branch, for nineteen yards and a first down.

Mario and I looked at each other with the same looks of amazement that we had exchanged three minutes earlier after the Welker drop. The Patriots were suddenly back in business.

I started pacing up and down the sideline, again.

On the very next play, he connected with Hernandez for eleven more.

The Patriots were driving down the field and I couldn't do anything to stop them. I felt completely powerless, much like I did when DeSean Jackson returned the punt and I was in street clothes on the sideline back in 2010.

But it was out of my hands now. All I could do was watch.

After a pair of incomplete passes, Brady broke from the huddle for the final play of Super Bowl XLVI.

The entire season would come down to a Hail Mary pass.

The last time we'd seen a Hail Mary thrown, Hakeem came down with it in the end zone in Green Bay. The play didn't work very often, but we'd all witnessed one being pulled off just three weeks earlier. It wasn't impossible. Both sidelines knew it.

Brady took the snap out of the shotgun, danced a few steps behind the line of scrimmage, and evaded JPP's outstretched paw.

He cocked his arm back and heaved the ball fifty yards for the end zone.

As it sailed through the air, I saw a sea of defenders dressed in white surrounding a handful of Patriots in blue.

"Knock it down!" I screamed, hoping to will the ball to the ground.

Deon, Kenny Phillips, and Jacquian Williams all jumped alongside Aaron Hernandez, Brady's reliable tight end.

The pass was thrown exactly where Brady intended for it to go—right in the middle of the end zone. The Lombardi Trophy was truly up for grabs.

Kenny leaped over Hernandez's back and swatted the ball with both hands.

Rob Gronkowski, Brady's other tight end, dove for it off the deflection but was too far away.

The ball hit the ground and trickled out of the end zone.

Incomplete.

Game over.

We'd just won Super Bowl XLVI.

As I ran onto the field looking for someone—anyone—to hug, I screamed like a little kid on Christmas.

I sprinted to Deon Grant and embraced him. Deon had been my big brother on the team for the past two seasons and now, after eleven years in the league, he was finally a Super Bowl champion.

I found Chris Canty, the ex–Cowboys star who had come to the Giants three years ago with dreams of winning a Super Bowl. "I told you we'd do it, Chris," I screamed, still giddily jumping up and down. "I told you we'd get you one!"

I wanted to hug every single person I saw wearing a white jersey.

D. J. Ware. He'd been the guy who told me all about "Cut Day" and praying for the phone not to ring. He was a Super Bowl champion now.

Michael Boley. The guy who always was the first one to greet me on the sideline after a touchdown. He was a Super Bowl champion now.

I saw Chase Blackburn off in the distance. The guy kept a suitcase packed by his bed *just in case* the Giants gave him a call in the middle of the season. He'd made arguably the biggest play of the Super Bowl and was now getting his second Super Bowl ring.

Justin Tuck, Brandon Jacobs, Corey "CWeb" Webster, Antrel Rolle—I embraced them all.

Running around the field, just looking for more guys to hug, I thought about Rhett Bomar. What if Rhett hadn't thrown me the ball on just about every play of the final drive in that "meaningless" preseason game against the Ravens? Would I even have made the team? Rhett was probably with his family in a living room somewhere in Texas, but I knew he was watching the game. I knew he was rooting me on. I knew he was pumping his fist in triumph, just like he did after tossing me that touchdown pass.

I thought about all of my old roommates. Tim Brown and Duke Calhoun with the Giants. Shawnn Gyles and Liam Coen up at UMass.

I thought about Courtney Greene, my best friend at Bridgton Academy. I thought about T. J. Tillman, Adrian Rodriguez, Kit Pommels, Rashawn "Rocky" Ricks, and Tymier Wells.

I thought about Jordan Cleaves.

I'd crossed paths with so many teammates. They'd each played a different role in my journey. They were all in some way partially responsible for me being on that field, celebrating a Super Bowl championship.

As I bounced from one guy to the next, I saw Elaina and my mother running onto the field.

They weren't alone.

Malik, Ebony, and Andrea had somehow made it down there, too.

I posed for a picture with Malik and Ebony, my father's two other children, and we looked at each other as the confetti fell from the Lucas Oil Stadium roof.

"You know, Dad would have loved this," Malik said to Ebony and me. "He would have been jumping around, hugging more people than you, Vic. He would have been the loudest guy in the stadium right now."

Ebony laughed and kissed me on the cheek. "He would have been so proud of you, Victor."

Elaina and my mother were beaming. They'd both been by my side for the whole entire ride. All the ups and all the downs.

Elaina wrote my e-mail to the UMass admissions office when I was kicked out of college for the first time. My mother drove me up to Amherst without a second's hesitation when it happened again just one year later.

They were two of the strongest, smartest, most beautiful women in the world. I looked at them and smiled, knowing my baby daughter had two wonderful women to watch and learn from.

Someone from the NFL called me up onto the podium and I got to be one of the first players to hold the Lombardi Trophy. I grabbed it with both hands and just shook my head in amazement. Was it all really happening?

I looked over at Eli and he was cool and calm Eli, as always. He nodded at me and smiled. He was probably already thinking about off-season workouts in April.

Before we left the field, I made sure to take a few pieces of the confetti.

I'd been watching the Super Bowl since 1996, and the one thing I always remembered was the confetti after the games. I was bringing that Super Bowl confetti back home to Paterson no matter what.

LATER THAT EVENING, Elaina and I went back to our hotel room and kissed Kennedy good night. We got into bed and briefly talked about the game, the season, and how blessed we were to have met each other on that summer evening in 2004.

I shut the lights off and told Elaina I loved her.

Then I reached over to the nightstand and grabbed one of the pieces of confetti.

I held it tightly in my hands. I needed to feel that confetti just one more time.

It was real.

Everything was real.

I just wanted to make sure.

EPILOGUE

SIX WEEKS AFTER our team enjoyed a parade down New York City's Canyon of Heroes and received a glorious welcome from our fans back at MetLife Stadium, I was driving my car around Paterson and decided to drop by my old high school.

In 2010, Paterson Catholic shut its doors, but the building had since reopened as a charter school called Paterson Charter School for Science and Technology. I didn't know what I wanted from the experience or what even compelled me to make the visit, but when I pulled into the parking lot, a wave of emotions washed over me.

I looked at "The Swamp," our old football field, and remembered all of those endless autumn afternoons, practicing my routes with Coach Wimberly screaming in the background. I thought of those glass cases in the hallways, filled with framed photographs of Tim Thomas and all of the Paterson Catholic greats before him, and remembered the rush of adrenaline I felt the first time I saw my face in one of the pictures. I thought of homeroom with Father Murphy, lunches in the cafeteria, and the thrill of walking into junior year biology class with my varsity jacket wrapped around my shoulders.

I no longer knew anyone inside of the building, but I wanted to walk those halls.

I got out of my car, walked through the building's front doors, and popped my head inside the school's main office unannounced.

Everything looked the same as it did eight years earlier, but *smaller*.

"Victor Cruz!" one of the women working in the main office shouted.

"Son, take a photograph with me! You must! You're my husband's favorite player on the Giants!"

I complied, but feared that I was interrupting a school day. I considered dipping back out, crawling into my car, and driving home. I'd gotten a taste of the school. That's all I really needed. I didn't want to cause a disturbance.

The school's principal then came out from his office. He introduced himself and, instead of asking me to leave, urged me to take a walk around the school with him.

"These kids need to see you," he said. "They've got to see you in the flesh, walking these halls."

I wasn't quite sure what he meant by the comment, but I nodded politely in return.

As we strolled through the building once known as Paterson Catholic, the memories came flooding back to me. I loved this school—regardless of what it was called now—and it felt good to be back.

Then the bell rang. End of period.

Within seconds, a wave of hundreds of students emerged from different classrooms and collided as one. They saw me, I saw them, and the reaction was sheer chaos. They slapped me five, they screamed, and they asked me for autographs. At one point, it got a little scary. There were thirty teenage kids—boys *and* girls—swarming me, just wanting to touch me. I looked at the principal, and he was smiling.

"This is nuts!" I shouted to him over the mob of hysterical students.

"Yeah, I had a feeling they'd get a kick out of this," he screamed back.

After a few minutes and several dozen autographs, we ducked back into the main office, shutting a glass door behind us. I hadn't bobbed and weaved so hard since the NFC Championship Game. I was out of breath.

"That was insane," I said, as I leaned against a bookshelf, sipping from a bottle of water.

"Sorry if that was a bit overwhelming, but they needed to see you here," he said. "By seeing you in person, they know that your story is not some myth. They know that journeys like yours are, in fact, possible."

He, then, said something I'll never forget. "These kids now know you didn't just come from out of the blue. They know that you came from within these walls and from these hallways. They know you came from Paterson."

He was right.

It may seem to football fans like I came completely out of the blue in 2011. But, my road was long, windy, full of hurdles, and even included some dead ends. I lost family. I lost friends. And on multiple occasions, I even lost my way.

When I reached what felt like rock bottom, I found a purpose to fight for my dreams. I realized I had a responsibility to the players that inspired me, the teammates who motivated me, everyone who believed in me, and to kids, like me, who just needed a chance.

I had to do it. I gave myself no other option.

The 2011 season was one I'll never forget, but it doesn't tell my whole story. It's just one piece of a narrative that's only twenty-five years in the making and still being written today.

What's most important in moving forward is not so much how I got here but, more so, what my journey has taught me:

You can't wait for your chance. You can't expect it. You have to earn it.

And, when you do, it's always with the help of others. So when you *do* get your shot, you carry on your shoulders the responsibility of validating the sacrifices everyone's made for you, the faith everyone has in you, and the trust you have in yourself to make the most of it.

This is my opportunity. And I'm playing to win.

ACKNOWLEDGMENTS

VICTOR CRUZ

At first, I thought all that went into writing a book would be over-whelming. I envisioned it being a slow and tedious process. I also feared that I wouldn't remember everything that's occurred in my life and that some key moments of my journey would go miss-ing from the overall narrative. But as I started to talk with Peter about my childhood, it all started to come to me rather easily and we ended up having a lot of fun.

Writing this book turned out to be a great experience and I'd definitely do it all over again if I had to. If my life story can inspire one kid or change just one life, all the hours and all the hard work that went into this project would be more than worth it.

First, I want to thank Peter Schrager. He is, in my opinion, one of the best young writers today and we worked incredibly well together. Upon meeting him, I learned that not only did Peter already know most of my story, but he was genuinely enthused about being given the opportunity to share it with the world. I was confident that he'd do a great job and he did. We had a great time writing this book together.

I'd also like to thank Carlos Fleming and everyone at IMG for making this book a reality. Thanks to Scott Waxman for help-ing us in putting all the pieces together. Thank you, Ray Garcia, Mark Chait, and the rest of the Penguin/Celebra team, including Kara Welsh, Craig Burke, and Julia Fleischaker.

Finally, I'd like to thank the special people who've helped make all of my life's dreams come true.

Coach Wimberly, Jim Salmon, and the rest of my coaches and teachers growing up—thank you for your guidance and constant belief in me.

My mother, Blanca, you're the strongest woman I know. Everything I do, everything I achieve, is a reflection of you.

My sister Andrea, my sister Ebony, my brother Malik—you've always been there and we've been through a lot. Our experiences together have shaped us into the people we are today. We've shared all of the highs and all of the lows, and you'll be with me for all that's still to come.

Abuela, you've dedicated your life to ensuring your family is happy and their lives are fulfilled. You taught me the salsa, yes, but that's just a tiny part of the impact you've made on me.

Kennedy, you're my angel and my inspiration. You'll always be Daddy's Little Girl and my life's greatest accomplishment.

Elaina, I love you. I've been yours since the first night we locked eyes and you've been with me for every step along the way. This book would have never come to fruition without your and Brand Infinite's determination and vision. I'm not the man I am today without you by my side.

PETER SCHRAGER

Vic, thank you for the opportunity of a lifetime. You're a tremendous person and I'm forever changed from having met and worked with you on this project. You said that you were in awe of the effect Michael Strahan had on those Giants fans at the mall back in 2007. You don't even realize how much you've impacted the lives of the individuals you've crossed paths with over the course of your twenty-five years. You're just getting started, my man, and I can't wait to see what's next for you. That next slice of bruschetta pizza (covered in crushed red pepper, of course) is on me. Keep on "peacocking," Mr. *GQ.* Keep on loving life.

Elaina, thank you for so graciously opening the doors to your lives to me. Kennedy, thank you for being so amazingly well behaved when Daddy was juggling "writing duty" with "baby duty."

Carlos Fleming, Scott Waxman, and Ray Garcia—thanks for taking a shot on a first-time author with big-time dreams. Mark Chait, you're an incredible editor and an even better handholder. Your late-night pep talks could rival Coach Coughlin's best locker room speeches. Kerri Kolen, thank you for being my own personal Chris Pettit. I never would have gotten this opportunity without your encouragement and faith. Eric Gillin, thanks for your eyes, your red marker, and our shared appreciation for early morning Dunkin' Donuts runs. Rick Jaffe, Jeff Husvar, Jed Pearson, Steve Miller, Nancy Gay, Alex Marvez, and Todd Behrendt at FoxSports.com—thank you for all the wonderful opportunities and experiences over the years. Devin Gordon and Sean Fennessey at *GQ*, Matt Sullivan at *Esquire*—the same goes to you guys. Dave, Abbie, Arleen, Bruce, and the rest of the Edelman gang—thanks for your unwavering support. John Bolster and Tom Seeley, we're long overdue for drinks. One of these years, I promise. Thanks to Steve Sobol, Jason Weber, and the rest of the NFL Films team for lending Vic and me the keys to your castle for a day.

Mom, Dad, and Justin—thanks for tolerating all those rides up to Grandma Rhoda's house where I recited made-up stories I'd written about Drazen Petrovic, Derrick Coleman, Kenny Anderson, and the 1992 New Jersey Nets. Then, now, always—you've been champions.

Most important, thank you, Erica, for being my everything. I'm not sure how this—or anything—gets done without you cheering me on. I love you.